Survival Skills for the Principalship

Survival Skills for the Principalship

A Treasure Chest of Time-Savers, Short-Cuts, and Strategies to Help You Keep a Balance in Your Life

John Blaydes

CORWIN PRESS
A Sage Publications Company
Thousand Oaks, California

#53138742

3-15-04

For information:

Corwin Press
A Sage Publications Company
2455 Teller Road
Thousand Oaks, California 91320
www.corwinpress.com

Sage Publications Ltd.
1 Oliver's Yard
55 City Road
London EC1Y 1SP
United Kingdom

Sage Publications India Pvt. Ltd.
B-42, Panchsheel Enclave
Post Box 4109
New Delhi 110 017 India

Printed in the United States of America

Library of Congress Cataloging-in-Publication Data

Blaydes, John.
Survival skills for the principalship : a treasure chest of time-savers, short-cuts, and strategies to help you keep a balance in your life / by John Blaydes.
    p. cm.
Includes index.
ISBN 0-7619-3860-5 (Cloth)—ISBN 0-7619-3861-3 (Paper)
  1. School principals. 2. Educational leadership. I. Title.
LB2831.9.B575 2004
371.2'012—dc22

                        2003021395

This book is printed on acid-free paper.

04 05 06 07 08 10 9 8 7 6 5 4 3 2 1

Acquisitions Editor:	Robert D. Clouse
Editorial Assistant:	Jingle Vea
Production Editor:	Julia Parnell
Copy Editor:	Toni Williams
Proofreader:	Theresa Kay
Typesetter:	C&M Digitals (P) Ltd.
Indexer:	Jean Casalegno
Cover Designer:	Tracy E. Miller
Graphic Designer:	Lisa Miller

CONTENTS

ACKNOWLEDGMENTS

Thank you to my fellow school administrator colleagues who contributed their expertise and talents to this book:

Judy Smith
Former Principal, McGaugh Elementary School
Los Alamitos Unified School District

Karen Lovelace
Assistant Superintendent
Los Alamitos Unified School District

Carol Hart
Superintendent
Los Alamitos Unified School District

Susan Van Zant
Former Principal, Meadowbrook Middle School
Poway Unified School District

Thank you to the Los Alamitos Unified School District for achieving and maintaining a high standard of excellence. A special thank you to former Superintendent Mike Miller for his visionary leadership. I am indebted to the Los Alamitos Unified School District and its extraordinary school administrators for the many outstanding programs, materials, and processes implemented in the district and that are shared in this book.

I gratefully acknowledge the dozens of outstanding, award-winning school administrators who, over the years, have been kind and gracious enough to share their stories, ideas, materials, and experiences that have contributed to the development of this book.

My personal gratitude and appreciation is extended to the "family" of staff and parents at McGaugh Elementary School, in Seal Beach, California, whose dedication and talents over the years have created an extraordinary school environment for children that is unique in education.

And a special thank you to my wife, Mary Alice, for her help and support while writing this book.

Corwin Press gratefully acknowledges the contributions of the following people:

Lystra Richardson
Associate Professor
Department of Educational
    Leadership
Southern Connecticut State
    University
New Haven, CT

Myrna W. Gantner
Director of P16 & School
    Collaboration
College of Education
State University of West
    Georgia
Carrollton, GA

Ronald P. Weiss
Associate Professor
Department of Educational
    Leadership
Minnesota State University,
    Mankato
Mankato, Minnesota

Patrick J. Bingham
Principal
David A. Harrison Elementary School
Disputanta, VA

Cheryl C. McFadden
Professor
College of Education
    Department of Educational
    Leadership
East Carolina University
Greenville, NC

Daniel P. Gaffney
Principal
Howard R. Yocum School
Maple Shade, NJ

Betty Hollas
Consultant, Staff Developer for
    Educators
Former Principal
The Woodlands, TX

David Hulsey
Professor
Department of Educational
    Leadership
State University of West Georgia
Carrollton, GA

Fran Madison-Cohee
NAESP California Representative
Principal
White Oak Elementary
Westlake Village, CA

Deborah Jenkins
Executive Assistant
Baltimore City Public Schools
Elementary Area III
Baltimore, MD

Jane Foley
Vice President
National Educator Awards
Milken Family Foundation
Santa Monica, CA

ABOUT THE AUTHOR

 **John Blaydes** is one of the nation's foremost experts in the field of school administration. He is an inspirational leader, author, motivational speaker, seminar leader, and educational consultant. In recognition of his innovative leadership, John has been honored with both the National Distinguished School Principal Award and the prestigious Milken Foundation National Educator Award. John also received the Kennedy Center for the Performing Arts National School Administrator Award for his dedication to arts education and California's School Principal Leadership Award from the California Librarians Association for his outstanding media center program.

In his role as inspirational leader, he has promoted a culture of excellence at his school. His school was twice selected as a California Distinguished School and has been honored with multiple awards for his outstanding visual and performing arts, media center, and math programs. Staff awards include the National School Nurse of the Year, the Presidential Award for Excellence in Mathematics Teaching, the California Media Center Teacher of the Year, the Sallie Mae First Year Teacher Award, the Orange County Teacher of the Year, and another recipient of the Milken Foundation National Educator Award.

John has a broad array of experiences in educational leadership, having been a classroom teacher, school site principal, district office administrator, and elected school board member in his community. John believes that the key to educational excellence lies in the ability of our nation's school administrators to be inspirational leaders.

Other Books Authored by John Blaydes

The Educator's Book of Quotes

Inspirational Leadership—Creating a Culture of Excellence in Times of Change

Providing Leadership for 21st Century Schools—Mastering the Changes, Challenges and Complexities of the Principalship

Enhancing Your Effectiveness as an Elementary School Principal

The Principal's Book of Inspirational Quotes

INTRODUCTION

Today's principals are finding the task of providing school leadership a highly political and complex task that challenges even the most experienced principal. The lives of students, staff, and parents lie in the balance. We have entered the era of high-stakes accountability and the principal, as the school's leader, is the one being held most accountable. No matter how hard you work, how much you do, or how well you do it, you are open to criticism and judgment. If principals are to survive in this challenging and complex environment, they will need to master the new three R's of school leadership—resiliency, renewal, and reflection.

WHY I WROTE THIS BOOK

As an experienced principal struggling to meet the increasing demands and stresses of the job, I was always on the lookout for any materials or resources I could use that would make my job a little easier. It seemed that too much of my time was spent composing letters, creating forms, or developing checklists that had already been written by principals at other schools. I felt like I was always reinventing the wheel as I sat composing a letter on school attendance when I knew that one of my colleagues had probably written a similar letter. If I could just borrow that letter, I could use it as a sample and then save time by modifying it to fit the situation at my school. So, whenever I could borrow a sample from a colleague, I felt that I had saved myself valuable time that could free me up to get out into the classrooms and do the important work of the principalship.

Because my day was incredibly busy with all the urgent tasks, problems, and interactions that I had to deal with, I never could find a few moments of quiet time to sit down at my desk and write the numerous memos, letters, and evaluations that required my undivided attention. So, they became the tasks that I took home to do at night and on weekends when I could create the uninterrupted quiet time I needed to get the job done. And I began to resent the valuable time this homework took away from my family and personal life. If I could just find a book of sample memos or borrow examples from my fellow principals, I could spend less time writing and more time with my family.

If principals are to survive as leaders in schools of the 21st century, they need to find ways to lighten their load by finding resources, materials, and support systems that will enable them to work more efficiently. Therefore, I wanted to write a practical book, jam-packed with easy-to-implement strategies, ready-to-use forms, and dozens of sample letters that could serve as a valuable resource.

WHO SHOULD READ THIS BOOK?

It is the goal of this book to provide principals, assistant principals, and aspiring principals with a treasure chest filled with over 500 powerful tips, shortcuts, time-savers, ideas, strategies, and sample letters and forms shared by award-winning principals from across the nation. This treasure chest will allow you to pick and choose those that would best fit your school. These concrete examples are designed to save you time and can be implemented immediately at your school. The book is organized into four chapters: Blueprint for Leadership in 21st-Century Schools, Mastering the Skills of Resiliency, Mastering the Skills of Renewal, and Mastering the Skills of Reflection. Each chapter is packed with school-tested samples and real-life examples designed to give you the survival skills that will save you time and allow you to work more efficiently.

Despite hundreds of interactions with people throughout a single day, when the dust settles the principalship is an isolated job. Your busy day allows little, if any, time for interaction and sharing with your fellow principals. It is hoped that the materials in this book can reduce some of that isolation by sharing what has worked for award-winning principals across the nation. These resources are based on the day-to-day reality of the job and the experiences of highly successful principals of what works and what doesn't work.

1

BLUEPRINT FOR LEADERSHIP IN 21st-CENTURY SCHOOLS

Mastering the Changes, Challenges, and Complexities of the Principalship

To know what to do is wisdom. To know how to do it is skill. To know when to do it is judgment. To strive to do it best is dedication. To do it for the benefit of others is service. To want to help others is compassion. To do it quietly is humility. To get the job done is achievement. To get others to do all of the above is leadership.

—Author Unknown

School principals are bombarded daily with a constant onslaught of urgent demands and pressures upon their time, energy, and resources. The challenges and complexities of the principalship require exceptional coping skills and can tax even the most experienced of principals. Add to the demands of the job the impact of ever-increasing standards, never-ending school reforms, and high-stakes accountability and the stress level of principals increases at an alarming rate. The expectations for high-level performance and demonstrated success are extremely high. To successfully lead schools of the 21st century, principals must be passionate, dedicated leaders who have a strong work ethic; demonstrate knowledge of learning theory, child development, and a variety of subject matter; and, most important, possess the ability to work successfully with all kinds of people. Effective school leaders need to know how to think, make decisions, solve problems, plan for the future, communicate successfully, use time efficiently, facilitate change, manage budgets, improve instruction, create a positive school culture, increase test scores, and inspire those whom they lead to achieve their greatest potential. And the most important skill needed to survive in this job is the ability to keep a healthy balance between work and a life outside of work—not an easy task, in light of working with the most culturally, socially, and economically diverse society in the history of the world.

The challenges and complexities of the principalship require exceptional coping skills and can even tax the most experienced of principals. Now more than ever, we need to be *inspirational leaders*.

We need to be positive, charismatic, dynamic, courageous, credible, enthusiastic, caring, compassionate, and competent. We need to be our school's best cheerleader, focusing on the positive miracles happening every day in our classrooms. We need to build upon and enhance student and staff self-esteem. We need to reinforce and support our teachers and build upon their competencies. We need to celebrate our successes. We need to have a set of fundamental principles in our lives that will guide our words, deeds, and decisions, even during times of adversity and controversy. We need to lead by example. What we say, we do!

We are in a very giving profession. We give, and we give, and we give, but we can't give what we don't have. It's impossible to be an inspirational leader on an empty spirit. We need to care for ourselves before we can care for others. We need to take the time for personal infilling and reflection so that we have the inner resources to continue to give to others. We sometimes get so caught up in the all-consuming work that we forget the importance of keeping a balance in our lives. For school principals, maintaining a balanced life between work and home is very difficult considering all the demands, expectations, and crises we face each day at school.

These unending demands and expectancies upon the time and energy of school principals begin to take their toll by creating stresses and conflicts as they try to lead their staff and community toward achieving the best for all children in their school.

The first step to managing the stress and demands of the principalship is to acknowledge the unrelenting changes, challenges, and complexities that principals face each day. Where in their busy day can principals find the time for self-care, self-reflection, and self-affirmation to keep them on the track to achieving their goals? If we are to survive as school principals in the 21st century, then we must master a new level of wisdom and skill by implementing the new three R's of school leadership—*resiliency, renewal,* and *reflection.*

Principals must develop a *resiliency* that will allow them to lead with a clear vision and purpose. Principals must be visionary leaders and establish high expectations for students, staff, and parents as a key to creating a positive school culture and to enhancing peak performance. By identifying how change creates incredible demands on their time and resources, principals will recognize that to survive as effective school leaders they must demonstrate the ability to understand and manage change. The role of the principal as an inspirational leader is to support and inspire others while at the same time monitoring and managing stress factors, thereby avoiding personal burnout.

Principals must find ways to *renew* their spirit, energy, and passion for the important work to be done so they can replenish the personal resources necessary to continue to be able to give to others of their time, energy, and leadership. Principals need to avoid burnout by keeping a balance between their professional and their personal lives.

Principals can maintain a sense of personal well-being by keeping their actions focused and aligned with their vision for their schools. To help accomplish this goal, principals need to touch the wisdom within through scheduling blocks of time within each day for silence and *reflection.*

MASTERING THE NEW THREE R'S OF SCHOOL LEADERSHIP

- RESILIENCY—The ability to recover quickly from a change or misfortune or to resume original shape after being bent, stretched, or compressed.
- RENEWAL—The act of becoming new again, of replenishing, restoring, or regaining physical or mental vigor.
- REFLECTION—The act of taking time for careful consideration, contemplation, and meditation.

The Impact of High-Stakes Accountability

I would hypothesize that the greater the emphasis on academic achievement through high-stakes accountability, the greater the gap becomes between advantaged and disadvantaged students. The main reason for this is that poor performing students do not need more pressure, they need greater attachment to the school and motivation to want to learn. Pressure by itself in this situation actually demotivates poor performing students.

—Michael Fullan

The role of the principal has changed significantly in the past few years as a result of the impact of high-stakes accountability in schools. Principals need to develop the skills to survive the changes, the school reforms, and the high-stakes accountability that schools are facing. Wave after wave of change flows over the schools, never allowing full implementation and success before the next wave of change inundates teachers and classrooms. The parade of school reforms never ends. There is always someone out there telling us how to best educate our children, again never allowing for full implementation of one reform before the next one begins. The mandates for ever-increasing standards continue to set the bar higher and higher, coupled with less and less money to help students achieve those standards. And, most important, this is the era of high-stakes accountability. Every school across America is being held to the goal of increasing test scores. Schools are being held accountable for improving test scores every year, so naturally the focus of instruction turns to test-taking skills. Many states have established rewards and sanctions systems for schools.

Those who fail to meet the standard of increasing test scores are placed on remediation plans and timelines for improvement. Failure to meet the improvement goals can then result in sanctions, where schools may be closed, principals removed, or teachers transferred. Rewards can vary from citations of excellence to financial rewards. California, in the first year of its rewards and sanctions system, rewarded teachers and principals at the highest-performing schools where significant gains were made in test scores each with personal checks for $25,000. The following year there was a budget crisis and there were no funds for high-performing schools so they just got a certificate and a simple thank you.

So as the pendulum swings toward high-stakes accountability with the focus on improving test scores, school leaders will need to find ways to improve scores and still maintain a balanced curriculum for their students. The very structure of schools and the way we do business is under scrutiny and the pressure to perform is impacting the job of the principal. If principals are to provide effective leadership during this time of high-stakes accountability, they will need to sharpen their skills of leadership and master the new three R's: resiliency, renewal, and reflection.

FRAMING THE POWER OF THE PRINCIPALSHIP

It's the action, not the fruit of the action that's important. You have to do the right thing. It may not be in your power, may not be in your time, that there'll be any fruit. But that doesn't mean you stop doing the right thing. You may never know what results come from your action. But if you do nothing, there will be no result.

—Mahatma Gandhi

To effectively utilize the power of the principalship, you must first build a framework for your leadership. Current thinking on the principalship has identified several characteristics that form the framework of sound leadership. The principal of a 21st-century school

- Does the right thing and is not just doing things right
- Recognizes teaching and learning as the main business of the school
- Inspires in others a shared vision
- Communicates the school's mission clearly and consistently to staff members, parents, and students
- Fosters standards for teaching and learning that are high and attainable
- Provides clear goals and monitors the progress of students toward meeting them
- Spends time in the classrooms interacting with students and observing teachers
- Promotes an atmosphere of trust and sharing
- Builds a good staff and makes professional development a top concern by creating a community of learners

LAYING THE FOUNDATION OF YOUR PRINCIPALSHIP

Learning is the essential fuel for the leader, the source of high-octane energy that keeps up the momentum by continually sparking new understanding, new ideas and new challenges. It is absolutely indispensable under today's conditions of rapid change and complexity. Very simply, those who do not learn, do not survive as leaders.

—William Bennis

Creating School as a Community of Learners

An important step for laying the foundation of your principalship is creating your school as a community of learners. Principals must recognize that, if they want student achievement to improve and test scores to increase, the key lies with the personal and professional growth of teachers. Help your school become a learning organization—a place of professional growth and renewal, where teachers feel a need to continue to learn, to share problems *and* successes, and to have stimulating, meaningful interactions. Such topics as homework, discipline, full inclusion, gifted programs, or retention can be the subject of informal discussions among teachers. Create a "teacher as learner" culture by formalizing the discussions through teacher readings and discussion groups of current articles and research.

With the volume of paperwork and mail that comes across the principal's desk, it is a monumental task to read or process all the essential articles and information. However, when you do find a great article on a topic that teachers should know about, share it at a staff meeting using the expert group or jigsaw methods to facilitate learning. Sharing the latest educational literature with teachers not only helps to provide them new information and research on important topics, but can also stimulate intellectual discussion, lay the foundation to support change, or clarify why several points of view are valid. Keep a lifelong learning environment at your school by creating a community of learners.

Teacher growth is closely related to pupil growth. Probably nothing within a school has more impact on students in terms of skill development, self-confidence or classroom behavior than the personal and professional growth of their teachers.

—Roland Barth

The key to effective professional growth for teachers is based on the relationships developed within the school between teacher and principal and between teacher and teacher. The quality of adult relationships will reflect the quality of instruction, the character of the school, and the achievement of students. The atmosphere of collegiality reflects a culture in which teachers and principals talk with one another, share their knowledge and skills, and help each other learn. Principals need to personally model, promote, and engage in learning if they are to build a community of learners at their school.

Here are a few simple strategies that will help principals strengthen the professional learning community at their school:

1. Since finding time is always an issue, build in time at staff meetings for reading and discussion of professional articles. It's unrealistic to assign an article on peer mediation and expect teachers to read it on their own time and come to a staff meeting ready to discuss what they've read. Instead, demonstrate that you value their time and their input by providing a brief period of sustained quiet reading during a staff meeting followed by a short staff discussion.

Divide teachers into small groups and number the paragraphs in the article. Assign each teacher in the group a number and he or she reads that paragraph in the article. Then provide a 5- to 10-minute reporting and discussion period for teachers to share the key learnings or points from their paragraph with their group at large. Everyone then gets the essence of each paragraph without having to read the entire article.

2. Hold faculty meetings in the classrooms of teachers. Start the meeting with the host teacher sharing something about his or her curriculum, effective instructional strategies, or a story about a particular success with a student.

3. Provide opportunity for cross-grade-level or interdepartmental staff discussions. Let people pair-share or discuss key ideas and concepts and brainstorm their application to the classroom. One strategy for mixing up these discussions by grade levels or departments is to use the Dance Card Partners activity (**Treasure Chest Sample #1**).

4. Promote shared leadership by giving all staff members the opportunity to be involved in the dialogue and planning of curriculum and instruction, as well as the day-to-day requirements of school life. Too often leadership of the school falls to the few who are interested. They soon burn out after years of always assuming the leadership role. To ensure that the leadership roles are shared by all members of the staff, use the Professional Responsibilities Staff Interest Survey (**Treasure Chest Sample #2**) to assess the areas in which they have an interest and then assign every staff member several responsibilities. You can avoid burning out those teachers whom you always rely on to volunteer and begin to build capacity and skill in those who are reluctant or resistant to lead.

5. Promote a voluntary after-school teachers' book club for both recreational and professional readings and discussions. Many teachers are voracious readers and would look forward to discussing their most recent book with fellow teachers. Don't look for large numbers—start with a few interested teachers and build from there.

6. Demonstrate your respect for the time and talent of your teachers by budgeting funds to release teachers to plan, write, or adapt curriculum for their grade level by providing half-day or full-day substitutes during the school year or budget a stipend for teachers to work in the summer.

7. For many teachers, the best part about working on a committee on released time is the opportunity to go off campus for lunch. It is a real perk to eat lunch out at a favorite local restaurant. During these informal lunch

TREASURE CHEST SAMPLE #1

DANCE CARD PARTNERS

Sign up a different partner for each of the four dance card slots so that your dance card is full.

	Waltz	
Twist		Tango
	Jitterbug	

TREASURE CHEST SAMPLE #2

PROFESSIONAL RESPONSIBILITIES

STAFF INTEREST SURVEY

In order to ensure that leadership responsibilities are shared among all staff members, please complete the following interest survey. Staff responsibilities require varying amounts of time. One committee may require many more hours than another, making it difficult to equate time and number. Having staff members on the same number of committees is not equitable in the amount of time required; however, there are many jobs to be done and many roles of leadership available. In order to accommodate requests and also get all the jobs done, please select five responsibilities under each section, numbering them in your priority order from 1 to 5, with 1 being your first choice.

School-Level Leadership

Priority   Responsibility

_____ Department/Grade-Level Chair
_____ School Site Council Faculty Rep
_____ School Site Council Faculty Rep Alt
_____ Communication Council Rep
_____ Communication Council Rep Alt
_____ Emergency Preparedness Committee
_____ Supply Room Committee
_____ Faculty Chairperson
_____ Xerox Committee
_____ School Calendar Committee
_____ Faculty Lounge Committee
_____ Social Committee
_____ Discipline Committee
_____ Duty Schedule Committee

Curriculum Leadership

Priority   Responsibility

_____ School Leadership Team
_____ Student Portfolio Rubrics Committee
_____ Reading Is Fundamental Committee
_____ Media Center Committee
_____ Technology Committee
_____ Special Education Committee
_____ Reading Incentive Program Committee
_____ School Safety Committee
_____ Authentic Assessment Committee
_____ Bilingual Advisory Committee
_____ Attend PTA Meetings Staff Rep
_____ Human Relations Committee
_____ Staff–Principal Advisory Committee

School-Level Leadership		*Curriculum Leadership*	
Priority	**Responsibility**	**Priority**	**Responsibility**
____	Esteem Team	____	I'd like to serve on a District Curriculum Committee: Subject area:
____	Event Chaperone		
____	Student Club Sponsor		

Please select your 1st and 2nd choice of responsibilities listed below for your part in the Emergency Preparedness Team:

____ First Aid   ____ Parent/Community   ____ Accounting

____ Sweep and Rescue   ____ Security

discussions, often some of the best ideas are shared. Also, going off campus for curriculum planning can be a positive perk. Nothing says you have to stay on campus to work—let one of the teachers or you volunteer your home for a more informal and relaxed setting.

8. Principals don't have to have all the answers. There are times you need to model that you are also a learner. You don't always have to be the leader of staff development. Sometimes allow teachers to represent you at trainings or inservices and use the free time to stay at school and visit classrooms. When the teachers return to school and present the information at a staff inservice, you join the teachers as a learner.

HOLDING A GRAND CONVERSATION

Values are the foundation of our character and of our confidence. A person who does not know what he stands for or what he should stand for will never enjoy true happiness and success.

—Lionel Kendrick

As instructional leaders, principals need to be visionaries, set goals, and lead the way. Goal setting is an important component in clarifying our values and beliefs. If teachers have a clear vision of where they're going, they're more likely to get there and more likely to effectively communicate it to parents. As school administrators, we can work with teachers to write goals in the personal and professional growth areas.

Build a positive, professional relationship with teachers by listening to what they have to say. But, when do you ever have time to just sit and talk with each of your teachers about their values, beliefs, and practices as a teacher?

Begin with a *grand conversation* with teachers. In early fall, schedule a roving substitute to release teachers for a 45-minute to 1-hour meeting with you. Use this time for a grand conversation in which you both share your beliefs and values about education and share personal anecdotes about why you chose this profession. Use this time to make connections and get to know each other at a more personal level. It's the personal stories that connect people.

You can ask teachers to bring to the conversation their professional growth goals and samples of student work as points for discussion. Let them know that this grand conversation is not tied to the evaluation process but is just an opportunity for professional dialogue about teaching and setting personal goals for the year. Teachers will appreciate having your undivided attention and will be excited about sharing what goes on in their classrooms. Once the concept of annual grand conversations is embedded as part of your school culture, you can begin to use the time to guide and monitor curriculum implementation and improve instructional strategies.

The principal can control the conversation by focusing on a specific curriculum area or instructional strategy. You can ask teachers to bring specific lesson plans and sample student work to the conversation that reflect implementation of new curriculum or instructional strategies by asking teachers to write classroom goals that support the school's priority curriculum areas. By having teachers define specific objectives and a time line for completion, as principals we can monitor progress through classroom observations or mid-year planning conferences (February–March) to informally assess progress, give assistance, or provide encouragement or applause for work well done.

An important step in goal setting is often omitted when we fail to celebrate our successes. A word of appreciation or a note written at the end of the year acknowledging growth, accomplishments, and successes is greatly appreciated and provides value, meaning, and closure to the goal-setting process.

MASTERING RESILIENCY

The First Step—Building a Climate of Caring

The Principal's Role as Climate Creator

> *We all need it. The deepest principle in human nature is the craving to be appreciated.*
>
> —William James

As principals we are the *climate creators* in our schools. We have the power to consciously create the kind of climate or environment we want for our schools.

• Our daily moods create the weather in our school and classrooms. Our challenge, then, is to be aware of how we can create a positive climate by our very actions and responses. Others look to us for leadership and direction. What we say and do has a tremendous influence on the feeling tone of the school. It can place a heavy responsibility on the principal's shoulders to always "be up," but if we give in to our negative feelings and reactions it will reflect to our staff.

• Our personal approach to students, staff, and parents can have a significant impact on the lives of others. Haim Ginott points out, "We possess the power to make a teacher's life miserable or joyous. We possess the power to humiliate or humor, to hurt or heal. In all situations it is *our response* that decides whether a crisis will be escalated or de-escalated, or a person humanized or de-humanized." As principals, whether we're working with students, staff, or parents, we have the power to become a tool of torture or an instrument of inspiration. We can encourage or discourage, criticize or praise, set low expectations or inspire to a higher level of excellence.

• As principals, we need to recognize the impact we have in creating our school's climate and accept the responsibility that comes with affecting others with our moods and reactions.

In the time we have, it is surely our duty to do all the good we can to all the people we can in all the ways we can.

—William Barclay

Teacher Pick-Me-Ups: Some Quick Tips for Reinforcing Your Staff Throughout the Year

• Provide treats from the principal in the teacher's lounge. Be sure and take credit—a signed card and a compliment lets them know it's from you.

• When a teacher has had a particularly rough day and you've been impressed with how well he or she has handled it, try a different but simple way of saying thank you or giving praise for a job well done. While the teacher is at school, call home during the day and leave a positive message on his or her answering machine. Then, when that teacher gets home, your positive comments are waiting to be heard. Not only will the teacher be surprised when he or she gets home but that teacher's supportive family also gets to share in the praise.

• Compliment a teacher where all can see. Let him or her arrive at school and find a positive comment from the principal written on the blackboard.

• Let the teacher know you really valued what he or she did enough to send a copy of the letter of appreciation you wrote to the superintendent. Add "cc: Superintendent" at the bottom of the letter.

• Use candy-grams as a great reinforcement and morale builder for your teachers. Visit your local supermarket and buy a variety of candy bars using the guide in Treasure Chest Sample #3. It's a fun way to recognize the efforts of teachers during times of stress by dropping a candy bar and note in their boxes.

TREASURE CHEST SAMPLE #3

CANDY-GRAMS

I "**MINT**" to tell you how much I appreciate all that you do. Keep up the work!	You're a real "**STAR**" at our school! Thanks for your "**BURST**" of good energy! Your teaching is out of this world!
We appreciate you "**BEARY**" much! Thanks for making our school great!	Thanks for helping us through the "**CRUNCH**"!
We really appreciate the "**MOUNDS**" of work you do. Thanks for a great job!	You "**SKOR**" high in our book! You're terrific!
An "**APPLE**" a day will brighten your way. We appreciate appreciate the excellent teaching we see each day.	Extra! Extra! Read All About It! We the "**EXTRA**" effort you put in your day!
You're the greatest—"**BAR NONE**"!	We couldn't survive a "**SOLITARY**" day without you on our staff!
You deserve an extra "**PAY DAY**"!	Thanks for a "**CRACKER JACK**" job
You deserve a "**KISS**"! Thanks for all you do!	Thank you for helping us "**NOW AND**" we hope to see you "**LATER**"—Thanks for being our sub.
You've been a "**LIFE SAVER**"! Thanks for being our sub.	

Birthday Greetings

Birthdays are a special day for each and every employee on your staff. A birthday greeting from the principal is greatly appreciated and helps build that feeling that "I'm important." Be sure to include a handwritten note for that personal touch.

- Don't forget summer birthdays. You can celebrate half-birthdays for July and August birthdays by sending a card on the date of their birthday in January for July birthdays and in February for August birthdays. Teachers with July and August birthdays are always surprised to get a half-birthday card.

- Listing staff birthdays in the weekly calendar or providing staff a list of birthdays for the year helps others celebrate the day also.

- Each month, celebrate all staff birthdays at one time with special treats in the teacher's lounge at recess or refreshments right before your staff meeting.

Assessing School Climate

What we want for your children . . . we should want for their teachers; that schools be places of learning for both of them, and that such learning be suffused with excitement, engagement, passion, challenge, creativity and joy.

—Andy Hargreaves

Every school has its own culture with traditions, celebrations, and programs that are unique to that school. If the principal has been at that school for any length of time, the climate of the school will reflect the leadership style of the principal. When there is a new principal assigned to a school, whether an experienced principal or one new to the profession, the climate and culture of the school must be determined. The new principal must determine the traditions, sacred cows, and programs that are an essential part of the culture of that school before trying to implement any changes. One of the biggest mistakes a new principal to a school makes is to initiate changes without assessing the culture and climate of the school.

Simple assessment tools that determine staff morale and attitudes can help us keep our finger on the pulse of our school climate, thereby enabling us to create a climate of positive self-esteem. Use the assessment tool in Treasure Chest Sample #4—Parent–School Climate Questionnaire—to measure the climate at your school. Identify where the biggest discrepancies exist and determine the steps you can take to narrow the gap between the actual and the ideal. Use the same tool with staff and parents and then reflect on where your perceptions and ratings match theirs. Want to measure staff morale? Use the Assessment of Staff Morale in Treasure Chest Sample #5 to identify issues of staff morale and cooperation.

Measurement is the first step that leads to control and eventually to improvement. If you can't measure something, you can't understand it. If you can't understand it, you can't control it. If you can't control it, you can't improve it.

—H. James Harrington

TREASURE CHEST SAMPLE #4

PARENT–SCHOOL CLIMATE QUESTIONNAIRE

For each of the 10 school climate dimensions described below, place an **A** for actual *above* the number that indicates your assessment of the school's current position on that dimension and an **I** for ideal *below* the number that indicates your choice where the school should ideally be on this dimension.

1. Warmth and support. The feeling that friendliness is a valued norm in the school and that staff and parents trust one another and offer support to one another. The feeling that good relationships prevail in the school environment.

There is no warmth and support in the school.	Warmth and support are very characteristic of the school.

1　2　3　4　5　6　7　8　9　10

2. Responsibility. Staff and parents share responsibility to achieve their part of the school's goals; the degree to which home and school share responsibility in the education of children.

No responsibility is shared in the school.	There is a great emphasis on sharing responsibility in the school.

1　2　3　4　5　6　7　8　9　10

3. Standards. The school emphasizes quality performance and outstanding achievement. The degree to which the staff and parents feel the school is setting challenging goals and communicating these goals and performance expectations to the community.

Standards are very low or nonexistent and the community is unaware of what they are.	High challenging standards and achievement are evident and are communicated to the school community.

1　2　3　4　5　6　7　8　9　10

4. Rewards. The degree to which staff members feel that they are being recognized and rewarded for their efforts and dedication to achieving school excellence. The degree that staff and parents feel valued and appreciated for their involvement and contributions to the school.

Staff and parents are ignored or their contributions go unrecognized or unrewarded.	Staff and parents are valued and rewarded positively.

1　2　3　4　5　6　7　8　9　10

5. *Organizational clarity*. The feeling among members of the school community that things are well-organized and school goals are clearly defined rather than being disorderly, confused, or chaotic.

The school is disorderly, confused, and chaotic.	The school is well-organized, with clearly defined goals.

1   2   3   4   5   6   7   8   9   10

6. *Communication*. The school promotes two-way communication by providing formal and informal opportunities for parents and staff to communicate on student progress, as well as on school policies, goals, and activities. School provides translation to assist non-English-speaking parents.

There is sporadic, ineffective communication among school community. Parents are unsure of school's goals or child's progress.	There is effective, clear communication with a variety of opportunities for two-way communication.

1   2   3   4   5   6   7   8   9   10

7. *Shared Decision Making*. The school encourages the inclusion of staff, parents, and community members in all decision-making and advisory committees. There is shared decision making when setting school goals and developing or evaluating programs, policies, or performance data. Parent participation is promoted and staff treats parent concerns with respect and demonstrates genuine interest in developing solutions.

Decisions are made by principal or a few staff members. Parent participation and input are seen as meddling by staff. Parent opinions are not valued or respected.	All members of the school community have an opportunity for input in decisions affecting school and students. Parent input is highly valued and seen as essential to student success.

1   2   3   4   5   6   7   8   9   10

8. *Parent–School Partnership*. School encourages parent volunteers and provides volunteer training. Parents unable to volunteer in classroom are given options for helping in other ways. School shows appreciation for parents' participation and values their diverse contributions. School reaches out to all families, including reluctant parents, recognizing the variety of parenting traditions and practices within the community's cultural and religious diversity.

(Continued)

(Continued)

Parent help is seen as a threat and not welcomed in classrooms. Most parents are viewed as not capable or able to learn.	Parent involvement is viewed as valuable and staff pursues a variety of ways to involve all parents. Parent contributions are rewarded and diversity valued.

1   2   3   4   5   6   7   8   9   10

9. Community Collaboration. The school pursues partnerships with local businesses and service groups in order to advance student learning and assist school and families. Student participation in community service is encouraged. School disseminates information to the school community, including those without school-age children, regarding school programs and performance.

Staff sees its role as the educators and resists outside influences. Little effort is made to establish business partnerships or communicate with the community.	School reaches beyond schoolhouse doors, promoting community partnerships and collaborations. Effective communications help build community pride in local school.

1   2   3   4   5   6   7   8   9   10

10. Leadership. The willingness of the staff and parents to accept leadership and direction from qualified others. As needs for leadership arise, staff and parents feel free to take leadership roles and are rewarded for successful leadership. Leadership is based on expertise. The school is not dominated by, or dependent on, one or two individuals.

Leadership is not rewarded; school is dominated by a few based on power and not expertise. People resist leadership attempts.	Staff and parents share a variety of leadership roles based on expertise.

1   2   3   4   5   6   7   8   9   10

Adapted with permission from Bob Reasoner.

High Visibility

Example is not the main thing in influencing others. It is the only thing.

—Albert Schweitzer

High visibility as a principal can help build trust and confidence that you are a knowledgeable school leader. If teachers are working hard and feel they

---

TREASURE CHEST SAMPLE #5

ASSESSMENT OF STAFF MORALE

In front of each statement place the number of the phrase that best describes how true the statement is for the teachers in your school.

1 = True for less than 30% of the staff
2 = True for 30%–60%
3 = True for 60%–90%
4 = True for 90%–100%

_____ 1. Teachers on the staff are in close agreement on discipline standards.

_____ 2. Teachers are clear about what is expected of them.

_____ 3. Procedures to be followed are well defined.

_____ 4. Classroom observations by principal are welcomed.

_____ 5. The staff displays trust in their administrator.

_____ 6. Teachers accept weaknesses pointed out to them without making excuses.

_____ 7. Inservice sessions are received positively.

_____ 8. Teachers openly seek help from others on the staff.

_____ 9. Staff members feel free to use their own individual teaching styles.

_____ 10. Teachers readily use new materials and try new approaches to improve teaching skills.

_____ 11. Staff members enjoy being together.

_____ 12. Teachers are supportive of one another rather than being critical of others.

_____ 13. Materials and ideas are freely shared.

_____ 14. Genuine concern is expressed for others.

_____ 15. The staff works as a cohesive group rather than in factions.

_____ 16. The staff is in agreement on the kind of school it wants to achieve.

_____ 17. Teachers set individual goals that support a common purpose.

_____ 18. There is a shared feeling of responsibility for the total school program.

_____ 19. Staff members put forth extra effort to correct problems identified by others.

_____ 20. The personal goals set each year are carefully selected to address identified needs.

_____ 21. Teachers capitalize on the unique talents and skills of other staff members.

_____ 22. Teachers monitor student growth to assess their own effectiveness and make adjustments accordingly.

_____ 23. Feedback from other staff members is used to assess personal effectiveness.

_____ 24. Staff members are convinced they can make significant improvements in student achievement.

_____ 25. Staff members talk about their enjoyment of teaching and their great sense of satisfaction.

Reprinted with permission from Bob Reasoner.

are doing a good job, they want their principal to know. High visibility gives the staff the knowledge that you have been in their classrooms frequently enough to know that they are doing a good job. We lead by our example. We are judged not by what we say but by what we do.

• The one trait that makes for an exceptional principal is the ability to manage by walking around (MBWA). Managing by presence means that you have high visibility—your presence is evident everywhere in the school. You're seen circulating around the school every day—in classrooms, the line-up area, playground, bus-loading area, dismissal area—wherever teachers, parents, and students gather.

• MBWA needs to become a habit. Once you've made it part of your daily routine, you will find it is an effective way of keeping your finger on the climate and pulse of your school. You will be able to nip problems in the bud, gain the respect of students who see you everywhere, and increase your credibility with parents and you will know what's happening in your school.

• We expect our teachers to be up and walking around their classrooms helping students and not to be sitting behind their desks. The same holds true for principals. We cannot remain desk bound and be effective. High visibility and presence will enhance our credibility and reassure teachers, parents, and students that we are effective and knowledgeable school leaders.

Principal Accessibility

The successful principal makes sure that he or she remains accessible to teachers. Teachers need to have easy access to their principal to communicate their concerns and problems.

• The five most common words heard by a principal are "Have you got a minute?" And of course, it's never just a minute! Teachers know you are busy but they still demand a piece of your time. Some days it just seems as if everyone wants a piece of your time and it feels as if you don't have enough pieces to go around.

• Accessibility before and after school, as well as in the teacher's lounge at lunch and recess, is crucial. The open-door policy is time consuming but important to good communication. Make sure that your door is always open just before school begins and right after school gets out, so teachers can just pop in for a brief chat. If it seems like your chat is becoming a discussion, then set a time to meet later.

• By being accessible to teachers in the lounge at recess or at lunch time, many small problems can be addressed or resolved in a few minutes, thereby preventing them from becoming full-blown problems later. Being available to teachers during their free time at recess or lunch can often save you time in the long run. These informal mini-conferences can be effective in helping to reach quick decisions or solutions because they are within the time frame of the recess. If teachers were to stop by your office or make an appointment to discuss the problem, it might take considerably longer to resolve.

Inspirational Messages

Principals can help motivate and inspire their staff by sharing inspirational messages. Keep your eyes open for motivational messages that you might come across in professional journals, newspapers, magazines, and, yes, even in Dear Abby. Look for poems, sayings, or quotes that help to honor the teaching profession and focus on the value of education. Have an inspirational quote of the day or week and post it in the office where everyone can see it. Reproduce these messages and share them with teachers and parents to inspire and reinforce the positive impact that teachers can have on children's lives. Powerful words about the importance of teaching in our society can inspire teachers and motivate them to reach out to and touch their students' lives. One example of an inspirational quote highlighting the impact a teacher can have on a student's life is the following tribute to a teacher written from a student's point of view:

TRIBUTE TO A TEACHER

To a special person in my life. Thank you for reaching deep into the corners of my being and seeing a part of me I did not know existed and others never saw. Thank you for your faith in my abilities and my future even when I did not believe. Thank you for sharing a part of your humanity and for the spark that glows warmly inside of me. Thank you. Your influence is etched in my soul forever. *From a student.*

—Dr. Susan Parks

Caring and Sharing

During times of personal illness or tragedy in a teacher's family or special times of celebration, it is important to show our concern and caring.

• When there is a bereavement or personal tragedy in the teacher's family, make a phone call, visit, or send flowers to show that you care and are thinking of them. A card with a personal note of compassion and caring is greatly appreciated at a later date.

• When a teacher is hospitalized, find time to send a potted plant or make a personal visit. Teachers are always surprised to see you at the hospital but really appreciate and value the time you took to come. Follow-up cards and phone calls are always appreciated by teachers.

• Upon the birth of a new baby, instead of sending flowers, give the new baby his or her first book with a personal dedication inside.

Compassionate Counselors

Our chief want is someone who will inspire us to be what we know we can be.

—Ralph Waldo Emerson

People want their leaders to behave with compassion. The ability to empathize, to put one's self in another's shoes, is an essential characteristic of an educational leader.

• Principals spend a considerable part of their day engaged in an activity for which most of us have not had an inservice, course, or training—counseling students, staff, and parents. Within our day we may counsel a student regarding a discipline problem, a teacher about an alcoholic spouse, or a parent with a parenting problem. As an authority figure in the school, and by our very accessibility, we sometimes find ourselves in the position of confidant and counselor for staff members and parents who may be experiencing personal problems in their lives. Staff members often share personal information about their lives that we'd really prefer not to know. Often we are the one they turn to in times of personal crisis or turmoil. They seek us out as a confidant—someone they believe can help them by listening, giving advice, or providing assistance or resources.

• We must always take the position of advocating what is best for children, even when it places us in conflict with a parent or colleague. We can demonstrate our compassion by helping the staff focus on the importance of seeing the good in *all* children and especially the value of seeing the good in the difficult, disruptive child.

Grief Counselor

As school principals we are sometimes called upon in times of personal loss. When a student, staff member, or parent at our school has lost a loved one, that person often seeks out the principal for support and counseling. It never entered many principals' minds that they would have to deal with death as part of the job. We need to be aware that sometime in our career we will be called upon to provide grief counseling to a student, parent, or staff member who has lost a loved one. We may even have to deal with the death of a student or staff member and everyone will turn to the principal for guidance and leadership. We will observe that people grieve in a wide variety of ways. We may be sought out in our leadership role in times of death and grieving and be asked to attend or speak at a funeral.

Longevity Recognition

It is important to recognize those teachers and educators who have dedicated their lives to children and served our schools over a long period of time.

• We need to honor all employees for their years of service in the school district. Such recognition can help build teacher pride and self-esteem and serve to model the importance of length of service to those teachers new to the profession.

• All employee groups including teachers, teacher assistants, cafeteria workers, clerical staff, and custodians should also be recognized for their length of service.

• You may want to schedule a special meeting where you or the superintendent present some form of recognition such as longevity pins, engraved miniature school bells, or certificates of appreciation. Include a special student performance that will add special meaning for those being honored. Invite the middle school or high school choir to perform, giving the elementary teachers the opportunity to see some of their former students perform.

The Second Step—Building a Climate of Commitment

We Can and Do Make a Difference!

There is no more noble occupation in the world than to assist another human being—to help someone succeed.

—Alan Loy McGinnis

Many of us entered education because we believed we could make a difference in children's lives. As educators, we cherish and value the process of education. From our own childhood we can remember teachers who took us by the hand and guided our steps, who gave us support and enhanced our image of ourselves, and who gave us the challenge to think for ourselves. For many of us school represents the transition from ignorance to knowledge, innocence to awareness, and childhood to maturity. As school administrators, we believe there is no greater path to knowledge and understanding. Therefore, we need to celebrate our profession and honor those dedicated teachers with whom we work by affirming that as educators we *can* and we *do* make a difference in children's lives.

Maintaining High Expectations

Whether you think you can or think you can't, you're right.

—Henry Ford

As the climate creators at our schools, we can create a climate of high expectations and performance. Our actions, more than our words, will establish the model of what we expect from others. We need to recognize the power of our expectations. What we expect is often what we get. Have a clear vision for your school and communicate it repeatedly to your students, staff, and parents in words and deeds. Look for ways to help others achieve your vision and then celebrate when your goals have been reached.

Enabling Teachers to Teach and Students to Learn

• As administrators, our focus should be *to enable teachers to teach and students to learn*. We need to examine how our decisions impact classrooms and instruction. Brainstorm ideas for reducing interruptions during instructional times, such as announcements over the intercom and requesting students be sent to the office.

• Provide your staff with lots of positive feedback when they rise to meet your expectations. Let them know you appreciate the extra effort it took to achieve the results. Recognition of a teacher's efforts and growth can be a strong motivator for further achievement.

• Look for ways to make the teacher's job easier by managing the school to limit classroom interruptions and avoiding voluminous or unnecessary paperwork whenever possible. Help them work smarter—not harder.

Celebrating Our Achievements and Successes!

In an era of catastrophic budget problems, declining public support, increasingly diverse student populations, school bashing by the media, and a general doom-and-gloom atmosphere, teacher morale can be devastated. It is crucial that we, as instructional leaders, help our teachers focus on their positive achievements and successes. We need to celebrate and compliment them when they do well. Let people know they've often achieved miracles, even under the most trying conditions and difficult restraints. Keep the positives in the forefront!

RAISE THE PRAISE!

MINIMIZE THE CRITICIZE!

Principal's Advisory Committee

Set up a principal's advisory committee to meet with you periodically to give you suggestions or feedback. Committee members should be able to meet on short notice so you can get input when you have to make a quick decision. Be sure to balance the committee with your supporters as well as your critics. When a serious school problem arises it can also serve as an informal problem-solving group that can resolve the issue before it becomes formalized into a grievance. It's important to keep union issues out of this committee; otherwise, you end up with your own mini-negotiations group. Keep it in the informal problem-solving mode.

Marketing Your School

The price of success is hard work, dedication to the job at hand, and the determination that whether we win or lose, we have applied the best of ourselves to the task at hand.

—Vince Lombardi

It is essential in today's educational climate that school principals look for ways to enhance the public image of their school in the community. We need to understand that schools shouldn't be talking about public relations but about public relationships. Effective principals recognize the importance of marketing their schools and establishing relationships with their parents and community. Parents are one of your strongest allies in marketing your school. Parents love to brag about their children, their teachers, and your school. So give them something to brag about.

Marketing your school is the intentional planning of ways to tell your school's story to the community it serves. Here are some ideas for marketing your school:

• Develop a marketing plan for reaching all segments of your school community. People tend to believe what they read in the newspaper so give them something good to read about. Your local newspaper can be an important source for information about your school.

• Make your own video or slide show telling the story about your school for parent check-out and presentation in the community. A picture speaks a thousand words.

• Take every opportunity to write articles about special school events or activities. Be sure to include lots of photos of teachers and kids. Have your PTA board select a parent to handle publicity or photos for you. Utilize clip art to provide professional illustrations for your parent communications. You can create sharp, attractive flyers and newsletters with clip art and the copy machine or special computer programs. The professional presentation of your curriculum programs, written materials, or parent handbooks can go a long way to projecting a positive image to your community.

• Speak at local community service groups such as Rotary, Lions, or the Chamber of Commerce and tell them the good things that are happening in your school. Invite a teacher to join you to say a few words about your school.

• Prepare a school brag sheet that highlights the exceptional programs at your school. List any honors or special awards the school or staff has received. Hand out the brag sheet to new or prospective parents as well as the local realty companies.

• Build a relationship with the local newspaper reporter. Invite the reporter for an escorted school tour. Send the reporter your monthly school events calendar or call once a month with possible school or classroom news stories.

The Third Step—Building a Climate of Belonging

Reducing Teacher Isolation

> *You quietly get the job done, and you do so with incredible dedication, perseverance, and dignity in an environment of steadily diminishing resources and escalating criticism of schools. Why do you do it? I believe the answer is very simple. You love children. You want to help give children the best possible start in life.*

—Nancy Keenan

Teaching is a very isolated profession. Teachers have limited contacts with other adults during the day. School principals can use a variety of strategies to facilitate teacher interaction and intellectual stimulation. Encourage teachers to work and plan together and then provide them many opportunities for collaboration.

• Use staff meetings for grade-level articulation meetings in which teachers meet and discuss curriculum topics, proposed educational reforms, and changes.

• Provide interactive tasks at staff meetings that encourage cooperation and engage teachers in discussing school philosophy and goals. Use articles from professional magazines and brainstorm with expert groups to generate thinking and discussion.

• Have a share fair where everyone shares at a staff meeting one successful activity or lesson in a subject area or your school's curriculum priority.

Escorted School Tours

> *Schools are like a jigsaw puzzle. Each edge piece of the puzzle interlocks with two others to form the puzzle's framework and give structure and support to the puzzle as a whole. Each piece has a unique design and cut that ensures just the right place to fit within the puzzle. Each morning, staff members form the edge pieces that interlock to create a safe environment and give support to one another and the whole. Each morning, they provide just the "right place" for every student to fit safely and securely. The staff members are strength and stability, and like the edge pieces, they do not stand alone in this responsibility. There are always others to support and assist, ensuring that every student has a place.*

—Karen Hegeman

One of the joys of being the principal is the wonderful lift we get when we visit classrooms. Teachers seldom get a chance to see what goes on in their colleagues' classrooms due to their own isolation in the classroom. One of the best ways to inservice your staff about your school is to take individual teachers on a school tour. What better way for them to see what goes on in other classrooms, grade levels, and departments? Since teachers' view of the school is usually limited to their own classroom, the escorted tour can give teachers the big picture of the school. The school tour is a wonderful way to share the joy of our job with our teachers!

• At elementary school, start with kindergarten and move up through the grades to see an overview of curriculum continuity and expectations throughout the school. Secondary teachers should have the chance to see other teachers in their department, if not the whole school. The one-on-one tour provides you the opportunity to individualize and inservice each teacher by using the teachable moment, pointing out where appropriate a specific classroom management technique or instructional strategy being observed. Point Out Positives Only!

• Be sure to visit *every* classroom and program as part of your walk-through. Teachers tend to think that everyone else teaches like they do. They are often amazed to see that not every classroom is like theirs. Teachers need to see what you see when you walk through classrooms. They need to see the great classrooms as well as the not-so-great classrooms. If you have one or two not-so-great teachers, the teacher-escorted tours can put subtle pressure on them to improve since they may not want to look not-so-great when their colleagues visit their classrooms.

• Schedule any new staff members early in the fall as part of acclimating them to your school campus and special programs. This can be especially helpful to new teachers as a perfect orientation to your school.

• Explore ways to provide release time for the tour—be creative! Have teachers buddy-up classes or use any extra substitute time to release teachers for their tour.

• The escorted school tour can be one of the most important team-building activities and positive builders of teacher self-esteem that you can do! Visiting classrooms is one of the most rewarding parts of a principal's job and it's a pleasure to share that joy with a colleague. The payoff with teachers is powerful!

Celebrating the Day of the Teacher

One of the best ideas for recognizing teachers on Day of the Teacher is to invite parents and students to send notes of appreciation to teachers to your office prior to that day. Collect the notes and organize them in individual remembrance books and present them to the teachers in a special ceremony on Day of the Teacher. The book of affirmations will provide teachers memories they will cherish a lifetime. The letter sent home to parents requesting letters of appreciation is found in Day of the Teacher—Remembrance Book (Treasure Chest Sample #6).

• Arrange for a school or parent group to place a flower and a note or card of appreciation on each teacher's desk upon his or her arrival in the morning.

• Arrange for your parent organization room mothers to provide a special box lunch or potluck lunch for the day.

• A special recognition assembly could include students reading essays, student council banners (Our Teachers Have Class! or Teaching Is the Best Job There Is!), special choir music, or even the mayor addressing the student body on the importance of an education.

TREASURE CHEST SAMPLE #6

DAY OF THE TEACHER
REMEMBRANCE BOOK PARENT MEMO

It has long been clear to me that teaching is at once the most difficult and the most honorable of professions. We have all been touched by the example, guidance, and motivation of a teacher whose often reluctant pupil we were. We can each recall a moment of insight or truth when caught in the act of learning. None of us owe larger debts for whatever we may have become, for whatever we may have been able to accomplish, than we owe to teachers in our past lives whose total devotion to young people and their discipline has been their chief reward and the reason we honor teachers and the teaching profession.

—William Friday

Dear Parents:

May 10 has been designated as Day of the Teacher. This tradition has its roots in the Spanish custom of "El Dia de la Maestra" and has been celebrated in California for the last 25 years.

At Star Vista School, we are planning several activities to recognize our teachers. Throughout the week, our wonderful PTA will provide special snacks and food during recess and lunch. Our staff really appreciate the ongoing, year-round support of parents and community members. Your praise and comments of encouragement inspire them to continue to provide a quality educational program for all the children in their class.

One of the greatest gifts for a teacher are words of appreciation. Teachers really appreciate it when students or parents take the time to write a note of thanks. This year I would like to ask your help to create a special memento for each of the teachers. As a gesture of appreciation for their hard work and dedication to your child, please write a letter of thanks. I am including a piece of blank stationary for you and your child to write a letter to your child's teacher and illustrate it—an expression of thanks, or to share memories, anecdotes, or personal thoughts. I've also enclosed an extra sheet if you would like to write a letter to one of our wonderful specialist support staff: media center teacher, school psychologist, art lab teacher, speech teacher, music teacher, reading lab teacher, or our resource specialist teacher. Additional letter forms are available in the office if you would like to write additional notes of appreciation to any of the wonderful teachers and specialist staff at our school.

I will then bind the letters for each teacher together and create an individual teacher remembrance book. I hope to present the remembrance books as a surprise, so please help keep the request and letter a secret. Please be sure that your letter is addressed to a specific teacher so that I may place the letters in the correct teacher's book. Hopefully you will have time over the Spring Break to write your letters. The letters can be returned anytime after April 17. It would be great if you or your child could return the letter directly to the special box in the school office no later than Wednesday, May 3. I will then have the time needed to prepare each book for presentation on Wednesday, May 10, the Day of the Teacher. Thanks for your help in making this celebration a special one!

Slide Show—School Video Presentation

• Add that special touch at your fall Back-to-School Night presentation. Introduce your staff members to the parents by developing a slide show of your staff.

• With today's sure-shot cameras, putting a slide show together is relatively simple. A specially prepared tape of beautiful background music (Pachabel's Canon in D or Danny Wright CDs) can add a professional touch to your presentation. You can narrate the slide show and introduce each staff member as their picture appears.

• Make sure each adult is photographed with a child, preferably with a hug or their arms around each other. When you see photos of teachers and kids with their arms around each other, it communicates that here is a warm, caring environment for children. Seeing their children up on the screen is always a sure-fire hit with parents. Pictures are tied to egos and the slide show can be an effective way to build parent pride and enhance teacher self-esteem. They say a picture is worth a thousand words and it's true.

• Video can be a wonderful and easy way to communicate what's happening at your school in the most visual way—*live action*. Prepare a video presentation of your school to show parents and community members your school successes. What better message can you send your parents about the warm, caring relationship that exists between teacher and child at your school than with an inspirational and touching slide show or video presentation.

The Fourth Step—Building a Climate of Safety

Making School a Safe Place

> *A mind that does not feel safe will never step out of its ignorance.*
>
> —Noah benShea

It is important to create a safe and comfortable environment in which students and teachers feel protected and secure. Schools need to address the safety concerns of teachers, which vary greatly depending on school location and community issues. Safety issues, such as where can I park my car safely or how late after school can I work alone in my classroom, are key factors in teacher morale. In this era of uncertainty and unknown dangers, schools are especially vulnerable targets for violence and terrorism.

• You need more than a sign saying that "Visitors Must Report to the Office." Staff, students, and parents need to be reassured that their school has a comprehensive plan for dealing with any kind of emergency, especially for an intruder on campus. Be prepared to handle an emergency before it happens!

• Establish a *school security committee* drawn primarily from the school's staff, including two or three parents. This committee would have the responsibility for assessing any potential dangers for your school, contacting local agencies and organizations for advice and help, and drawing up a security plan for the school.

Schoolwide Discipline Plan

If you want to get the best out of a man, you must look for the best that is in him.

—Bernard Haldane

Establish a schoolwide discipline plan. Establish a discipline committee to determine the school's standards and procedures. Inservice staff and students on conflict management, conflict resolution, or peer mediation strategies. Have each teacher complete a classroom behavior management plan (Treasure Chest Sample #7) with a copy on file in the principal's office and one placed in the substitute teacher's folder. That way you have a copy of the plan for when students are sent to your office for discipline and you know which steps have been followed. The substitute gets the third copy so there are no questions about the rules and rewards in the classroom, eliminating a "get the sub" attitude among students.

A Tip for Handling Students Sent to Your Office for Discipline

Often students are sent to your office for discipline and you are out in classrooms or a meeting and are not immediately available. In many cases students will just sit in the office area until you return and are ready to see them. It's not much of a negative consequence for the student who gets to sit and watch all the exciting things going on in the office. Therefore, students need to be actively involved in reflecting on why they were sent to the office. The Discipline Problem-Solving Record Card (Treasure Chest Sample #8) can provide just that activity. While waiting to see you, students can complete the following form. Review the record card before interviewing the student. Sometimes you just might get information that you wouldn't have discovered in an oral interview. The record card can also be a helpful tool in dealing with difficult parents who challenge your decision regarding consequences. When the parent challenges you and says, "My child would never do that!" you can show them the record card, which provides black-and-white documentation, in the student's own handwriting, of their admission of guilt.

TREASURE CHEST SAMPLE #7

SAMPLE ELEMENTARY CLASSROOM
BEHAVIOR MANAGEMENT PLAN

Please complete the steps in your Classroom Behavior Management Plan. Please make three copies: one for you, one for the substitute folder, and one for the principal's file.

Teacher: Joy Goals   **Grade: 4**

A. The five major rules in my classroom are
    1. Respect yourself and others
    2. We are a "hands-off" school! Keep your hands, feet, and objects to yourself
    3. Follow directions and clean up after yourself
    4. Listen carefully and work with quiet voices
    5. Make your own responsible choices

B. The sequence of consequences in my classroom is
    1. Verbal reminder or warning
    2. Name on behavior chart or yellow card pulled
    3. Loss of recess time or red card pulled
    4. Note sent home to parents or phone call home
    5. Parent conference scheduled
    6. Sent to principal's office

C. I use the following positive reinforcement techniques:
    Individual—Verbal praise, awards, stickers, VIP of the Week award, daily awards, weekly book drawing (they get a ticket for the drawing each day if no card is pulled or step 3 is not necessary), positive phone calls, or notes home

    Small Group—Super Table award, Monthly Lunch Bunch for 100% homework completed

    Whole Class—Dragon Puzzle points earned for each piece of puzzle for positive class behavior

---

Principal's Report Card

As principals, we need feedback from our staff as to our effectiveness as a school leader. Design a report card that gives the staff an opportunity to evaluate your services as their principal. Avoid a lengthy form for soliciting input. A simple but effective form can include three statements, *Do More, Do Less, Continue,* and a space after each for teacher input. Distribute the principal's report card to the staff and make sure it is anonymous to ensure honest input. When you tally the results you will be surprised at how well the report card helps build and strengthen rapport with the staff. Share the results with them. You might even want to draw up a plan of action in response to their input and share that plan with your staff. They will be impressed with your responsiveness to their evaluation and appreciate your willingness to solicit their input on becoming a more effective principal.

TREASURE CHEST SAMPLE #8

DISCIPLINE PROBLEM-SOLVING RECORD CARD

Student Name:

Date:

Names of those involved:

Where did this happen?

Did anyone see what happened? Who?

What happened?

How do you feel about what happened?

How do you think the other person feels?

Why do you think he or she feels that way?

List two ways you could have solved this problem or something you could have done so that it would not have happened.

1.

2.

Student Signature: _____

Monitoring Staff Stress Levels

It's important to keep your finger on the stress level of teachers and see what you can do to enable teachers to teach and students to learn. Staff meetings can be a good indicator of teacher stress levels. Here are several ideas for your staff meetings to help relieve the stress and build a climate of support and caring:

• Use music to add excitement to your staff meetings. As teachers enter the staff meeting, have songs like "YMCA" by the Village People, "I Will Survive" by Gloria Gaynor, or "Let's Twist Again" by Chubby Checker. These are favorites at any party and will get the staff meeting off to a fun start.

• Here's a great stress reliever when the staff is getting uptight and difficult. Go to a party store and buy rolls of those party streamers you throw at a ship's sailing or New Year's Eve parties. Have dozens of them sitting out on tables when the teachers enter the meeting. Put on great dance music, like a Brazilian samba or the latest dance hit, and people will start dancing around and throwing the streamers at each other. Soon they are laughing and having fun and stress flies out the door.

• Create an "Unsung Heroes" book to honor those special people at your school. Dedication page can read:

The people in this book are people we know. They are people who make us laugh, pull us through a bad day, undertake huge tasks each day, do small things that may go unnoticed, inspire us, make our work just a little bit easier, and touch the hearts and minds of children. The people in this book are our Unsung Heroes!

The Fifth Step—Building a Climate of Personal Competency

Generating Generous Teacher Praise

I expect to pass through life but once. If, therefore, there be any kindness I can show or any good things I can do to fellow human beings, let me do it now, and not defer or neglect it, as I shall not pass this way again.

—William Penn

• As school administrators, we need to enhance teacher self-esteem by providing positive feedback and reinforcement. We need to celebrate individual achievements. Letting teachers know what a good job they are doing and that you appreciate their dedication and hard work can be a powerful motivator to continue a tradition of excellence at your school. We all respond to praise. It's easy to praise those teachers who are doing a great job; however, you probably have some teachers on your staff for whom it's difficult to find something to praise. George Matthew Adams points out, "Encouragement is oxygen for the soul." You need to remember that you may have teachers on staff who are asphyxiating! You need to make sure that you provide praise to all your teachers.

• Share the accomplishments of outstanding staff members with other staff and your community. Encourage teachers to try new ideas and develop new curriculum. Reward and actively support those who strive to improve their instructional abilities and to make their classrooms a better place for their students.

Notes to Teachers

• You can enhance peak performance in your teachers by reinforcing the good teaching you see with praise and recognition. You need to praise profusely, and if you can provide teachers with that praise in writing it's even better. Praise is a great motivator and lets teachers know what it is that you value. When you write notes of praise it communicates to the teacher what it is you expect to see when you visit classrooms and reinforces your high expectations.

• Teachers appreciate notes from their principal that recognize the good job they are doing. Teachers want to feel that what they're doing is important and that their contribution is recognized and appreciated. Notes that are specific and personal, not written to everybody, are those most valued. Even though you *say* you appreciate them, the handwritten statement has more meaning for them because you took the *time* to do it. Budget a portion of time each week to sit down and write notes of appreciation for a job well done. They can be one of your strongest motivational strategies for keeping a high level of performance in your school. Everyone likes to be praised for doing his or her best.

Giving Feedback Following Classroom Walk-Throughs

One of the joys of our job is visiting the classrooms in our schools. Teachers often wonder what we think about the lesson or their teaching when we walk through their classrooms. We know it is important to provide feedback to teachers as often as we can after we have walked through their classes, but it seems there is never enough time to sit down and write a note to each teacher. Besides, by the time you get back to your office after walking the campus you have been interrupted with questions to answer, problems to solve, emergencies to handle, and so on and so forth, and you've completely forgotten what it was that you observed, let alone what you were going to write.

• A solution to that problem is to take a notepad and folder with you on your walk-throughs. When you see something great going on in a classroom, take a second and jot a quick note and leave it on the teacher's desk. Teachers really appreciate the instant feedback!

• In your walk-through folder keep a checklist of all staff members so you can make sure that you chart each teacher and classified staff member as well as the date the note was written to ensure that you provide feedback to everyone on your staff. Before each walk-through glance at your checklist to note the white spots. The white spots tell you which teachers haven't received a note from you yet.

• By using NCR notepaper you can also keep a copy of the note for your files and use it later on as a reference when writing teacher evaluations.

• You may even want to carry your Dictaphone on your walk-throughs and dictate comments and observations as you visit classrooms. You can then drop the tape off with your secretary, who can type up the notes and they can be in teachers' boxes that afternoon.

Teacher Recognition Awards

School principals play a key role in the recognition of teacher excellence at their schools. There are many local, county, state, and even national awards for which principals can nominate their teachers or school. Keep your eyes posted on magazines such as *Educational Leadership, Teacher,* or *Principal,* as well as other professional journals and publications. There are national awards such as the Reader's Digest American Heroes in Education, *Teacher* magazine's A+ Schools, and your State Teacher of the Year Awards. Professional organizations often recognize outstanding teachers in their field. County, state, and national professional curriculum organizations are excellent sources for nominating your staff for recognition. Teachers appreciate the honor of being nominated for an award by their principals. Let your parents and community know that a teacher from your school has been *nominated* for this award. They will be impressed and the publicity can help you communicate to the community at large that your school is a school of excellence.

Teacher of the Year

Select a teacher from your staff as your school's nominee for Teacher of the Year as part of your district, regional, state, and national Teacher of the Year Award programs. Have a professional portrait taken of the teacher and display it in a prominent location along with those selected in previous years. Let parents and the community know of the teacher's honor through your newsette or newsletter and by utilizing your local newspaper to feature an article on the nominee.

Encouraging Parent Praise

In a completely rational society, the best of us would aspire to be teachers and the rest of us would have to settle for something less, because passing civilization along from one generation to the next ought to be the highest honor and the highest responsibility anyone could have.

—Lee Iaccoca

The school principal can play an important role in helping parents recognize the importance of praising the good works of teachers. Many parents don't recognize the importance and impact their words of praise can have on motivating a teacher.

• Principals need to communicate to parents the importance of praising teachers and the resulting positive impact on the morale and climate of the school and the most important benefit for their children—a satisfied teacher who knows his or her efforts are appreciated. Publicly encourage parents to write notes of appreciation to the teachers at your school. The next day teachers will be buzzing in the lounge about all the wonderful notes they received. The end result is a staff that feels their efforts are valued and appreciated by parents and they are invigorated and energized when their efforts are recognized.

• Encourage parents to make a donation to the media center to purchase a book that is dedicated to a favorite teacher with a specially designed bookplate designating appreciation for their child's teacher. What a great way to increase and update the volumes in your media center at no cost to the school.

• Principals can meet with PTA or other parent groups and brainstorm ways parents can honor the teaching profession. Discuss ways your school can say thank you to teachers (banners, bookmarks, T-shirts, etc.). Encourage parents to write notes of appreciation to staff members. Pass on to teachers any positive comments of parents or colleagues that you hear.

• Create a Wish List notebook with a page for all teachers that identifies items for their classrooms that they wish they had. Have the Wish List notebook available in the school office for parents to check the page for their child's teacher and to purchase items as a gift for the classroom. What a great way to say thanks!

Encouraging District Office Praise

The principal can urge the district office personnel, as well as school board members, to write a personal note to the staff after a school visit. Let them know how much the staff appreciates hearing from the school board and district administration that they are doing a good job.

The Good Note File

Today in education it is sometimes difficult for educators to be sure they have done the right thing. How do we measure our success as school administrators? The clues we use to measure our successes as educators are more obscure than ever before. Sometimes we may never know the influence we have had on a student's life. Other times a parent or student will be so touched by something we've done that they will write us a note of appreciation. When we get those positive notes it reaffirms the good job we are doing each and every day. Notes of appreciation can be an effective measure of our success. It is important that we keep our notes of appreciation in a special file.

• Every staff member should maintain a Good Note file. The Good Note file consists of notes or letters of praise from students, parents, colleagues, and supervisors. It is important to save the good notes and throw out the negative ones. Whenever we get a negative note we always take it more personally than it was usually meant and we get angry, hurt, or defensive. Rather than spending a lot of time beating ourselves up, we need to focus on the positive influences we have had on others. That's when the Good Note file comes in handy.

• Every time we get a positive note we need to put it in a Good Note file. The Good Note file should be in your desk for easy access. Sometimes principals, and even teachers, experience one of those terrible, horrible, no-good days when nothing goes right, just like Alexander in the well-loved book. You may have just conferenced with a hostile parent or today that "special" student has exhausted all your "catch 'em being good" strategies. You may be exhausted, depressed, and feeling that being in education may not be worth all the hassle.

This is the time to pull out the Good Note file and reread those positive notes. There affirmation after affirmation confirms that you have made a difference in children's lives. The reading of these affirmations helps us to focus on the *positive* impact we have as educators. Most days it's just comforting to know that the Good Note file is close by, but on some days you may want to take out the whole file and reread each note. There's not a better way to end your day than reading those wonderful notes that people, whose lives you've influenced, wrote especially to you! Yes! It's all worth it! You have made a difference!

STRENGTHENING YOUR INFRASTRUCTURE

The School Secretary—The Key to Your Success as a Principal

Alone we can do so little, together we can do so much.

—Helen Keller

There are two important support systems that hold up the infrastructure of your school—the school secretary and the school custodian. These key positions are vital to your success as a school leader. The key to your success will depend upon your working relationship with these essential positions. It is imperative that you work together as a team. Here are some tips for strengthening your infrastructure and making the relationships highly productive and satisfying.

• Work as a team! Treat your secretary as an intelligent and highly skilled professional colleague—not as a gofer. Make your own phone calls and get your own coffee. Discuss what your secretary does best and what you do best and then decide how you can share responsibilities to get the job done.

• Communicate your priorities to your secretary and let your secretary do the same for you. Do not forget to communicate changes in priorities when they happen. Open the door to honest dialogue. Ask the question "Is there anything I'm doing that is getting in the way of your doing your job effectively?"

• Let your secretary know your whereabouts throughout the day and about any scheduled special events or meetings. Keep your secretary informed! Meet periodically to review budget expenditures and allocations.

• Schedule meetings periodically to set up your calendars and to discuss issues and priorities. Use this time to compliment and thank your secretary for the support and backup you have received. Let your secretary know when he or she has done a good job. Praise frequently—don't wait until Secretary's Day!

• Remember that the school secretary is often the first contact most of the parents and public have with the school. First impressions do count! Discuss phone procedures and what you would like the secretary to say when answering the phone. Answer questions such as, How many times do you want the phone to ring? Do people at the school counter take preference over people on the phone? What is the image of the school office when you walk in the door? These expectations need to be discussed and defined so you and your office staff can provide the best possible services and environment for your school.

• The secretary is at the hub of the school, and his or her impact is felt at all levels of the school community. It is often very difficult for the secretary to get free of the demands of the front desk and the volume of tasks, crises, and problems he or she handles each day. Give the secretary a break and ask him or her to join you on an escorted tour of the school several times throughout the year. Find a way to cover the secretary's job for the time you're gone and share the joy of your job! By visiting all classrooms and programs in the school you can give your secretary the opportunity to see the school in action. Then it will be easier to connect what happens in the office with what goes on in the classroom. The personally escorted tour helps the secretary put it all in perspective and see that his or her job in the office has an important impact on students and staff in the classroom.

• An efficient secretary can save you considerable time by screening your mail—getting rid of the junk mail and sorting the important mail for you. Sit down with the mail and train your secretary how and where to sort your mail. Establish color-coded folders for sorting the mail: a pink folder for immediate attention items, a red folder for district office memos, a yellow folder for parent communications, and so forth. Have your secretary sort the mail into these folders so you can select the priority folders for quick access to important information and you don't have to rummage through large stacks of mail.

• It is essential to set aside a specific time each day for daily planning to establish priorities for handling the workload. Help your secretary understand that his or her job is really Interruptions Facilitator. As principal and secretary, you both share days that are fragmented and frustrating, making it difficult to achieve any sense of completion. Daily planning and effective communication are an essential part of the teamwork that will enable you both to experience some sense of success.

Coming together is a beginning. Staying together is a process. Working together is success.

—Henry Ford

The School Custodian—The Key to a Safe and Clean School Environment

If a man is called to be a street sweeper, he should sweep streets even as Michelangelo painted, or Beethoven composed music, or Shakespeare wrote poetry. He should sweep streets so well that all the hosts of heaven and earth will pause to say, here lived a great street sweeper who did his job well.

—Martin Luther King Jr.

The school custodian is a key member of your infrastructure and literally maintains your school as a safe and clean environment for learning. The day and night custodians need to be an important part of your infrastructure team. Here are some tips for strengthening that team.

• Communicate your priorities for school and classroom maintenance and grounds upkeep to the custodian. Meet periodically to discuss issues, schedules, and long-range goals. It's easy to get busy and not feel an urgency to schedule a meeting with your custodian. However, by meeting when there is not an urgent issue, you will be able to prevent problems from occurring or address them before they reach crisis stage. Safety is always the issue. Develop safety checklists for the custodian to submit on a monthly basis to keep you informed of any potential safety issues and demonstrate that your approach to school safety is preventative.

• At least three times each year do a thorough walk-through of the school campus and grounds with the custodian. Ask him or her to identify issues and concerns. Take notes or develop a checklist to identify any current or potential problems. Identify any safety issues. Use this opportunity to compliment and praise your custodial staff for a job well done.

• Research shows that when the public wants information about any aspect of school life it's not the teachers, the principal, or the school secretary that they seek out. It is the school custodian. If the public wants the real story, the school custodian is the most trusted source. Remember this and keep the custodian in the loop.

• Include the custodial staff in staff parties and school social events. Invite them to join the staff at parties, T.G.I.F.'s, or special events. Make them feel welcome. Hold a special day each year where the students, staff, and parents recognize and honor the custodial staff.

Building the Family–School Connection

Our neighborhoods represent the best and last frontier in our collaborative efforts to advocate for and improve the lives of children. It is within the structure of neighborhoods that children develop, incorporate values, and eventually learn the skills necessary for responsible citizenship.

—Charles De Leo

A Family of Families

The children who attend our schools today come to us from many different kinds of families. Gone is the era when most families consisted of Mom, Dad,

Dick, Jane, Spot, and Puff. Today's families are made up of a wide variety of configurations: two-parent families, single-parent families, blended families, same-sex parents, grandparents who are raising their grandchildren, and even children who have no family, who come to us from a foster home. Recognizing that all children bring with them the unique influences of their own home environment, it is imperative that we create a family of families within our school community.

School staffs need to explore ways of involving all the adults in a child's family by having them make a commitment to support their child's education. Commitment to excellence is accomplished by families and schools working together in the pursuit of educational excellence for their children. To strengthen parents' willingness to become involved in their children's education, schools must promote a collaborative environment in which parents are valued and recognized as essential partners in their child's life. Schools must develop family involvement programs that train and support parents in dealing with the multiple pressures of rearing children in today's complex world.

Parental involvement takes on new meaning as schools explore creative ways to reach out and involve those hard-to-reach parents or those parents who feel uncomfortable in a school environment. Schools need to try ideas such as home visits, incentives for attending parent education programs, or scheduling family nights in which parents and their children participate together in a school-directed activity. Consider establishing a parent center at your school where parents have a place to meet and learn together. Involve parents in booster club activities where they work together to paint posters or banners promoting school pride, help keep a clean school environment, or reach out to local businesses for incentives to reward students for their academic success.

Research shows that parent and family involvement play a significant role in determining children's intelligence, competence, and achievement. Therefore, it is incumbent upon schools to bring together each family within their school, of whatever configuration, into a coalition of families focused on meeting the diverse and challenging educational needs of all children.

Reaching Out to Our Reluctant Families

The home environment is a most powerful factor in determining the level of school achievement of students, student interest in learning, and the number of years of schooling the children will receive. It accounts for more of the student's motivation in learning than does the school curriculum or the quality of instruction in our schools.

—Benjamin Bloom

Not all families have the ability or desire to become involved in school-related activities. Being a parent is demanding, especially for single-parent families or when times are hard. Time and energy can be in short supply for many parents. Some parents may want to become involved in their child's education, but lack the knowledge, language, or skills they think are necessary. Others simply don't know how best to support their children in school. Some parents may not feel comfortable at a school due to differences in education, language, or socioeconomic status. Other families may experience challenges in mobility that make it difficult to sustain close ties. The challenge for schools is to explore resources and strategies for providing meaningful involvement for the reluctant parents.

Some parents choose to remain anonymous or uninvolved at school. School may remind them of unhappy memories or feelings of failure in school that they carry over to you as the school principal. They may be uncomfortable about their child's lack of success in school reflecting on them as parents. Many parents would never interrupt your day with an appointment—they believe you're too busy to meet with them or they are intimidated by the school authority.

To make your self more accessible to reluctant parents, schedule a "Chat with the Principal." Set aside a specific time each month for parents to drop in and meet with you informally. The best times are right after school starts, right before school ends, or a brown bag lunch. Let everyone know that you are available to answer any questions—no appointment necessary. Be sure you meet in a neutral space, not your office, to establish a relaxed, informal environment conducive to effective communication. Set aside this time with no interruptions and bring some paperwork to do in the event only a few parents show up.

Another way to bring in those reluctant families and help them feel comfortable at school is to open a parent center. The parent center can provide parents a place to sit down with other parents and in a relaxed, comfortable environment discuss concerns or ask questions. The center can provide support for parents by serving as a place for parent inservices. The center can also serve as a resource for information regarding referral services and provide information to parents in need. The center can be staffed by a part-time community liaison and supported by parent volunteers. Baby-sitting can be provided for school events and workshops to encourage attendance.

Decorating the Refrigerator Doors of America

Communication between home and school is a crucial link to ensure school success. When concerns or problems arise, parents need access to teachers and teachers to parents. Schools need to define communication channels that make it easy for immediate communication between home and school.

In homes all across America, the refrigerator door serves as the family message center, art gallery, story display, photo album, and weekly calendar. Refrigerator doors have become centers where families share and communicate with each other. They contain samples of children's artwork, spelling tests, or special stories. They are cluttered with school notices and calendars of upcoming events.

Schools should explore ways to capitalize on this effective communication tool. Refrigerator door magnets with your school name, logo, or the absence phone number can help parents easily access important information about your school.

Sending all school notices home the same day each week or on the same color of paper can make it easier for parents to know which are the school's flyers and when to check their child's backpack for school notices. A monthly calendar that identifies the important events happening that month at school well in advance will help busy parents organize and plan their involvement in school events.

Parent newsletters, parent conferences, kindergarten orientation or welcome conferences, parenting workshops, parent surveys, phone calls, notes home, and student behavior contracts are a few of the many ways schools have traditionally worked toward effective home–school communication. We are on the cusp of an expanding field of technology that will provide us exciting new ways to connect and communicate between home and school. However, we need to always be looking for new and effective ways to keep communication open between school and our families.

PUTTING THE HOME BACK IN HOMEWORK

As part of our partnership with the home, schools can help put the home back in homework by having a clearly defined homework policy for parents and identifying the important role that parents can play in the success of their child in school. Teachers need to design homework activities that can stretch student thinking and help them apply what they have learned to real-life situations, while helping busy families experience an enjoyable time together.

Homework assignments need to challenge students to think, reason, and apply skills to specific situations. Periodically, assignments should provide students practice and drill on specific learnings, but if all homework assignments consisted of skill and drill, then homework would become a chore and not a powerful learning experience. Homework assignments need to avoid activities that can create power struggles between parents and student that could end in family conflict and tears. Thought-provoking family homework assignments can create opportunities for family interaction, discussion, and dialogue and help parents discover what their children know and think. The school's homework philosophy should be clearly stated and shared with parents. It needs to be consistent from classroom to classroom at each grade level. Emphasis should be on the *quality* of the homework experience rather than the *quantity* of work.

The school's homework policy needs to be communicated clearly to parents, students, and teachers. Determine your school's homework policy and then send home a brochure defining expectations, procedures, and policies (Treasure Chest Sample #9).

(Text continues on page 47)

TREASURE CHEST SAMPLE #9

PARENT HOMEWORK BROCHURE

Homework Philosophy

Homework is an integral part of the educational process. In addition to reinforcing specific subjects in the classroom curriculum, homework can and should be used to

- Develop responsibility and good study habits
- Encourage growth of the individual student to his or her full potential
- Enhance communication skills
- Apply knowledge to real-life situations in a meaningful way
- Logically connect or challenge facts and ideas
- Provide each student an opportunity to develop independent judgment
- Think critically and problem solve

The assignment of homework serves several purposes. It provides opportunities for students to reinforce and practice newly acquired skills or apply recent learnings to real-life situations. Homework may also consist of assignments that help students prepare for class participation. Extended homework assignments provide students the opportunity to apply time-management and organization skills in order to monitor and complete within the allotted time frame.

Equally important and often overlooked is the important fact that homework is an exercise in developing responsibility and good study habits. These are skills that are essential to students being successful in school, as well as later in life. Accepting the responsibilities related to homework means the student needs to independently take direction, manage time, and complete the work to the best of his or her ability.

Homework is about learning to make choices about *when* to do homework, *how* to do homework, *where* to do homework, and *when* to turn it in. Homework assignments should be meaningful and clearly explained to students. Instructional materials must be clearly legible. Required written assignments should be collected, evaluated, and returned in a timely manner with appropriate comments. Teachers should avoid placing excessive emphasis on grading homework assignments because grades should reflect demonstrable achievement under controlled conditions. Sometimes homework reflects more of the parents' involvement than the student's.

The question of the role of homework and its impact on the family can result in different points of view. Some parents feel that schools do not assign enough homework. They expect more homework so they can help their children be more successful in school. They believe that homework helps reinforce the basic skills and develop good study habits. Some parents feel there are excessive amounts of assigned

(Continued)

(Continued)

homework which often conflict with other family priorities. Their children are often involved in after-school activities such as sports, religious instruction, private lessons, scouts, or other organized activities. Other parents see homework as a nightly battleground that ends in tears and frustration. Each family must confront the issues and determine where homework requirements and expectations fit into their lifestyle and values. Parent support of homework is an extremely important factor toward building positive attitudes and successful study habits. Parent interest in schoolwork reflects their belief that what their child is doing is important and that school is a family priority. It is evident that student, teacher, and parent needs and expectations vary. Therefore, flexibility must exist in the assignment of homework. Time requirements are difficult to establish because of the wide variation of reading and work speeds. There should in general be an evolutionary growth in student homework requirements between grades K–12, and consistency should be maintained throughout the school, from teacher to teacher and grade to grade.

Beyond these guidelines, but in keeping with the positive role that homework should provide, the following parameters are established as general guidelines (rather than as limits or requirements) in terms of the time spent by students:

- In Grades K–1, homework should not normally exceed an average of 10–20 minutes per day.
- In Grades 2–3, homework should not normally exceed an average of 20–30 minutes per day.
- In Grades 4–5, homework should not normally exceed an average of 30–40 minutes per day.
- For middle school students, homework should not normally exceed 1–2 hours per academic subject per week.
- For high school students, homework should not normally exceed 2–3 hours per academic subject per week.

The Purposes of Homework

1. Homework develops responsibility.
2. Homework builds good self-discipline and stimulates pride in work.
3. Homework prepares students for classroom participation and activities.
4. Homework develops independent study habits.
5. Homework reinforces and extends school learning experiences and provides practice, review, and application of basic skills.
6. Homework provides a structure for reaching closure on the skills and knowledge in the classroom.
7. Homework lays the foundation for students taking responsibility for their own learning.
8. Homework develops organizational and time-management skills.
9. Homework stimulates creativity and imagination while fostering student initiative.
10. Homework stimulates critical thinking and problem solving.
11. Homework provides practice, review, and application of basic skills.

Types of Homework

Homework may be assigned or student selected on a daily, weekly, or long-term basis from either of the homework categories given below.

Assigned Homework. Assigned homework is homework that has been assigned by the teacher and is to be completed, turned in by a specific date, assessed by the teacher, and returned with appropriate comments or marks. Assessment criteria and comments will vary, depending on the purpose of the assignment. Assignments may include such activities as

1. Spelling contracts
2. Vocabulary study
3. Handwriting practice
4. Research skills (note-taking, clustering, outlining)
5. Research reports and projects
6. Book reports
7. Completion of work missed due to absence
8. Proofreading activities
9. Math application problems
10. Reading, writing, and thinking experiences throughout curriculum
11. Social studies, science, and health assignments
12. Current event activities
13. Discussion topics
14. Preparation for classroom activities
15. Study and review for quizzes and tests
16. Problem-solving activities
17. Fine art activities
18. Math practice sheets
19. Assignments that have been started in class, but do not require explanation or help to complete

Homework: Home and School Working Together

A. Responsibilities of the Students
 1. Write down all homework assignments and due dates before leaving class. Use a notebook or folder to copy and keep all your assignments.
 2. Make sure you fully understand the assignment and the concepts to be practiced or applied. Ask your teacher to explain again if you're not sure.
 3. Organize your materials. Be sure to take home your homework assignment and all necessary materials (textbooks, special supplies, etc.).
 4. Demonstrate good study habits by budgeting the necessary time to complete the assignment.
 5. Demonstrate pride in your homework by doing your best work and working independently. Ask for assistance only after giving it your best.
 6. Demonstrate responsibility by finishing your homework neatly.
 7. Place your completed homework in a spot where you will see it before you leave for school and not forget it.
 8. Be sure you turn your homework in on time.

(Continued)

(Continued)

B. Responsibilities of the Parents

1. Demonstrate that homework is a priority in your family by establishing a *regular* time to develop a daily homework habit. If there are no homework assignments to complete then encourage your student to utilize this quiet time daily for pleasure reading. This reading could be done silently or orally as a shared experience.

2. Parents should provide the support and supervision necessary to see that their child organizes and completes homework for return on the due date.

3. Avoid family arguments or power struggles over homework. If a conflict occurs, please send a note explaining the problem to the teacher with the uncompleted homework. If continuing problems occur regarding homework assignments (such as homework takes too long, is too difficult, or creates tremendous frustration) please contact your child's teacher.

4. Arrange a quiet environment for homework that is in a private, personal area, rather than a public area like the family room or kitchen. Provide a table or desk, chair, proper lighting, and an area free from distractions such as radio, television, phone, or conversations.

5. Parents should be available to assist students with homework, but their proper role is that of *consultant.* Parents should not complete the assignment for their child. Parents who participate in the actual doing of their child's homework dilute whatever academic learning was intended but, more important, cause the child to become dependent upon his or her parents' continued presence and help where homework is concerned.

6. Teach independence by encouraging your child to *persevere* and complete the assignment without assistance. If your child has given his or her all and still is stuck, then step in as a consultant. Help should be brief! Parents can give examples, clarify directions, and provide guidance and support but should not actually do any of the homework for their child. Parents should be available to help only if the student asks of his or her own initiative, resisting the urge to interrupt or ask, "Need any help?" There will be specific homework assignments that require parent participation and family involvement is appropriate.

7. Encourage your child to report progress to you on long-term assignments. Help your child divide the project into manageable segments and have him or her report progress along the way.

8. Expect and encourage your child to do his or her best and neatest work.

9. Encourage your child to report his or her progress to you on long-term assignments.

10. Encourage reading for pleasure. Either read to your child or provide a time *every day* for pleasure reading.

11. Recognize that, since children have different needs, abilities, and interests, homework assignments will be given accordingly.

C. Responsibilities of the Teacher

1. Plan homework that provides practice, preparation, extension, or application and is directly an outgrowth of skills taught in the classroom.

2. Make sure assignments are meaningful and clearly explained to the students.

3. Collect all homework assignments, check for learning, and return to students regularly with appropriate comments or marks.

4. Check on progress of long-term assignments.

5. Recognize and reward students who successfully and consistently complete and turn in their homework assignments.

6. Reinforce good study habits and responsibility by informing parents when a student fails to complete homework assignments through phone calls, homework alerts, or parent notes home from the teacher or principal.

7. Homework should not be assigned to deprive children of adequate time for necessary recreation, free-play, or other out-of-school activities.

8. Teach students how to apply effective study skills and implement organizational and time-management skills.

9. Maintain high expectations of performance on all work assigned.

Parent Support Is Essential

Homework is an integral part of your child's educational process. Homework brings the school and home closer together. As the school and home share most of the responsibility for education in the years ahead, cooperation between home and school is even more imperative to develop a sound and sensible educational program for the student.

Parent support and supervision of homework is an extremely important factor in building positive attitudes and study habits regarding homework. The following suggestions are designed to facilitate our students' learning responsibility for homework without incurring family conflicts:

1. Homework provides the opportunity for practice and application of academic skills. However, homework is also an exercise in accepting responsibility, postponing reinforcement, perseverance, and independent accomplishment. For all those reasons, it's even more important that the student do it with little help from his or her parents.

2. Parents can, and sometimes should, be available to help with homework. When they do, it should be for one of two reasons:
   - First, because the child is stuck at some point, has given it his or her all, and legitimately needs adult guidance to get unstuck.
   - Second, because he or she has finished the homework, but wants someone to review or proofread it. In helping with homework the proper role for parents is that of consultant, not participant, and a fine line divides the one from the other. When parents help a student with homework, the help should be brief. Parents can give examples, clarify directions, and provide guidance and encouragement, but should not actually do any of the student's homework. Parents who participate in the actual doing of homework not only dilute whatever academic learning was intended but also, and more important, cause the student to become dependent upon their continued presence and help where homework is concerned.

3. If parents feel their children are asking for help simply because they want attention or want someone else to do their thinking for them, they should not hesitate to say, "I am sure you can think that one through on your own. Stick with it!"

(Continued)

(Continued)

4. Parents may need to set an upper limit time on homework. The super-conscientious student, wanting to turn in the perfect paper, may spend an inappropriate amount of time on homework. The student who is slow or has a learning problem may struggle for too long to finish the assignment. The student may be responsible for deciding when to begin, but parents should decide when to call time. The deadline should be consistent, say 7:30 P.M. every day, but can be temporarily suspended for special projects or assignments. The shortest route to a nightly never-ending homework marathon is to tell the child when to begin but not when he or she must be done.

5. Completion of homework is the student's responsibility. Parents need to let their child learn responsibility by experiencing the consequences at school for failure to complete the assigned homework on time. Parents should also decide upon an appropriate consequence at home.

6. When working with your child on homework, maintaining a relaxed, stress-free atmosphere will help to build positive attitudes about schoolwork and keep harmony in the family.

Student–Parent Homework Inventory Sheet

Student Name: _____

Dear Parents:

Please confer with your child and have him or her complete the following inventory on homework study skills and return it to your child's teacher. Thank you.

1. I understand that it is important to write down my homework assignments because:
2. I understand that it is important to bring home all materials I will need to complete my assignments because:
3. It is important to schedule for each day a regular time to complete my homework because:
4. I have arranged to do my homework in a quiet place which is located:
5. It is important to budget enough time to complete all homework assignments because:
6. I am proud of my homework when I:
7. When I turn my completed homework in on time I feel:
8. I feel it is important to proofread my work because:
9. I have a special place to put my completed homework so I won't forget to take it to school. It is located:
10. On days when I have no specific homework assignment, I will use my regularly scheduled time for homework to:

Student Signature: _____

Parent Signature: _____

HOMEWORK SURVIVAL KIT FOR TEACHERS

Shortcuts for Teachers

Teachers need new strategies and ideas for the assignment, monitoring, and correcting of homework in order to survive the incredible demands of teaching. Madeline Hunter advised teachers, "Inspire, don't perspire over paperwork."

Skilled and creative teachers can discover productive ways to avoid the paper mill, yet validate that student learning has occurred. The following shortcuts in Treasure Chest Sample #10 incorporate a variety of creative tech-

niques for validating learning through homework; however, each one must be taught to students. Students cannot be expected to use them until they have been instructed how and have had sufficient practice to perform them independently.

TREASURE CHEST SAMPLE #10

HOMEWORK SURVIVAL KIT FOR TEACHERS

Simple Homework Assignments Using Critical Thinking

A teacher can create critical thinking assignments that challenge students and are easy to evaluate. For example, if students were asked to list the five most important character traits of the hero in the story, the homework list could be brought to a reading group or conference, and students could be asked to share the two most important traits or the one trait they are least sure about. Other examples of higher-level thinking assignments students could be taught are as follows:

1. List 5–10 words in your story that you can touch (cat, tree, envelope) and 5–10 words that you can't touch (over, that, special).
2. List 5 ways the main character is like you and 5 ways you are different.
3. Make up 5 multiplication problems with a zero in the product.
4. Using the same facts in a story problem you've written, write a question that would require you to add to find the answer, a question requiring subtraction, another question for multiplication, and another for division.
5. Write 5 questions from the chapter on the American Revolution in your Social Studies book that would test whether someone had really understood the 3 major points in the chapter. Make sure the answers cannot be found in any one sentence. Star the question you think is best.

(Continued)

(Continued)

A creative teacher can think of endless possibilities that generate high-level thinking. "Star the one you think is best" enables a teacher to examine only one response, but others are available if needed for verification.

Tips for Reducing Time Spent Correcting Homework

Homework is assigned so students *learn* or apply the information, skills, or process. Madeline Hunter said teachers need to assign homework that "measure[s] the learning, not the doing." The important question to be gained from the homework assignment is "Has the student learned?" not "Has the student done?" In fact, with homework, the teacher never knows *who* has done the homework—the student, parent, brother, sister, or friend.

Unfortunately, countless hours of classroom time are wasted over the years when valuable instructional time is taken to correct daily homework. Sometimes it seems we have forgotten the purpose of homework and reward the *doing* and not the *knowing*. Teachers can use a variety of correcting techniques that still measure what students have learned or know. Teachers need to vary the strategies so students won't know which will occur on any one day, so they are stimulated to do their best every day. Also, they will view homework as a way of learning, not a chore to be done. Below are some simple strategies for teachers to modify their correcting techniques so they can measure the learning:

1. When students enter the classroom there are three similar problems from their homework assignment on the blackboard. Students are asked to quickly work each problem on the back of their homework assignment and turn it in. The teacher can then check the homework to see that it is done and then correct the three problems to measure the learning.

2. Before turning in the homework assignment, have students circle their best five answers, which you then correct to measure the learning.

3. Assign multiple questions for homework and then select a few of the questions for a test. For example, the teacher could assign a list of 10 questions for homework covering material in a social studies unit or reading story. Students are then informed that they will be tested on the material by the teacher selecting two or three of the exact questions for a short quiz after the homework is collected.

4. In math, students can select their favorite problem, turn their paper over, and write it as a word problem.

5. Each student can create a question or problem to be added at the end of their homework assignment. These could then be assigned as homework the next day.

6. Students can trade or exchange questions, problems, or activities that they have written (i.e., word searches, crossword puzzles, story problems).

When teachers begin to measure the knowing and not the doing strategies, which eliminates correcting volumes of papers, it is important to inform parents of the reasons for using these techniques and their accelerating effect of students' learning. Otherwise, these strategies will be viewed as the teacher getting out of work rather than ways to stimulate high-level thinking and increased student responsibility for learning.

Student Consequences

Some students have difficulty taking responsibility for completing their homework and turning it in on time. In an effort to help establish and reinforce good study habits, the school staff has identified the following sequence of consequences for students who fail to complete or turn in homework assignments:

LEVEL 1: Parents are notified by phone call or a Homework Alert sheet that is sent home with the student. The Homework Alert sheet must be signed by the parent and returned to school the next day. Failure to return the Homework Alert sheet will result in a phone call to the parents. Student must redo or complete homework and turn it in by specified date. Paper will be marked late.

LEVEL 2: Parents are notified by phone call or Homework Alert sheet. Homework Alert sheet must be signed by the parent and returned to school the next day. Failure to return the Homework Alert sheet will result in a phone call to the parents. Student must redo or complete homework and turn it in by specified date. Paper will be marked late. Student consequence will be to stay after school.

LEVEL 3: Parents are notified by Principal's Letter to Parents. The letter reviews the need for parental support and identifies parent responsibilities for seeing that student completes and turns in homework assignments.

LEVEL 4: A parent conference is requested with the teacher, student, and parents. Strategies are brainstormed to eliminate the problem. Parents and teacher agree upon an appropriate consequence.

Note: Parents can also help by establishing consequences at home for not completing homework. Parents usually find out after the fact that an assignment was not completed. However, a missed privilege or favorite TV program goes a long way toward teaching students responsibility for getting future assignments finished and turned in on time. Reasonable short-term consequences enforced *consistently* at home will help your child develop good study habits and responsibility for his or her own work.

However, it's much better to focus on positive ways to reward the student for completing his or her homework. In addition to reinforcing the intrinsic reward of feeling good that comes from a job well done, parents can help by establishing rewards at home as an incentive for their child to complete their homework assignments. When a child is having difficulty getting his or her homework completed and turned in, parents can help motivate by setting a weekly goal and rewarding the child with a special treat when he or she reaches that goal.

Keeping parents involved in the communication loop is crucial to holding students accountable. When students start failing to complete their homework or turning it in on time, parents need to be informed. The Homework Alert (Treasure Chest Sample #11) is a brief communication tool that lets parents know what's happening at school and requires student and parent signatures for accountability. If a student continues to have a problem with completing homework or turning it in on time, then a follow-up letter is sent to the parent from the principal that solicits parent support to correct the problem (Treasure Chest Sample #12).

TREASURE CHEST SAMPLE #11

HOMEWORK ALERT

Date: _____ Teacher: _____

_____ has failed to complete or turn in the following homework: _____.

Please see that the above homework assignment is completed and turned in by _____.

Please sign below to indicate that you have read this notice and have your child return it with the completed homework. Thank you for your support.

I promise to take this Homework Alert home and discuss it with my family.

Comments:

_____

_____

_____

Student Signature: _____

Parent Signature: _____

TREASURE CHEST SAMPLE #12

PRINCIPAL'S HOMEWORK LETTER TO PARENTS

Homework is an integral part of your child's educational process. The assignment of homework serves two purposes. The first and obvious is practice and application of academic skills. Equally important and often overlooked is the fact that homework is an exercise in developing responsibility and good study habits. These are skills that will be essential to being successful in school. Parent support and supervision of homework is an extremely important factor toward building good study habits and personal responsibility. We believe that, as parents and teachers working together, we can build success for your child. We need your help!

You have been contacted by your child's teacher to inform you that homework has not been completed or turned in on time. Unfortunately, the problem is continuing. Therefore, we are asking you to take a strong role in seeing that your child completes his or her homework and turns it in on time. Currently, your child's effort, study habits, and academic progress are being affected. Future grade reports may reflect an unsatisfactory effort or grade; however, if we jointly take action now, we can work together to instill a responsible attitude toward home and good study habits. Please contact the school if you need suggestions or have any questions. Please sign the section below and return to school with your child. Thank you.

Sincerely,

____ I will cooperate with the school by monitoring my child's homework.

____ I am unable at this time to work with the school in monitoring my child's homework.

Parent Signature: _____

2

MASTERING THE SKILLS OF RESILIENCY

RESILIENCY

Resiliency is a key survival skill. Resiliency is defined as the ability to recover quickly from a change or misfortune or to resume an original shape after being bent, stretched, or compressed. We've got to be able to bounce back when challenged by an angry parent, facing a budget crisis, or dealing with declining test scores. We must develop a resiliency that will allow us to lead with clear vision and purpose, despite urgent demands upon our time and attention. As inspirational leaders, we must support and inspire others while at the same time avoiding burnout by keeping a balance in our life between work and a life outside of work.

Despite hundreds of interactions with people throughout a single day, when the dust settles, the principalship is an isolated job. We need to rely on building relationships with our fellow colleagues. We need to share more with others who do the same job we do. Who better understands the difficulties and complexities of the principalship than someone who does the same job?

THE ROCK OF THE PRINCIPALSHIP

When we choose to become school administrators we pick up the rock of the principalship. We will carry that rock with us throughout our career. We will carry it with us wherever we go and whatever we do. What we don't often realize is what a tremendous weight it can become over the years. Often we suddenly discover that the rock of the principalship is no longer just a rock—it has grown into the size of an enormous boulder. We feel weighed down by its sheer size.

The Rock
Of The
Principalship

Today, for many principals the rock of the principalship continues to grow heavier and heavier. We keep taking on more and more responsibilities, adding little rocks to our pockets. We keep thinking we can handle it all. But we need to keep track of the rocks in our pockets. We need to find creative ways to get rid of the little pebbles and a few of the big rocks in our pockets. How can we make sure we aren't adding more and more rocks to our pockets? How can we avoid being weighed down?

Setting priorities is the first step to lightening the load. Selecting the important work and delegating to others the less important tasks can do a lot toward balancing the weight. Watch out for the pebbles and rocks we add to our pockets! Before we know it, we are carrying the weight of a boulder.

Hard work is often the easy work you did not do at the proper time.

—Bernard Meltzer

Working More Hours Is Not the Answer!

The work of a school administrator is all-consuming of our time, energy, and resources. If you had 24 hours a day to do the job of the principalship, you would still need more time because the needs to be met are so great. So, if having more time isn't going to solve the problem and help us get the job done, then we need to look toward using our time more wisely and working smarter, not harder.

How can we find the time to get it all done? We begin by extending our workday, working longer hours for short periods. We work longer and longer hours hoping to get it all done. We come in early a couple days a week. We stay late to get extra work done before we go home for the day. These periodic extensions of our workday soon become long term. It seems however much time we devote to the job there is always more to do. In order to find time to get the work done, we begin to take more and more time away from our personal life. We begin to abandon self-nourishing behaviors, telling ourselves that we don't have time to go to the gym, to garden, or to read recreationally. We delude ourselves with the hope that we can get the job done if we just work long enough hours, so we plod along working ourselves into exhaustion.

We start by making bargains with ourselves, saying "If I go in to the office a half hour early tomorrow I can get a lot done without any interruptions." You find going in a half hour early so successful you begin to make it a routine every morning. Going in early gives you quiet time to get the work done. Then people discover you are there early and they begin coming in and interrupting your quiet time. So now you've lost the purpose for coming in early—gaining extra quiet time to get the work done. But we still keep coming in early—not gaining the extra time we need but just extending our workday.

We also make bargains with ourselves, saying "If I stay late and get the job done then I can go home and have a life!" Staying late to get the job done before you go home doesn't work. Because of the exhausting hours you've put in since early morning, you find it more difficult to work creatively and effectively at the end of the day. Extending your day just adds to your exhaustion and the inability to think clearly or have the energy to complete the job quickly. By the time you do finish the job you don't go home and have a life—you go home, have dinner, and, exhausted, drop into bed.

Few of us can continue to work long hours forever. When we make it routine to come in early and stay late for the long term, we are adding rocks to our pockets.

We begin to pay the price as the job weighs us down. We find ourselves physically or mentally exhausted. Our health begins to deteriorate and our relationships with others outside of work begin to disintegrate. We are not happy in our work and we are less productive. We are beginning to experience the onset of burnout.

Everyone has the same number of hours in a day. It's your choice how to use them. Recognize the reality of your workday. Decide that you will create a work schedule that makes it possible for you to work less hours by prioritizing the important work you need to do and delegate the less important tasks to others. Be realistic! Recognize that you can't do it all. It's a question of choice. Choose to create a more even balance between your work life and your life outside of work.

For Principals Stress Comes From Four Directions

Stress comes to the principal from many directions. Sometimes it seems like the principal is in the middle of a vise and is trying to keep an equal balance between pressures from the four major points of the compass: north, south, east, and west. From the north come those pressures and issues related to the district office and the board of education. And from even farther north comes those issues mandated from the governor and state legislators. And way up north are those federal mandates from the president and Congress. Each

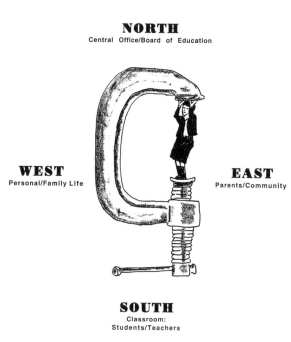

NORTH
Central Office/Board of Education

WEST
Personal/Family Life

EAST
Parents/Community

SOUTH
Classroom:
Students/Teachers

of these branches of government, federal, state, and district, bring political issues to the plate of the principal. In the south are those pressures and issues related to the classroom. Here we find the issues related to student learning, testing, special education, and discipline coupled with the teacher issues of contract management, hiring, supervision, evaluation, and dismissal. All of these issues add pressure to the life of a principal.

In the east we find the issues of parents and community with their expectancies and demands. Sometimes the parents bring their own agendas to the school and exert pressure to get the best teacher or challenge the principal on a school suspension. These demands and pressures take an emotional and sometimes physical toll. And in the west are the personal and family life issues that demand equal time. Here family and friends want equal time from you and you struggle to even find time for yourself.

As each of the four points exerts pressure, principals stand in the middle doing their best to fend off the issues that consume their life. What happens when the parents put on pressure not to suspend, the teacher's union is threatening a strike, or the board of education mandates a new program? When the demands of the north, south, and east become too much, the principal will often step over into the west and begin to take time away from family and friends in order to get the job done. We keep adding rocks to our pockets. Thus, the struggle to squeeze in time for family and friends challenges the principal who is under pressure to meet the demands of the three other quadrants.

Watch Out for Burnout

• We can delegate routine tasks. Things may not get done as well we might have done them—but at least they'll get done.

• Start a modest daily exercise program. The principal who exercises regularly is more apt to feel better physically and emotionally than one who doesn't.

We need to take time for self-care, reflection, and affirmation. We have a choice. We can allow the stress of the job to crush our ability to be the kind of inspirational leader we want to be or we can energetically and enthusiastically demonstrate that we are the positive climate creators at our school. Our challenge is that we get in touch with the joy in our job every day. Joy is an essential ingredient of inspirational leadership.

SURVEY RESULTS—STRESSORS

The job of the principalship can be very stressful. The expectations of self and others, added to the current focus on test score improvement, weigh on the principal. Mix in improving instruction and all the people issues of discipline, evaluation, and personal interactions and the result is overwhelming levels of stress. What are some of the issues that provide stress in your life? Take the Stress Inventory (Treasure Chest Sample #13) to identify your stressors. Then identify your top three stressors and write down the steps you can take to reduce the amount of stress they add to your life.

TREASURE CHEST SAMPLE #13

STRESS INVENTORY

Many factors contribute to principal stress. Identify those work-related factors that contribute to your stress level by evaluating each item on the following rating scale:

Rarely/Never Bothers Me   Occasionally Bothers Me   Frequently Bothers Me

1   2   3   4   5

_____ Time constraints
_____ Paperwork
_____ Telephone interruptions
_____ Visitor interruptions
_____ Parental complaints
_____ Staff conflicts
_____ Parent groups
_____ Teacher misconduct
_____ Allocating and managing budget
_____ Lack of parent support or involvement
_____ Teacher apathy
_____ Conflicts between teachers and parents
_____ Unrealistic workload
_____ Negative staff members
_____ Too many meetings
_____ School office organization
_____ Lack of social life
_____ Classroom observations
_____ Inadequate feedback
_____ No quiet time for reflection
_____ Fragmented day
_____ Lack of job security
_____ Technology changes
_____ High-stakes accountability
_____ Office management
_____ Contract management
_____ Unnecessary and unproductive meetings
_____ Lack of authority
_____ Lack of fun and humor
_____ Overscheduling
_____ Athletic programs

_____ Terminating staff
_____ Writing evaluations
_____ Assemblies
_____ Rumor control
_____ Gaining community support
_____ Lack of district support
_____ Vandalism
_____ Teacher unions
_____ State and federal regulations
_____ Dissatisfaction with salary
_____ Lack of resources and supplies
_____ Inadequate facilities
_____ Parent–Teacher organizations
_____ Nighttime activities
_____ Special education regulations
_____ Limited career advancement
_____ Urgent demands and decisions
_____ Underfunded programs
_____ Feelings of inadequacy
_____ Demanding parents
_____ Lack of respect for your position
_____ District office staff
_____ Focus on testing
_____ Paperwork
_____ Plant maintenance
_____ School board
_____ Meeting deadlines on time
_____ Long hours on job
_____ Implementing changes
_____ Cluttered workspace
_____ Evaluation by your supervisor

Of the highest-ranked items, select the top three that are the most stressful and write down steps you can take to reduce their impact on your life:

1.

2.

3.

The Tyranny of the Urgent

It seems that every task we have to do, and every problem we have to solve, needs to be done immediately. The urgency factor reflects the hectic lifestyle we lead today. Everyone wants instant action, instant resolution, or instant answers. The pressure on the principal to respond immediately is never-ending. Often the important work is set aside in order to find time to address the urgent issues. There is a constant tension between the urgent and the important work to be done. The important work does not need to be done today, tomorrow, or even this week. But urgent tasks demand instant action every minute of every day. These urgent tasks consume our time and energy. We push aside the important work and at the end of the day we feel that we have given in to the tyranny of the urgent. The important work of the principalship is getting out into the classrooms and interacting with teachers and students. Principals find it easy to neglect doing the important work because it does not demand instant action. With renewed commitment, principals need to make sure they do the important work of the principalship and get out into classrooms every day.

A PRINCIPAL'S LAMENT

I spent years working long hours, really believing that I was doing what a loving, responsible father and parent should do. I often felt torn because most nights I was attending a school function or community meeting and most weekends I had a briefcase full of paperwork to consume me. Somehow, I believed that one day it would be different—that I would get all the work done—but it never was. Now my children are grown. There are no more soccer games to coach or attend. No one is waiting, hoping that I will get home in time to shoot a few baskets. And the memories are more about the special times I missed than the special times that I shared with my kids. I missed moments I can never recover. I regret that I didn't weave more time for my kids and my wife into my work schedule. What I didn't enjoy then, I can never reclaim. I only hope others can learn from my story.

Anonymous

TUESDAYS WITH ME

Looking for a Way to Have a Life Outside Work?

Coming in earlier or staying longer at work is not the answer to getting the job done. The job of the school administrator is never-ending. It's a 24-hour-a-day job. There will always be more to do than there is time in the day. We need to make sure that the demanding challenges of our work do not totally consume our lives. We need to find a balance between our professional and our personal lives. We need to make time for a life outside of work!

Many of you may be familiar with the best-selling book, *Tuesdays With Morrie*, by Mitch Albom. The book tells the story of a sportswriter who reconnects with his college mentor, a former professor who is dying of cancer. The sportswriter makes the commitment to take time off from work every Tuesday to fly to Boston to visit with his dying friend.

Instead of Tuesdays with Morrie, I'm suggesting that you take time off from work for Tuesdays with Me! Make a weekly commitment for time with yourself. Give yourself time each week for getting to know yourself better and doing the things that bring you joy and rejuvenation. Reclaim time for yourself by setting a goal of leaving work on time one day a week and then go home and have a life outside of work! Since school environments and personal responsibilities vary, you will need to determine an appropriate time for leaving that works for you—a half hour after school gets out, the end of the contractual work day for teachers, or when the office closes.

Start with small steps. Decide that one day a week, let's say Tuesday, you will leave work on time and *not* take extra work home with you. The not taking work home might be difficult for some, so start with just going on time one day a week. Once going home on time one day a week and taking work with you becomes routine, try just going home on time and not taking work with you.

Try it for a month. You will find that on the day you pick, you will be more focused about what you want to get done. For some reason, once you've solidly made the decision to leave on time on that day, every cell of your body works in unison to help you accomplish your goal. You begin to use your time efficiently and you are more focused on the tasks to be done for the day. Subconsciously, your mind knows that you'll be leaving earlier and you work more effectively— thereby making it easier to go home on time and have a life outside of work.

Having a life outside of your workday is an important goal for maintaining a balance in your life. Scheduling one day a week to go home on time is not an unreasonable expectation! The only way you can make time for yourself is to schedule it. You're well worth it!

Recharge Your Battery

Sometimes a principal's life seems like an Ever Ready battery. It just goes on and on and on and on! But all batteries need recharging! We cannot continue to run on an empty battery. We need to recognize that there are people in our life who are our battery drainers. These battery drainers can be students, parents, staff members, or people in our lives who just suck the energy right out of us. If we have battery drainers in our lives, then we need to identify those people who charge our batteries. We need to charge our batteries to combat the battery drainers. We need to identify the battery chargers in our life, who we can call up on the phone and they make us laugh, inspire us, or give us words of comfort. We need to place these battery chargers on our speed dial so when we have a bad day we can just stagger into our office and we only have to push one button and there is the charge to our battery that will help lighten our load and get us through the day.

The Joy of the Job

Many school administrators suffer from a disease called *seriosity*. They're just too serious about work. It is serious and important work we do, but we've got to learn to lighten up and have some fun within our busy day. We all need to identify the things that bring us joy in our job and then make sure that we build them into our daily schedule. By keeping in touch with the joy in our job every day, we can keep focused on the positive impact of our work and sustain the physical energy and mental strength it takes to do the important work of the principalship.

What gives you joy on your job? What are the things that renew your spirit and boost your energy? Write down three things that give you joy as a principal.

1.
2.
3.

If you can't identify at least three things about your job that give you joy, then you shouldn't be doing it. The work we do is too important to be done without joy.

Miles of Piles—Cutting Through the Clutter

Piles of paper, if left alone will breed at an alarming rate.

—Harriet Schechter

Overwhelmed with the amount of paperwork that flows across your desk each day? Are you weighed down by the sheer volume of paper to be processed? How can you find the time to sort through the piles of paper overflowing your in-basket? Increase your efficiency and productivity by using the following shortcuts.

Want to Eliminate the Junk You've Acquired?

The number-one step to becoming more efficient and productive is to stop accumulating and start eliminating. Toss out the multitude of junk you've kept. Get rid of anything you don't use or want. As educators we have a tendency to be pack rats—keeping or storing things, just in case we might need them some day. The result is piles, files, or boxes of useless materials that we store in the corners of our garage or office for a time we might need them. If the time comes around when we need them again, there will have been so many changes that the materials will be out of date or useless. We need to clean out our work space and throw out the things we no longer need or use.

You may think you know where everything is, but it takes a lot of time to find it—wasted time. The real danger comes when something of value or importance ends up buried in one of those piles. The unfinished projects, reports, and papers demand your immediate attention, and too often they are forgotten or lost. They'll remain undone until someone calls asking for the information or you wake up in the middle of the night remembering some important project you never started. Now a crisis develops, and you have to drop everything and deal with it.

—Jeffrey Mayer

Want to Reduce Your Piles of Paper to a Manageable Level?

Does the "out of sight, out of mind" syndrome contribute to the miles of piles upon your desk? We tend to keep things on our desk so we won't forget about them. The result is huge piles of papers that are like rocks in your pocket—the sheer volume weighs you down. We tend to keep things in case we'll need them in the future. Our file cabinets are jammed full of papers that we never use. Research shows that 80% of papers stored in your file cabinets are never touched after filing them. This means that you only utilize 20% of the files in your file cabinet.

Are You a Hard Copy Addict?

Do you need to print out multiple copies of a letter? Stop printing out hard copies of everything that you create on your computer. You will just have to file it and, because you never seem to find the time for filing, it sits in a to-file pile that clutters up your desk. Instead, keep the data stored in the files on your computer and utilize back-up systems to protect your data.

If you are working off the in-box that is fed to you, you are probably working on the priorities of others.

—Donald Rumsfeld

Want to Reduce the Amount of Mail That Comes Across Your Desk by 50%?

You can dramatically reduce the amount of paperwork that you find in your in-basket. The first step is to set aside time to train your secretary on how you want your mail sorted. Ask your secretary to hold the delivery of all mail until the end of the day. Then after school schedule some time and have him or her bring the accumulated mail into your office. Together you sit down and sort it. For each piece of mail, identify how you would like it handled or where you would like it routed. Since the mail changes each day, you need to do the joint sorting at the end of each day for a week so you can identify the routings for the variety of mail you receive. Most principals face such a volume of mail because they have not taken the time to train their secretary on how to organize, handle, and route their mail.

As mentioned in Chapter 1, create color-coded folders for sorting the important mail. Then, when you sit down to sort the mail in your in-basket, you don't have to dig through all the papers to find the important information you need. You can just pull out the color-coded folders first and handle this information as a priority.

Want to Stop Putting Mail Back into Your In-Box?

When we are unable to make a decision of how to handle the mail in our in-basket we often just put it back into the basket, planning to deal with it at a later date. Sometimes we shuffle that same piece of paper 10–15 times across our desk or in and out of the in-box before we either throw it out or make a decision. We end up creating piles of postponed decisions. You can use the *three strikes you're out rule* to stop shuffling your mail back and forth and help you make a prompt decision. The three strikes rule states that by the third time you look at a piece of paper and you haven't taken action, then it's probably not a priority in your life. Each time you pick up a piece of paper from your in-box and can't make a decision what to do with it, put a check on the upper right-hand corner. The next time you pick up that piece of paper and still can't make a decision, put a second check in the corner. Now, when you pick it up for the third time you will see the prior checks and they will be a signal that it's three strikes, you're out! You either make it a priority and take action or throw it away!

Want to Create a System for Tracking Your Mail?

Keep a set of folders in your desk drawer or nearby file cabinet numbered from 1 to 31 to represent each of the days of the month. As you sort through your mail, determine the date you'll need to take action on an item and then put it in the folder for the day when you will need to deal with it again. This way it does not clutter your in-basket and reduces the constant shuffling of paper. For example, something that you need to handle on the 14th of the month goes into the folder numbered 14. For a report that is due on the 21st you put in the 18 folder, three days prior to the due date to give you time to complete it by the 21st. Review each day's folder first thing in the morning and there are your priorities for the day.

Want to Get Your Staff to Pause Before They Interrupt You?

A closed door to your office gives the message do not disturb. An open door to your office gives the message come on in. Are you tired of having teachers walk into your office when you're on the phone with a confidential call and they just stand and wait for you to finish? For an alternative strategy, try leaving your office door ajar or halfway open during busy periods. It's not completely open or completely closed, which makes the teacher stop and think about interrupting you. It signals that you should not be needlessly interrupted but could be interrupted for something important.

The Above-the-Clutter Signboard

The above-the-clutter (ATC) signboard is a great prop to help keep you on track. The ATC signboard is a clear, legal-sized Lucite signboard for your Post-it notes. It can be purchased at any office supply store and stands up on a base, thereby rising above the clutter and confusion of your desk. It's not likely to get lost or buried and you can move it with you all day long. It can appeal to your playful visual side. Spatial placement on the ATC signboard is important. You can organize it in a variety of ways. You can move the most important tasks to the top left corner while the least important tasks move to the bottom right. You can categorize topics such as projects, phone calls, and family. You can shift priorities and easily move the Post-its into new positions, creating a game that is whole-brained fun.

Avoid Meeting Mania

It seems that as school administrators we often "meet" ourselves to death. We're always scheduling a meeting, attending a meeting or wishing how we could get out of the meeting we're in.

—Author Unknown

If the main reason you have scheduled a meeting is to impart information that is not open to input and discussion, then cancel it. You can share the same information in writing and you won't take people's time simply to talk *at* them.

Do you have to attend every and all meetings? What would happen if you didn't go? Ask yourself the purpose of the meeting you're expected to attend and if you cannot discover a purpose that is central to your highest priorities, then do not attend the meeting. You don't have to attend all meetings. Sometimes you can send a delegate or someone to represent you and have them report back to you with the findings or issues. This gives the delegate an opportunity for shared leadership, building his or her capacity and knowledge base, and in the long run it saves you time.

Be more productive by starting your meetings with an agenda and specific purpose—what you expect to accomplish at the meeting. Setting the goal or task helps to keep people focused and productive.

What is the message we give when we hold a meeting and provide no ending time, just an open block with no time limits? The message is talk all you want, take all the time you need, and let's hear everybody's opinions, stories, and suggestions. People work better when they know the parameters of making a decision and understand that they need to use their time efficiently. *Set an ending time* for input and discussion on the topic. Designate a timekeeper and when the time is up, if you've not reached a decision, then have the members vote to stop the meeting and set a date and time to come back again or set a new time limit and try to reach consensus.

Try holding a short *stand-up* meeting. It's amazing how quickly things can get done when people aren't sitting down comfortably. The message communicated by holding a stand-up meeting is that this meeting will be brief and productive. Let's make a decision and move on.

Try the *SC (schedule and cancel)* method. Schedule a meeting you never intend to have and then cancel it. Say something like "I know that everyone's busy so I've cancelled our 2:00 meeting." Everyone will love you for it!

Very often the greatest value of an administrative meeting comes from the time before and after the meeting or the break time. These are the times when principals can get together in pairs and small groups and talk about the reality of their jobs. We have meaningful dialogue when we get to share ideas, solve problems, and discuss mutual concerns. To us, that is quality use of time and often the most productive time we spend at meetings.

TIME MANAGEMENT TIPS FROM AWARD-WINNING PRINCIPALS

Time plays no favorites. Everyone gets the same amount to start with. What he or she does with it is up to each individual. Leaders don't have more time than anyone else. They just make better use of their time on and off the job. Time management is simply making choices. Better choices mean better time use.

—Robert Ramsey

What is the best shortcut or time management tip you've found most helpful? This was the question asked of 200 award-winning principals from across the nation. The following strategies come from award-winning principals from across the nation who have been recipients of state Principal of the Year Awards, the National Distinguished Principal Award, or the Milken Family Foundation's National Educator of the Year Award:

• When I return phone calls, I write the information on a steno pad—message, phone numbers, and any notes. (I can easily carry it with me and make calls from the cell phone when driving to meetings.) It's also a great resource for referring back to dates, times, and finding phone numbers quickly. *Judy Smith, Seal Beach, CA*

• Make a commitment to a walk through all classrooms each day so staff can catch me rather than have them waste time lined up at my office door. (Always carry a note pad!) *Patsy Higdon, Candler, NC*

• Closing my office door for 1 hour a day. *Georganne Rollaus, Russellville, AR*

• In a "normal" 12 hour day, I try not to handle a "job" twice. Where I can delegate, I do with key employees. I maintain a master calendar of events up to 4 or 5 weeks in advance and meet with key employees once a week. *Wayne Tanaka, Las Vegas, NV*

• Forcing myself to clean off my desk at the end of the day—this *always* keeps me from feeling befuddled and less productive the next morning. I also mentally prioritize and re-prioritize every day as necessary. I never go in to work without visualizing the tasks I need to do (even though I often don't get them all done). *Laurel Telfer, Los Alamitos, CA*

• Sort all mail over a recycling bin and only place on your desk what you'll take action on within the next week. *Lee Schmit, Tacoma, WA*

• Put together a team of highly knowledgeable individuals with an expertise in specific aspects of school program. Give these staff members authority to make decisions on my behalf. This frees up hours as well as builds leadership capacity. *Patricia Brooks, Ft. Washington, MD*

• Think of all my classrooms as my office. Use computer to type all correspondence from classrooms. E-mail myself notes from observations. Open/respond to all mail from classrooms. *Todd White, Greenville, SC*

• One of my most helpful practices was when my wife bought me a Palm organizer. I can instantly check and update my calendar, make notes and access information. It fits in my pocket and is easy to carry around. *Manuel Valenzuela, Tucson, AZ*

• Focus on what is essential. Do that best. Give other tasks that aren't so important to others, and in some cases just don't do some things that are not important. *J. Lynn Jones, Spanish Fork, UT*

• Putting "First Things First." We are constantly inundated with demands on our time. I make sure I prioritize the use of my time by trying to clean out the junk. *Steve Woolf, Tonganoxie, KS*

• Hmmmm—I absolutely, positively have an end time for my day and I go home and don't take it with me. I give my job 100% but once I'm home it gets 100%. *Delice Hofen, Olathe, KS*

• I found that if I visit classrooms informally while I open my mail, I can get a feeling about the classroom, see what is going on and support teachers. This informal knowledge makes my formal evaluations more meaningful. *Susan Van Zant, Ramona, CA*

• Time Management—As simple as making a list of the things to get done at the end of the day so that the next day when I come in I know exactly what I need to accomplish. *Denise Potter, Carlsbad, NM*

• NEVER procrastinate. I'm a closure type of individual. Prioritize your day, check off items on your "to do" list, and utilize technology and the support people around you to help you accomplish your task. Don't just pass work on to others, but don't think you have to do it all, either. *Roger Wilcox, Waverly, IA*

• There are no shortcuts in our field. We must plan purposefully and maintain/organize our schedules by identifying our priorities. *George McCullough, South Bend, IN*

• Realizing that you can't do it all. It is ok to have something you haven't gotten finished yet. Leaving it at work is ok. *Howard Jay, Glenwood Springs, CO*

• Organize information into loose-leaf notebooks—standardized test scores, minutes and agendas, data, etc. Each kept current—cuts down on hours of searching. *Deborah Drugan, Chicopee, MA*

• Writing all tasks down and then dividing them into three categories: (1) those that must be done now; (2) those that have deadlines, but are not immediate; and (3) those that can wait until 1 and 2 are done. This focuses all my energy where it needs to be. *Stephan Shepperd, Kellogg, ID*

• Empower leaders at every grade level. Have these leaders take on special projects. *Juliette Romero Benavidez, Belen, NM*

• Prevent problems! If I can catch a child being good or doing the right thing, I mention or notice it. Children want to be noticed, and noticing the good seems to prevent the bad, or problems. *Nancy Moga, Covington, VA*

• Just get out of the office. The classrooms, hallways, gym, cafeteria, playground and media center are the places to be. Other work will get done. Principal teachers need to be with children. *Doug Pierson, North Kingstown, RI*

Forgive what remains to be done.

—Unknown

BUILDING THE
PARENT–SCHOOL PARTNERSHIP

With children, there is no substitute for parental time periods of unhurried, undivided attention. Often, even the best parents forget that need or develop lifestyles which provide no room for it. We find ourselves so problem-oriented as parents that we spend most of our time with our children as troubleshooters. When our child needs our help, whether to tie his shoe or get a driver's license, we address the problem, help as best we can, and move on. But often there is no particular thing our children need from us; what they need is just for us to be there.

—Dr. Charles Paul Conn

Time Poverty

There has been a significant decline in the amount of time a child spends with a parent due to the increase of single-family homes, blended families, and dual-income homes. This decline has been identified as *time poverty*. Recent studies showed that the average American mother spends less than half an hour a day talking or reading to her children. Fathers spend even less time— only 15 minutes a day. Little conversation occurs in homes and parent–child communication consists mostly of commands ("Be quiet, turn down the TV, stop hitting your brother"). It is very rare to find a family in which there is active dialogue between children and their parents with an exchange of ideas, information, or opinions.

The school must keep in mind that there are many time demands on families today and design school activities that promote family activities. Schools need to create programs in which children come with their parents and participate, rather than perform, along with their parents in workshops such as Family Math, Family Reading, or Family Science. Schools can create school–family team-building events such as a Family Ice Cream Social, Multicultural Family Night, or Family Sports Day.

Recognizing Parents as Educational Partners

Parent volunteers are an integral part of the educational process. Volunteering gives parents the opportunity to contribute to their child's education and work with the school to provide the highest-quality education for their children. Schools need to explore a variety of strategies for building a large cadre of parent volunteers, of both working and nonworking parents, to support the instructional program. A personal letter from the principal inviting parents to volunteer to support their child's school indicates to parents that the school welcomes their active participation (Treasure Chest Sample #14).

TREASURE CHEST SAMPLE #14

PARENT VOLUNTEER SURVEY LETTER

Dear Parents:

The parents at Star Vista School have a close partnership with the classroom and school. Our parents support our school in a variety of ways. We have a large cadre of parent volunteers who help in the classroom or with special events and programs. This year we hope to provide opportunities for our parents and community to volunteer at Star Vista with the

PEP Program
Parents as Educational Partners.

A PEP volunteer is a mother, father, grandparent, or other interested adult or member of our school community who is willing to give his or her TIME and TALENT to help out at school as a member of the Parents as Educational Partners Team!

The staff at Star Vista School would like to invite you to become a PEP volunteer!

Your participation as a PEP volunteer supports our instructional program and school goals, and students will reap the benefits.

While no magic formula exists, the ideal PEP volunteer demonstrates a love for children and is dependable, flexible, and dedicated to support the school in its efforts to educate each child to his or her highest potential. Our PEP volunteers will also reap benefits by experiencing

1. The joy and excitement of working with young children
2. The personal satisfaction of making a difference in children's lives
3. The knowledge that by contributing your time and talent you are helping the school continue its outstanding programs despite any financial cutbacks
4. The personal growth that comes from being needed and the opportunity for updating skills

(Continued)

(Continued)

On the following pages you will have the opportunity to volunteer for school events or your child's classroom for the school year. Please look at the PEP Classroom Volunteer Survey and the PEP School Volunteer Survey and consider how you could offer some of your time. We encourage adults in the community other than parents to also fill out the surveys, so if you know of a relative or someone in your neighborhood who would be a good school volunteer, please ask for another volunteer survey.

All first-time volunteers are invited to attend the following:

PEP volunteer training session held in the Community Room

Basic Techniques for First Time Volunteers

Friday, October 9 from 9:30 to 11:30 a.m.

PEP volunteers who will be working with students on a regular basis in the classroom do need to submit proof that they are free of tuberculosis. If you have already done this, it only needs to be updated every four years. If you have any questions, please contact Hazel, the health clerk in the school office.

Thank you for your wonderful support and cooperation!

Please return the surveys by Friday, September 25.

A Tip on Effective School Volunteer Programs

Many schools bemoan the fact that they can't get parents to volunteer in classrooms while others experience dynamic parent volunteer programs with enormous classroom support. One of the keys to a successful volunteer program is *specificity*. The more specific you are in requesting volunteers, the more likely people will volunteer. Schools are often too general in their request for parent support. Many parents are unsure of the time commitment or teacher expectations and therefore hesitate to volunteer. Schools that are very specific in their requests are more likely to get their requests met. If you were a parent and were asked to help out in your child's classroom once a week you might be anxious about what you would be doing and hesitant about volunteering. However, if you were asked to help out on Tuesday mornings from 8:30 to 9:30 and administer the spelling tests and help students input their stories in the computer for publication, you now know the time constraints and responsibilities. You can then make a decision if that's a good time or a task you would enjoy doing. When asking for school event volunteers, be sure to identify the dates so they can check their calendars for availability. Many parents appreciate knowing school event dates well in advance so they can arrange their schedules to attend. The following parent volunteer survey (Treasure Chest Sample #15) provides parents with specific requests so they can choose to volunteer for those schoolwide activities that interest them as well as for specific responsibilities in their child's classroom.

TREASURE CHEST SAMPLE #15

PEP CLASSROOM VOLUNTEER SURVEY

Name:_____ Phone:_____

Child's Name:_____ Room Number:_____

Best time to contact: _____

I am interested in volunteering as a PEP volunteer assistant in my child's classroom in the following areas:

____ Working with individuals or small groups

____ Working with students who need help in special areas

____ Attending and helping with classroom parties

____ Willing to do at-home work for the teacher such as clerical tasks and cutting letters

____ Willing to help make instructional materials for classroom

____ Willing to read to students

____ Willing to coordinate classroom supplies

____ Willing to work in ANY classroom where there is a need

____ I have the following skills that may be of service to the teacher: (List any that apply)

The following days are best for me to volunteer. (Please circle those that apply)

Morning	Monday	Tuesday	Wednesday	Thursday	Friday
Afternoon	Monday	Tuesday	Wednesday	Thursday	Friday

I work outside the home: __ Full-time __ Part-time __ No

I have small children at home: ____ Yes ____ No

Comments:

Working With Parents as Educational Partners

Schools need to emphasize the role of parents as educational partners and work closely with home to provide the necessary support for student success. We must work together, as neither of us alone can do the job. Many parents would like to volunteer in their child's classroom or for school events but their working schedule prevents their participation. Other parents will find a way to get off from work to be there when needed. When surveying parents for ways they can be involved in and support the school, we need to include activities for both working and nonworking parents. When asking for volunteers it is important to provide parents with a list of specific activities so they will be more likely to make a commitment. The more specific the request for support, the clearer the commitment and the more likely someone will volunteer. Surveys can be developed that ask for volunteers in the classroom (such as Treasure Chest Sample #15) as well as for school events (Treasure Chest Sample #16).

TREASURE CHEST SAMPLE #16

SCHOOL VOLUNTEER SURVEY

The PEP Program—Parents as Educational Partners

Volunteer Name: _____ Phone: _____

Circle one: Parent   Grandparent   Community Member   Other: _____
My children attending Star Vista Elementary School are:
(List name, teacher, and room number)

The following days are the best available times for me to volunteer (please circle those that apply):

Morning	Monday	Tuesday	Wednesday	Thursday	Friday
Afternoon	Monday	Tuesday	Wednesday	Thursday	Friday
Evening	Monday	Tuesday	Wednesday	Thursday	Friday

Best time to contact: _____

I work outside the home: __ Full-time __ Part-time __ No

The time needed as a volunteer in the PEP Program varies from 1 to 3 hours a week depending upon the task or responsibility. I would enjoy helping Star Vista School as a PEP volunteer by (please check each line for the areas or responsibilities where you would like to volunteer)

____ **1. PEP Squad Leader Classroom Mother**
    Responsibilities:
    a. Coordinate and schedule classroom
       volunteers and school PEP volunteers
    b. Coordinate classroom parties
    c. Coordinate and organize materials and
       supplies for classroom
    d. Call parents in classroom to volunteer
    e. Meet monthly with the principal

____ **12. Volunteer—Media Center**
    ____ Reading to children
    ____ Help students with research
       projects in REACH
    ____ Shelving books
    ____ Donate books for library
    ____ Clerical tasks
    ____ Assist student book checkout
    ____ My child's class

___ **2. Volunteer—Classroom Instruction**
___ Collect/organize student supplies
___ Assemble games, charts, sentence strips,
    instructional materials for the classroom
___ Help put up bulletin boards in classroom

___ **3. Volunteer—Computer Lab**
___ Assist with whole class
___ Assist with small groups (3–6)
___ Donate computer software
___ Donate computer equipment
___ Other expertise:

___ **4. Volunteer—Student Publishing Center**
___ Help students publish their works
___ Assist students with computer skills
___ Coordinate publishing center volunteers

___ **5. Volunteer—PAL Tutoring Program**
___ Volunteer once a week to meet with
    and tutor one child who needs one-on-one
    attention. A year-long commitment.

___ **6. Volunteer—School Events**
___ Assist with school activities on special
    schoolwide events or theme days
___ Assist on school pictures day
    Tuesday, October 13
___ Assist with Halloween activities Oct. 31
___ Assist with Pageant of the Arts
    Thursday, April 20
___ Costumes
___ Scenery
___ Backstage supervision
___ Student supervision
___ During rehearsals
___ During performance

___ **7. Volunteer—PE**
___ Organize ballroom equipment
___ Assist teachers with PE activities
___ Work in ballroom at recess
___ Donate PE equipment

___ Any class
___ Assist in student publishing
___ Assist with video production
___ Videotape school events
___ Present donated class books
___ Coordinate volunteer schedule

___ **13. Volunteer—Parent Center**
___ Coordinate parent center
___ Provide baby-sitting for
    school daytime meetings
___ Volunteer in parent center
___ Coordinate parent ed materials
___ Assist parents in locating
    referral and social services
___ Conduct parent ed workshop
    Topic:

___ **14. Volunteer—Guest**
    Speaker
    I would like to do a presentation
    or activity for students in the
    area(s) of:

___ **15. Volunteer—Book Fair**
    Week of May 17–21
___ Assist in set-up May 17
___ Assist with sales
___ During school - Day(s):
___ After school - Day(s):
___ Open House evening May 20

___ **16. Volunteer—Bilingual Students**
___ Work one-on-one with students
    in English
___ Work with small groups in English
___ Assist with interpretation
    Language spoken:

___ **17. Volunteer—Health Aide**
___ Assist health clerk with vision
    and hearing screening
___ Assist in verifying TB tests
___ Check students Outdoor Camp

(Continued)

(Continued)

___ **8. Volunteer—Lost and Found**
___ Coordinator of Lost and Found
___ Lost and found helper
___ Take to Consignment Store
___ Wash clothes
___ Put clothes out at Open House

___ **9. Volunteer—Disaster Preparedness**
___Assist coordination of school supplies
___Assist in disaster drill
___Have CB license and will relay messages

___ **10. Volunteer—School Publicity**
___ Take photos of school events
___ Deliver press releases to local newspapers

___ **11. Volunteer—Drama/Music**
___ Supervise students at rehearsals
___ Supervise students backstage
___ Stage manager
___ Rehearsal accompanist
___ Assist with scenery
___ Assist with costumes
___ Assist with dance
___ Assist with ticket sales
___ Assist with publicity
___ Assist with bake sale

___ **18. Volunteer—Family Math**
___ Assist teacher at Family Math, Science, or Reading sessions
___ Help with organizing materials
___ Baby-sit

___ **19. Volunteer—PROS (Parent Resource Outdoor Support)**
___ Assist with playground supervision
___ Help with cafeteria line
___ Morning or afternoon recess
___ Lunch recess
___ Help with lunch supervision

___ **20. Volunteer—Art Lab**
___ Assist students in art lab
___ Any classroom
___ My child's class
___ Prepare art materials for lab
___ Assist with art gallery setup
___ Matting student artwork

___ **21. Volunteer—RIF (Reading Is Fundamental) Committee**
___ Assist in distribution of books
Dates: ___ Nov. 23–24
        ___ Feb. 22–24
        ___ June 14–15

School Volunteer Training

Schools need to emphasize the role of parents as educational partners and provide volunteer training before they enter the classroom. Once schools have identified a cadre of school or classroom volunteers it is important to provide volunteer training to ensure success and guarantee continued involvement. Schools can schedule a brief one- to two-hour training session and review the standards and expectations for classroom and school volunteers. You can put together a Parent Volunteer Handbook (Treasure Chest Sample #17) that includes a welcome letter from the principal, confidentiality expectations, responsibilities of the volunteer, a code of ethics and do's and don'ts, a first day checklist, a list of effective ways to work with children, and simple group control strategies.

(Text continues on page 78)

TREASURE CHEST SAMPLE #17

VOLUNTEER HANDBOOK WELCOME LETTER

Dear Volunteer:

Welcome to our school. On behalf of all the students and their teachers, I want to thank you for volunteering to help us provide the best possible education for our students. You are an important component in the success of our students. Your presence in the classroom will provide the teacher with valuable help in giving individual and small-group assistance. In whatever way you choose to help, whether in the classroom, media center, computer lab, or other school programs, you can be sure your contribution is needed and valued.

This handbook was prepared to give you assistance in your role as a school volunteer. The role and responsibilities of the school volunteer listed in this handbook will provide you with the guidance for making your volunteer experience an enthusiastic success. Basic techniques and strategies you can use to help children learn are discussed briefly. Naturally, the teacher will always be nearby to provide directions and to answer your questions.

Please feel free to discuss any aspect of the school volunteer program with me or other members of our staff. I am most appreciative of the time and talents you are donating. I know you will experience the joy of working with young children. Your contributions will make a difference in their lives. We hope you will be rewarded by the love and appreciation of the students and staff. Thank you very much for your caring and support.

VOLUNTEER HANDBOOK

School Volunteers Make a Difference!

Across the nation, mothers, fathers, grandparents, businesspeople, and senior citizens are finding that their involvement as school volunteers is having a positive influence on student achievement. Volunteers are making a difference in schools!

School Volunteer Tips—Remember to Be

- *Honest* in your approach and attitude, which will aid in developing trust
- *Patient* when working with students because when they are having difficulty with a subject they do not need additional pressure
- *Flexible* in responding to the needs of students
- *Friendly* because with a smile and a thank you, you can accomplish miracles
- *Respectful* by treating individuals in the same manner you wish to be treated
- *Confidential* because it is very important that what is observed in the classroom remains confidential and student performance or behavior is not to be discussed with other parents

(Continued)

(Continued)

The Three R's for School Volunteers

Responsibility—The effective volunteer is

- Dependable and recognizes the vital importance of regular attendance
- Appreciative of the efforts of the school to educate all children and to provide maximum learning opportunities for each
- Supportive of the administration and teaching staff
- Aware of the importance of planning
- Sincerely concerned about the students
- Able to generate enthusiasm about each child
- Willing to be discreet, dedicated, and punctual
- Professional in his or her commitment, dress, and manner

Rapport—The understanding volunteer

- Recognizes the child's need to improve self-image and independent study habits
- Supports the child by offering genuine friendship
- Recognizes the individuality of each student
- Provides a relaxed, friendly, and caring atmosphere with students
- Respects the teacher and school's ultimate responsibility for the health, welfare, and education of each student
- Provides opportunities for each child to be successful
- Cooperates, coordinates, and communicates continually with teachers, school administrators, and classified staff
- Is comfortable asking for clarification and is willing to express concerns and questions with school staff
- Recognizes the essential need for confidentiality and will not comment or gossip about individual students, staff members, or the school

Rewards—The successful volunteer

- Shares with the child the warm personal satisfactions that result from successful human relationships
- Provides the teacher or staff member with the satisfaction of knowing that the student's needs are being met and that quality education is being promoted, extended, and enriched
- Receives the sincere gratitude of the school community
- Celebrates in the knowledge that he or she has made a difference in a child's life

(Continued)

How Children Learn

Children learn by doing, not by observing. Children learn by asking questions and by searching for answers to their questions. They learn by discovery and experimenting. They learn by using all their senses when possible. They learn by sorting and combining objects and ideas. They learn by repeating experiences. They learn by building confidence in themselves. Children learn behavior by observing people they respect.

How You Can Help Children Learn

1. Let children participate in activities as frequently as possible.
2. Ask children questions that may lead them to the correct answer instead of telling them directly.
3. Let children explore and discover by themselves.
4. Encourage children to feel, smell, taste, and listen, as well as look at objects.
5. Let children try new methods of doing things even though you already know an easier way. Avoid making models for children when they use art media.
6. Let children sort and combine according to their own ideas.
7. When speaking to children

   - Praise their good efforts
   - Use a tone of voice that will encourage them and make them feel confident
   - Avoid comparing children and their work
   - Give children a choice only when you intend to abide by the choice
   - State directions in a positive form ("We use blocks for building" rather than "Don't throw the blocks")

8. Let children observe you as a model for appropriate behavior (sharing, showing respect, talking quietly, taking turns, etc.).

Classroom Volunteer First-Day Checklist

____ Find out where you are to set your things down and where your work station is located.

____ Determine the way in which the teacher will communicate with you.

____ Find out classroom standards and how you are to enforce them.

____ Meet and develop rapport with children.

____ Try to learn names of children or have name tags.

____ Assist pupils when possible.

____ Be punctual. Call the office if you need to be absent.

____ Find out where equipment and supplies are kept and how they are obtained.

____ Be patient when dealing with children.

____ Pupil successes and efforts should be praised.

(Continued)

(Continued)

Code of Ethics for Volunteers

1. Classroom and student work is always confidential. Please don't discuss student problems with anyone except the teacher.
2. Try not to compare children within the classroom.
3. Since there are as many different methods as there are teachers, please do not compare different methods of teaching. There is no one best way to do anything.
4. Work positively for the good of the school. Constructive criticism should be directed only to the supervising teacher or school administrator.

The Do's and Don'ts of a Volunteer

What a Volunteer does	What a Volunteer does not do
Praises and encourages	Berates or belittles
Tells the child good things about him- or herself	Acts in a cold or indifferent manner
Tries to understand how the child feels	Criticizes the teacher
Commits to regular attendance and arranges own parent substitute	Fails to call and let school know he or she is going to be absent
Builds caring and supportive rapport	Gets physical with a child
Speaks directly to teacher about any concerns regarding student performance	Violates confidentiality by passing on information to the community
Is considerate of teacher's time	Loses control and says something that is inappropriate or might be regretted
Makes a difference in a child's life!	

Effective Ways to Work With Children

1. Be warm and friendly—learn the children's names and show interest in what they are doing and telling you; you are very important as a listener.
2. When working with children, encourage them to do their own thinking. Give them plenty of time to answer. Silence often means they are thinking and organizing what they want to say or write.
3. If you don't know an answer or are unsure of what to do, admit it to the children and work it out together—feel free to ask the teacher for help when you need it.

4. Use tact and positive comments. Encourage children and seek something worthy to compliment, especially when children are having difficulties. (Catch them being good!)

5. Accept each child as he or she is—you do not need to feel responsible for judging a child's abilities, progress, or behavior.

6. If a child is upset, encourage him or her to talk the problem over with you. You need not solve the problem, but by listening and talking you help the child feel you care.

7. Respect a child's privacy—if a child or teacher reveals personal information about a child regard it as a confidence. Keep it confidential!

8. Maintain a sense of humor.

9. Be consistent with the teacher's rules for classroom schedules and behavior.

10. Wear comfortable clothes and don't hesitate to get down to a child's level.

11. If parents and friends ask about what you do at school, tell them you enjoy working with the children and discuss the activities you do rather than specific information about a child, the teacher, or the school.

12. Keep your commitment. The children expect you and look forward to you coming. If you know you will be gone, tell them in advance.

Tips on Discipline Strategies

1. Call each child by name (name tags or cards are helpful at first). The best techniques are preventative. Know the standards. Set them before every lesson. "Today we will walk slowly to the media center." "You will raise your hand when you finish with your work." Then instruct the children as though you expect them to comply.

2. Give positive, specific praise—"I like the way Suzy is working quietly." "What good math workers. You are doing a great job of working cooperatively." State positive actions—"Walk quietly" instead of "Don't run!"

3. Give sufficient warnings and time. Here are some examples:
   "Morgan, in 5 minutes you'll need to stop painting and put your apron away, wash your hands, and then come sit on the rug."
   "Chantelle, I asked you not to play with the headsets. Now you need to leave the listening post and go to the book corner. Tomorrow you can work with the listening post again, but you'll need to remember the rules."

4. Keep your voice as low as possible. The children will get louder as your voice gets louder. Have an unhurried attitude. Enjoy them and they will enjoy you.

5. Offer each child a chance to participate. Quiet children are sometimes ignored.

6. Count slowly from 1 to 5 when you want clean-up to occur.

7. Keep lowering your voice to a whisper to be heard and to quiet the group. If students don't respond to a soft voice use group body action. Handclap a signal for quiet. "I'll know you're listening if your hands are on your shoulders" (touching head, folded in your lap, etc.).

8. Be sure a child understands what you're saying. We sometimes use words that children do not know. Ask them to repeat directions to check for understanding.

9. Excuse child from group by who is wearing blue, has blond hair, has two dogs, and so forth, saving the best for last.

Parent Classroom Observations

Many times when parents have concerns about their child's teacher or have a complaint, they will often want to visit the classroom and see for themselves. They want to visit the classroom unannounced in order to really see what goes on in there. Some parents will want to camp out the whole day in the classroom to observe the teacher. Teachers need to welcome parent observations but they must not be unlimited in length and disruptive to the classroom. It's unfair to the teacher to have a parent camped out in the back of the room on a witch hunt. To accommodate a parent's wish or need to observe in their child's classroom and to protect teachers from abusive parents spending the entire day, specific classroom observation guidelines should be established. Parents should be welcomed anytime to classrooms but should know if they are visiting for a specific reason it's better to schedule a specific time to visit.

As a principal dealing with an angry or difficult parent who wanted to observe in the classroom, I would always schedule a time for both of us to observe together. With both of us observing it's a protection for the teacher, and the other benefit is that both the parent and I are seeing the same situation. This prevents the problem when the parent says one thing and the teacher reports something different happened.

The following sample of parent classroom observation procedures (Treasure Chest Sample #18) identifies the standards and expectations for the parent. It also is the pass that allows the parent into the classroom and if a teacher feels threatened he or she can request the principal's presence during the observation. The form also provides space for feedback from the parent on the observation.

TREASURE CHEST SAMPLE #18

PARENT CLASSROOM OBSERVATION PROCEDURES

We want parents to be a part of the school setting whenever possible. Parents are encouraged to participate in our classroom volunteer program that helps to reduce the adult–student ratio.

When parents visit a classroom to observe, they should consider the following points:

1. Please check in at the office before visiting the classroom so we can account for who is on the school campus. Be sure to check out this form and return it to the school secretary at the end of your observation. The teacher will ask to see this form to verify you have checked in at the office.

---

2. Please limit your observation to 30 minutes. Extended observations tend to distract children from learning activities. If you want to spend more time in the classroom, call the teacher in advance to let him or her know you are coming. If you want to spend extended time in the classroom, your volunteer services of working with children would be most welcome. The teacher will plan for your active involvement and assistance during any extended time you wish to spend at school.

3. When entering the classroom, find an unoccupied chair and make yourself comfortable. Feel free to move around the room and observe quietly the children working independently. We ask that any observations regarding other children in the classroom remain confidential.

4. Please do not attempt to carry on a discussion or conference with the teacher when students are in the classroom. The teacher's responsibilities are to the pupils and the instructional program. Conference appointments with the teacher may be made in the office to discuss your observation.

5. Observations, even for a trained observer, provide a snapshot in time or a limited view of a complex series of interrelated experiences and activities. It is assumed that all observers will have the integrity to discuss questions and obtain clarification from professional staff. Our interests are mutual.

It is your responsibility to give us feedback regarding your observation.

QUESTIONS and/or COMMENTS:

Check if appropriate:

____ Please phone me   ____ Please arrange a conference

Parent Name: _____ Phone: _____

Child's Name: _____ Date of Visit: _____

Room #: _____ Teacher: _____

Parent Education Survey

To promote the parents as education partners, schools should recognize the importance and value of providing parents information that can keep them informed about school curriculum, expectations, and programs as well as provide parent education training. Keep parents involved and the inservices relevant by surveying parents as to their interest on a variety of parent education topics (Treasure Chest Sample #19).

TREASURE CHEST SAMPLE #19

PARENT EDUCATION SURVEY

Child's Name:_____ Grade level of child: _____

Parents Name:_____

In order to help us plan parent inservices that will be informative and worthwhile, we would like to ask interested parents to fill out this survey. It will help us to assess your interests and needs and to plan appropriate presentations.

Please indicate with a check mark any topic for which you would like to attend a presentation or discussion and return to the school office by November 15.

Parenting and Family Living Topics Survey

____ Child Growth and Development   ____ Discipline and Your Child
____ How to Prevent Drug/Alcohol Abuse   ____ Teaching Refusal Skills
____ Raising a Child as a Single Parent ____ Parent Effectiveness Training
____ Building Your Child's Self-Esteem   ____ Preventing Sibling Rivalry
____ Coping With Death/Illness in Family ____ Coping With Divorce
____ Family Communication Skills   ____ Building Good Study Habits
____ Homework Without Tears   ____ What to Say About Sex Ed
____ Conflict Resolution   ____ Positive Parenting
____ Guide for the Working Parent   ____ Other Topics:

School Curriculum Topics

____ Language Arts Instruction   ____ Science Instruction
____ How Children Learn to Read   ____ Family Life
____ Whole Language and Phonics   ____ The Writing Process
____ Mathematics   ____ Technology/Computer Ed
____ Technology in Our Schools   ____ Health Education
____ Kindergarten Readiness   ____ Physical Education
____ Music/Art Instruction   ____ Social Studies Instruction

School Procedures and Organizational Topics

____ Restructuring Schools   ____ Thematic Teaching
____ Teaching to the Multiple Intelligences ____ Cooperative Learning
____ Gifted and Talented Education   ____ School Budget Workshop
____ Full Inclusion/Special Education   ____ Teacher Staff Development
____ Student Assessment and Testing   ____ Student Portfolio Assessment
____ Developmental Report Card   ____ Other:

Please suggest any other topics that are of interest to you:
I can attend: ____day meetings only   ____day and/or evening meetings
                           ____evening meetings only

Kindergarten Parent Communication Tools

The greatest gifts you can give your children are the roots of responsibility and the wings of independence.

—Dennis Waitley

Entering kindergarten is an important milestone for most families. Many parents are excited, but also anxious, about what lies ahead for their child. They worry if their child will do well or struggle in school. They are unsure of what will be expected of their child. Schools can play a key role in reducing these anxieties and reassuring parents by providing a kindergarten orientation meeting. Following are a variety of parent communication tools that can help schools bring parents into an active and supportive role in their child's education. You'll find a principal's letter inviting parents to a kindergarten orientation (Treasure Chest Sample #20), a parent information sheet on the school's kindergarten philosophy (Treasure Chest Sample #21), a handout on kindergarten goals and what their child will learn this year (Treasure Chest Sample #22), and a handout on what parents can do to get their child ready for kindergarten (Treasure Chest Sample #23).

(Text continues on page 87)

TREASURE CHEST SAMPLE #20

PARENT INVITATION TO KINDERGARTEN ORIENTATION

Dear Kindergarten Parents:

Welcome to the Star Vista School family. Your child is standing on the threshold of one of the greatest adventures of life. Kindergarten is an important milestone in the life of a child. It is an exciting time for children; a whole new world opens up for them each day, bringing new experiences and developing skills as each child learns to live, work, and interact with others. This first year will have a lifetime effect on your child as kindergarten sets the foundation for school success and beyond.

When your child starts kindergarten you are entrusting the school with a great responsibility. We take that responsibility seriously and will use a highly individualized approach to meet the particular needs of your child while making learning a positive experience. However, this is a cooperative effort, requiring the support and encouragement of both the parents and the school.

We would like to invite you to Kindergarten Parent Orientation on Wednesday, Sept. 5 from 10:30 to 12:00 to provide you with the opportunity to hear an overview of the year's plans. On the morning of Kindergarten Parent Orientation you are invited to accompany your child to school. You can find your child's classroom assignment

(Continued)

(Continued)

posted in the school office window. Please locate your child's name and room number on the posted list and escort your child to the room assigned. Parent volunteers will be in the hallways to help you locate classrooms. Your child's name tag will be found on tables outside the door. Once your child is in the classroom, parents are then invited to attend the Parent Orientation to be held in the school auditorium.

If your child will be walking to school, this would be a good time to determine the safest route and practice walking to school. If your child will ride the bus, I encourage you to take the opportunity to ride the bus with your child. A bus pick-up schedule for the orientation is included in this letter. Please find the bus stop closest to your home and await the bus there at the time indicated. You will be returned to the same bus stop at the end of orientation.

Kindergarten hours for students for the first month of school (Sept. 5–Oct. 3) will be from 8:00 to 12:30. From Oct. 3 on, students will attend from 8:00 to 1:20 p.m. The first month of school is on a shortened schedule to provide teachers and parents time to meet each other in Kindergarten Welcome Conferences. Your child's teacher will give you an opportunity at the Parent Orientation to sign up and schedule your Welcome Conference.

We are happy to have you with us and look forward to meeting you personally. We are confident that it will be a rewarding and successful year for your child.

TREASURE CHEST SAMPLE #21

PARENT HANDOUT: KINDERGARTEN— A STATEMENT OF PHILOSOPHY

We believe the children are our future. Teach them well and let them lead the way.

It is a great day when your child enters kindergarten. It is an important milestone in the life of your child and represents an important step toward independence. With this step, he or she enters a bigger and broader world.

The school now becomes a partner with you in the education of your child. Kindergarten is an important period in the life of any child. It should be a happy adventure in living, working, and learning with a group. Kindergarten sets the foundation of skills and attitudes needed for success later in life. We take this responsibility seriously. Through the combined efforts of home and school, we will make kindergarten a time of great educational, personal, and social growth for your child.

Our kindergarten program is an exciting, challenging experience designed to meet the developmental needs of each individual child. Early school experiences should provide a child opportunities to mature intellectually, physically, socially, and emotionally at a rate of growth that matches his or her unique abilities and developmental progress. We believe in taking children where they are developmentally and then helping them engage in learning and skill acquisition according to their own developmental rate. Star Vista School appreciates and practices this philosophy.

Our instructional program is designed to develop the whole child, with emphasis on his or her unique strengths and needs. Our curriculum is designed to provide an individualized developmental program for each child based on his or her individual developmental rate of intellectual growth. We provide classrooms where your child will explore concepts and ideas and interact with his or her peers and teachers in a rich environment to allow the whole child to grow. We believe a child's learning experiences should be joyful and successful. Therefore, our top priority is building self-esteem and a joy of learning. We encourage and promote positive self-esteem and confidence by building on each child's strengths.

Our kindergarten program focuses both on your child as an individual and on your child as a part of both small and larger groups. While the kindergarten curriculum provides a strong foundation for future academic progress, it also emphasizes the many other kinds of lessons that boys and girls need to learn in order to get along well with others. We see each youngster as a unique being whose individuality should be accepted and valued. The kindergarten program is rich and varied. Much of our teaching is intended to provide for the three E's: *exposure*, *enrichment*, and *exploration*.

We want students to feel good about themselves as learners. Our goal is that our students will become self-reliant, independent thinkers, and problem-solvers, while learning to respect the rights of others. They will learn about conflict management and how to take responsibility for resolving minor conflicts through lessons and role-playing. We believe all children need to feel accepted as they are! Each child is valued as a separate and unique individual.

In a language-rich classroom, your child will have the opportunity to engage in learning and progress developmentally at his or her own rate. Our beliefs about how children learn are based on current research and we have positive expectations for all students to succeed. Social skills, as well as academics, are an important part of kindergarten. Your child will learn how to get along with others, how to share and work with others, and how to accept responsibility in a group.

Star Vista School strongly believes that the education of children is a partnership between home and school. Parent involvement is crucial to the academic and social development of students. Parents are encouraged to participate in the educational process. They need to read to their son or daughter every night to help them learn to read. Being read to is an important step in building an enriched vocabulary that will enable children to decode familiar words as they learn to read.

(Continued)

(Continued)

Parents need to help students with their homework, emphasizing the importance of establishing good work and study habits. Parents may serve as classroom or schoolwide volunteers or attend evening parent education programs offered by the school. They can be active in the Parent–Teacher organization or attend monthly Parent Council meetings in which parents and staff discuss school issues and programs. Parents can maintain continuous communication with the school through parent conferences and ongoing dialogue with their child's teacher.

Star Vista School wants every child to have a successful educational experience. Commitment to excellence is accomplished when families and schools work together purposefully, with mutual respect and trust, in the pursuit of educational excellence for their children. This goal becomes reality for a child when parents and school staff work together in an atmosphere of shared concern and cooperation.

TREASURE CHEST SAMPLE #22

PARENT HANDOUT: KINDERGARTEN GOALS—WHAT YOUR CHILD WILL LEARN

All children want to learn. They need to be successful at what they do so they will feel confident to try new things. Star Vista School's kindergarten program will offer many learning experiences to further the social, emotional, psychomotor, and intellectual development of your child. Through a diagnostic prescriptive approach, the pace of the learning will be determined by your child's developmental level.

Kindergarten will help your child in the following ways:

- **Learn to work, play, and share with other children** and to appreciate and respect other classmates by participating in group activities as a leader, observer, and contributor.
- **Develop self-esteem** through many successful experiences. Opportunities to increase confidence and self-esteem will be ongoing and based on student needs.
- **Increase language skills** by sharing experiences, retelling stories, participating in dramatic plays, learning to listen and observe for details, and studying other readiness skills. Children develop concepts of language through concrete experiences in which they use all their senses—touching, smelling, hearing, listening, and seeing.
- **Develop math concepts and skills** through meaningful experiences with concrete objects, pictures, and the use of math symbols.

- **Grow in responsibility** through learning the proper care of equipment and learning to follow directions.
- **Develop freedom of personal expression** while experimenting with such materials as clay, paper, paint, scissors, paste, crayons, and tools.
- **Increase physical development and coordination** through active participation in games, use of blocks and outdoor equipment, and perceptual training.
- **Enjoy music and begin to develop music skills** through rhythmic interpretation, listening to records and instruments, singing songs, and playing rhythm band instruments.
- **Develop science skills** by observing and studying plant and animal life and become more aware of weather, nature, and seasonal changes. Children's natural inquisitiveness will be used to develop the inquiry skills necessary to better understand the real world.

TREASURE CHEST SAMPLE #23

PARENT HANDOUT—GETTING YOUR CHILD READY FOR KINDERGARTEN

Parents as Educational Partners

Welcome to kindergarten! Just as seedlings need sun, fertile soil, and water to blossom, children need a positive, caring, and creative atmosphere in which to learn and grow.

All children need to feel accepted as they are. Only then can they be helped to reach their highest potential. We encourage positive self-esteem and confidence by building on each child's strengths and interests.

We help children to see how what they learn in school relates to everyday experiences. When children are understood and appreciated, they thrive.

We invite parents to become involved in school life. We believe in the importance of maintaining close communications between families and school staff.

There are many things you can do to prepare your child for school. It is important to reinforce at home what your child learns at school. Here are a few ideas:

- **TALK TO YOUR CHILD.** The more a child can say, the easier it is for him or her to learn to read.
- **LISTEN TO YOUR CHILD.** Encourage your child to tell you about the things he or she sees and does. Good talkers become good readers.

(Continued)

(Continued)

- **READ TO YOUR CHILD.** Reading aloud becomes fun for the child and he or she soon wants to read on his or her own.
- **MAKE YOURS A READING HOME.** If your child sees you reading books, magazines, or newspapers, he or she will know that reading is an important value in your family.
- **TAKE YOUR CHILD PLACES.** Going to parks, on walks, to museums, or to stores all help to give your child new interests. Make these outings valuable to your child by pointing out interesting sights and discussing them. Ask him or her questions and LISTEN to the answers.
- **PROVIDE OPPORTUNITIES** for your child to play with other children.
- **GIVE YOUR CHILD** a credit card for the future—a library card. Take your child to the library. Get the child his or her very own card and let your child pick out his or her own books.

Reading With Your Child

Literature can provide hours of enjoyment for both you and your children and can help your children understand themselves and others in a new way. Children love to be read to, and reading a book together out loud—enjoying both the pictures and the story—is a rewarding and educational experience.

Good books lead children to new places, new experiences, and other periods of time. This very early stage of reading is important to the development of the child's lifetime reading habits. It is also essential to success in school!

Appreciation for good literature grows as you and your children together experience literature. At the same time, as children listen to a selection, they are developing many important language skills. Research studies show that *reading aloud is the single most important activity* contributing to a child's ability to read later in school. Reading aloud contributes to the development of readiness skills for learning to read and reinforces any skill necessary to learning to read and write. Another important factor is the warm, supportive interaction between parent and child that nurtures a warm feeling and builds positive self-esteem.

The following are suggestions for using literature with your children:

- Plan a regular time for reading to and with your child.
- Find a comfortable place to read together. Select a book you think will be interesting to your child or let your child choose the book.
- Practice reading aloud. You will probably find that a soft reading voice is best suited to reading aloud.
- Let your child enjoy the illustrations of the book as you read.
- Children pick up repetition or pattern in a story very quickly. They may want you to read the story over and over. They may also want to join you in reading part of the story as they hear the pattern repeated.
- Become a model—when children see their parents reading and enjoying it, they will in turn consider reading a worthwhile and valuable activity.

Kindergarten Welcome Conference

During the first few weeks of school, kindergarten parents are most eager to hear how their child is doing. Kindergarten teachers are often inundated with parent questions, conferences, and drop-by visits. To help alleviate parents' anxieties, some schools schedule parent conferences in the first month of school. This Welcome Conference (Treasure Chest Sample #24) gives both the teacher and the parent an opportunity for good two-way communication. The Welcome Conference provides the teacher with the opportunity to solicit parents' input and expectations for their child and for the teacher to communicate his or her goals and expectations for the child.

TREASURE CHEST SAMPLE #24

KINDERGARTEN WELCOME CONFERENCE AGENDA

Purpose

The purpose of the Kindergarten Welcome Conference is to provide time for both the parents and the teacher to sit down together and discuss the hopes, goals, expectations, and concerns about the kindergarten year. It is the first step in establishing an important parent–teacher partnership. The Welcome Conference encourages two-way communication between home and school and allows parents to share their knowledge and observations about their child, at home and at school.

Welcome Conference Agenda

1. Introduction, Purpose, and Philosophy of the Kindergarten Program (5 minutes)

Philosophy: It is the belief of Star Vista School that children's learning experiences should be joyful and should meet their individual needs in social, emotional, psychomotor, and intellectual development. Therefore, our kindergarten program is intended to balance the social, emotional, psychomotor, and intellectual needs of students through a sequential, developmental approach to individualized learning. The academic content of kindergarten will vary according to each child's individual needs and abilities. However, all kindergarten students will explore concepts and will interact appropriately with their peers and teachers in a rich environment designed to allow each student to develop to his or her fullest potential as a happy, healthy, whole human being.

All children want to learn. They need to be successful at what they do, so they will feel confident to try new things. The Star Vista kindergarten program is based on a developmental curriculum that builds on students' prior knowledge and experiences. Teachers are aware that children grow through sequential stages of development and that they progress at different rates. All kindergartners will

(Continued)

(Continued)

participate in activities that are challenging and stress the development of cooperation and self-esteem. Kindergartners learn best through hands-on activities that have meaning to them. Students will be given many opportunities to interact with books, materials, and people in their environment. They will construct knowledge through guided exploration and meaningful dialogues. Major emphasis will be placed on developing a strong language based on reading, discussing, and writing books and writing in individual journals.

Play is a major contributor to children's growing knowledge base. It is through play that they manipulate materials, develop physically, mature emotionally, and become part of a social environment. Play also forms the basis for the use of symbolic, abstract thinking—a capacity that is critical to formal learning.

2. Discussion of Kindergarten Questionnaire (15 minutes)
3. Overview of Expectations and Goals (10 minutes)
    Sample Question: What Do You Expect Your Child to Learn in Kindergarten?
4. Closure

Back to School Night—Building Continuity

At the beginning of each year, most schools set aside an evening for parents to come back to school and visit their child's classroom. The purpose of this evening is to meet the teacher and hear of the teacher's expectations, goals, and special plans for the school year. Over the years, many teachers developed packets of materials to hand out to parents with units, goals, and expectations, while others just talked, making it a Back to Boredom Night. Comparisons by parents began to develop as teacher presentations varied in many ways and judgments were made about the quality of the teacher.

The standards and expectations of the school and classroom are best communicated when they are consistent in every classroom. It is important to provide an outline and structure for teachers to speak from so that the message to parents will be consistent from classroom to classroom at each grade level. The Back to School Night Parent Handout Form (Treasure Chest Sample #25) was developed to provide an outline for teachers of what to cover in their presentations and help to ensure continuity of presentation and material from classroom to classroom. Teachers at each grade level are given time in lieu of a staff meeting to complete the form cooperatively. The forms are given to the secretary who types them into the computer to be revised each year. The Back to School Night Parent Handouts are then duplicated for the teachers for their presentations. Parents appreciate leaving that evening with a written guideline of standards, expectations, and curriculum goals for the year. The form also becomes part of the teacher–principal fall planning conference and serves as the starting point for curriculum discussion.

TREASURE CHEST SAMPLE #25

PARENT HANDOUT—BACK TO SCHOOL NIGHT

Teacher: Mary Noelle   Grade: 5

1. Special School Programs

PEP—Parent Volunteer	McRIC Reading Incentive	Sea Lion Chorus
Math Problem Solving	Outdoor Science School	Computer Lab
Physical Education	Splash—Choreography Club	Speech Contest
Pageant of the Arts	Reading and Math Journals	Science Lab
Video Productions	School Musical	Student Council
Student Publishing Center	Night of the Stars	Spirit Day

2. Behavior Management Expectancies

Standards

1. Come into class quietly and have supplies ready

2. Keep your desk and area neat and clean

3. Be responsible for yourself and your belongings

4. Listen and follow directions

5. Use kind language and be kind to others

6. Remember—we're a "hands off" school!

Consequences

1. Verbal warning

2. Time out at recess—$5 deducted from checkbook system

3. Note home to parents to be signed and returned—$5 deducted from checkbook

4. Parent conference or phone call home—$10 deducted from checkbook

5. Sent to principal's office

Rewards!

Classroom Money	Notes Home
Verbal Praise	Principal's Award
Free Homework Pass	Good Citizen Award
Reading Star Award	Math Wizard Award
Class Star of the Week	Class/Table Points
Lunch Bunch With Teacher	Free Choice Time
Front of Lunch Line Pass	

(Continued)

(Continued)

3. Academic Program Highlights

A. Language Arts.

Our language arts program incorporates reading, writing, spelling, oral language, and phonics instruction as integral parts of teaching our children to read. Literature teaches students about the best of human character, the most admirable in human values, and the most articulate in human speech. It prepares them for understanding ideas and expressing themselves, both orally and in written form, effectively about human issues.

In a reading workshop format, the students will be reading many kinds of fiction, nonfiction, and traditional tales. The students will read independently as well as receive teacher-directed guided instruction. They will begin to analyze the plot structure and be introduced to themes of conflict. Students will be able to identify causes of a character's behavior. Students will appreciate figurative language and its literal meaning. They will use a variety of techniques to decode unfamiliar words.

Fifth-grade students will be able to write several cohesive paragraphs. In Writing Workshop, they will do writings in the sensory/descriptive, practical/informational, and analytical/expository domains. Students will practice peer revising and editing. Conventions of grammar will be taught within the writing process using directed teaching. Students will utilize word processing to publish their own stories and books. Students will have frequent opportunities to speak formally and informally before their class. All students will present two formal oral presentations for assessment.

B. Math

Students will receive instruction daily in mathematics with an emphasis on number operations, measurement, and application skills. Students will utilize problem-solving skills and apply mathematics to real-life situations. Students will record their understanding of mathematical concepts in their math journals.

C. Social Studies

Social studies will be an integrated literature-based program. The focus will be on American history with three major units of study:

- Discovery—Explorers and Colonization
- Independence—Colonial Unrest and the War of Independence
- Moving West—Pioneers and Expansion

Through the use of historical novels, social science text, and original sources, students will research and understand the formation of the United States government and appreciate the cultural diversity of its people.

D. Science/Health

The fifth-grade science program will focus on units incorporating the scientific method of investigation. In preparation for Outdoor Science School, the students will experience hands-on instruction in the areas of

Animals	Plants	Astronomy
Geology	Environment	Physical Science–Matter

Additional fifth-grade units will include family life and a drug education program taught by Officer Rick of the Seal Beach Police Department.

E. Homework Policies

Homework should not exceed 40 minutes per day. Homework is assigned four nights a week. Besides the assigned homework, any other classroom work that was not completed in class should be completed at home. Areas in which homework assignments can be expected on a regular basis are math, spelling, reading/writing, book projects, and nightly recreational reading as part of McRIC, our reading incentive program. During the year there will be additional assignments such as memorization challenges (states and capitals) and research projects (historical person report, historical person oral presentation, a state report, and explorer report and oral presentation).

F. Special Classroom Activities

Famous American Artists Unit	Class and Individual
Student Books	Guest Speaker Program
Poetry Lessons (various types)	Writing Workshop
Essay Contest	Reader's Theater
Reading Workshop	Life Masks
Class Meetings	Pioneer Day
Research Projects	Model Rocket Launch
Gifted and Talented Units	

CREATIVE MODELS—SPECIAL NEEDS STUDENTS

All children are gifted; some just open their packages earlier than others.

—Michael Carr

High expectations for student achievement and equal access for all students to a challenging, meaning-centered curriculum are the keys to success for *all* children in school. We often see children rise to what is expected from them and therefore teachers need to maintain high expectations for each student. Star Vista School houses special education students in five Special Day Classrooms from Pre-K to fifth grade and the school's goal for special education students has been to provide them access to the curriculum in the least restrictive environment. We believe *all* children can learn. Several groups of teachers got together and developed plans to achieve that goal. The Star Vista School Community of Learners Model is the creative result of their efforts.

The Community of Learners Model—A Multiage Full Inclusion Classroom

The Community of Learners is a multiaged classroom consisting of special education and regular education students in kindergarten through first grade. The Special Day Class students are fully included and have been combined with general education kindergarten and first-grade children to create a team-taught classroom. The two teachers team in an open-space classroom and their classroom instructional program is supported by a special education instructional assistant who works with all children. The Community of Learners classroom provides for the full inclusion of all special needs students in a general education classroom.

A typical day in the classroom would include students discussing, collaborating, and participating in a variety of activities in different curriculum areas. Each child has the opportunity to grow and learn at his or her own pace and develop good self-esteem and self-reliance through academic accomplishments. Children work individually or in small groups that vary sometimes based on student ability, grade level, or interest. The integration of special education and regular education students provides students opportunities to develop tolerance and understanding for each other's strengths, talents, and differences.

The Community of Learners classroom provides students with an excellent opportunity for continuity of learning in their classroom. Children who enter the program remain in the same classroom for two years. This provides teachers the opportunity to begin the first day of school with an in-depth knowledge about that child. Time at the beginning of the year is not lost to discovering what works or doesn't work in teaching that child so the teacher can begin immediately teaching, challenging, and supporting his or her learning.

The Community of Learners classroom provides parents a unique opportunity to become more actively involved in their child's education. Parents know that they are required to donate time and materials to support their child's classroom. A large group of parents volunteered to help the teachers in the late summer set up the classroom environment. The parent work crew stepped right in, donating materials, supplies, and their time and talent. They helped create a stimulating, exciting classroom environment that reflects the teachers' Community of Learners theme. Parents have continued to volunteer in the classroom, providing guidance and support for many of the small-group multiage activities throughout the day.

Children who are treated as if they are uneducable almost invariably become uneducable.

—Kenneth B. Clark

TIMESAVERS FOR REFERRALS AND INTERVENTIONS

The number of students requiring additional services and interventions due to learning difficulties is continuing to grow. As the special needs student population continues to grow, a greater amount of the principal's time is taken away from school leadership. Principals find themselves spending more and more time in student study team meetings or IEP meetings. This time must be used as efficiently and effectively as possible. Frequently time is wasted when the student study team begins questioning the referring teacher and discovers that no interventions had been tried in the classroom. Unless the classroom teacher has tried a variety of interventions and strategies to address the student's needs, it is premature to schedule a student study team meeting. The Special Needs Interventions Inventory (Treasure Chest Sample #26) provides an intervention inventory for the teacher's use in determining strategies and interventions to address the student's needs. For each of the interventions listed, the teacher must identify those that were successful, not successful, and not tried. Before referring a student for a student study team meeting, the teacher must submit a completed Special Needs Interventions Inventory form along with the request for a team meeting. When the team meets, it now has the data of which interventions have worked and which have not worked, or were not tried, and can more effectively plan how to meet the needs of the student.

TREASURE CHEST SAMPLE #26

SPECIAL NEEDS INTERVENTIONS INVENTORY

Date: _____

Name of Pupil: _____ Teacher: _____

Birth date: _____ Age: _____ Sex: _____ Room: _____ Grade:_____

Address: _____ Home Phone:_____

Parent/Guardian: _____ Work Phone: _____

✳✳

Please circle each intervention listed below:

*** NT = Not Tried   S = Successful   U = Unsuccessful ***

1. Parent/Guardian Contact
NT	S	U	a. Face-to-face conference
NT	S	U	b. Telephone conversations
NT	S	U	c. Written messages/progress reports
NT	S	U	d. Other:

2. Learning Environment
NT	S	U	a. Change seating
NT	S	U	b. Change groups

(Continued)

(Continued)

NT	S	U	c. Reduce distractions (study carrel, isolation, sit in front)
NT	S	U	d. Provide opportunities to release energy
NT	S	U	e. Provide increased routine

3. Instruction

NT	S	U	a. Modify instructions
NT	S	U	b. Tutor (student, parent, PAL–Partners at Learning)
NT	S	U	c. Student writes down directions/assignments
NT	S	U	d. Reduce degree of difficulty (content/amount)
NT	S	U	e. Give immediate feedback on task
NT	S	U	f. Allow more time for task
NT	S	U	g. Extra help given by volunteer
NT	S	U	h. Extra help given by cross-age-tutor
NT	S	U	i. Teach to student's strengths
NT	S	U	j. Use timer
NT	S	U	k. Break assigned tasks into small steps
NT	S	U	l. Use different learning approach (visual, auditory, etc.)
NT	S	U	m. Individual instruction
NT	S	U	n. Small group instruction

4. Behavior Management/Reinforcement

NT	S	U	a. Individual conference with child
NT	S	U	b. Positive reinforcement: __ verbal __ nonverbal __ written __ concrete
NT	S	U	c. Contracting/charts/work for points
NT	S	U	d. Timeout in room or at recess
NT	S	U	e. Ignore behavior to extinguish
NT	S	U	f. Instruction in conflict management
NT	S	U	g. Student writes letter to parent
NT	S	U	h. Provide special recognition or responsibility
NT	S	U	i. Use student's interests to motivate/reinforce
NT	S	U	j. Modeling
NT	S	U	k. Suspension/systematic exclusion
NT	S	U	l. Detain after school
NT	S	U	m. Sent to another room
NT	S	U	n. Maintain proximity
NT	S	U	o. Set up with a buddy who is a positive role model
NT	S	U	p. Sent to principal's office

5. Non-Special Education

NT	S	U	a. Reading specialist
NT	S	U	b. Learning specialist
NT	S	U	c. Other interventions

6. Contacts With Support Team

NT	S	U	a. Nurse
NT	S	U	b. Learning specialist
NT	S	U	c. Speech and language pathologist
NT	S	U	d. Psychologist
NT	S	U	e. Principal
NT	S	U	f. Assistant principal
NT	S	U	g. Former teachers

Priority Needs

Please identify the top three specific areas of concern or behavior for this student that would require additional interventions.

1.

2.

3.

The team now has the data from the classroom teacher about interventions but it needs general background information on the student's life, so considerable time at the beginning of each meeting is often devoted to reviewing the history and background of the student. This litany of the history of the student's life and obstacles they've faced in the past begins to take more and more meeting time. Teachers love to tell the story of the student, thereby taking valuable time away from focusing on a plan of action to remediate the problem. The Special Needs Student Background Form (Treasure Chest Sample #27) can facilitate effective use of the team's time by helping it focus directly on developing strategies that will help the student rather than reviewing the student's history. The Special Needs Student Background Form is submitted with the referral form and is duplicated in advance of the meeting for all team members. Each team member will come to the meeting having reviewed the student's history and ready to use the valuable planning time to develop a plan that will address the learning needs of the student.

TREASURE CHEST SAMPLE #27

SPECIAL NEEDS STUDENT BACKGROUND FORM

Name of Pupil: _____ Teacher: _____

Birth date: _____ Age: _____ Sex: _____ Room: _____ Grade:_____

Address: _____ Home Phone:_____

Parent/Guardian: _____ Work Phone: _____

****

1. Attendance: ___Absences ___Tardies

2. Previous retention: __ yes __ no

3. Number of former schools:

4. Cumulative record has been reviewed? __ yes __ no

5. Primary language if other than English _____

6. Is child currently in any special programs?
   __ Learning Disability __Special Day Class __ Speech/Language
   __ Gifted __Limited English __ Bilingual __ Other (name)_____

7. Parents have been contacted regarding concerns? __yes __no

   Comment/Reactions:

8. Background Information (If known. Please do not ask child or family directly)
   ____ Attendance problems   ____ Lives with someone other than parent
   ____ Latch-key child   ____ Child discusses concern about home
   ____ Group or foster home   ____ Known medical problems
   ____ Death in immediate family   ____ Previously referred
   ____ Divorce or separation   ____ Previously involved with counseling
   ____ Unemployment   ____ Currently involved with counseling
   ____ Single-parent household   ____ Involvement with community agency
   ____ Takes medication (list below)

   Use the space below for additional comments (home structure/routine, siblings, etc.):

9. Reason for consultation referral (please check specific areas listed below that reflect current concerns regarding this student's performance and behavior):

   A. Health
      ____ 1. Frequently absent due to illness.
      ____ 2. Records indicate the following known medical problems:
      ____ 3. Is receiving medication?
              What and why?
      ____ 4. Are there nutritional concerns?
              If so, what?
      ____ 5. What is the current state of hygiene? __healthful __unhealthful

___ 6. Vision

___ 7. Hearing

___ 8. Other concerns in health area:

___ 9. Home supervision/care:

B. Academic Performance

   1. Reading

      ___ a. Reading Book Instructional Level ___

      ___ b. Individual Reading Inventory ___

      ___ c. Reading Recovery Level____

      ___ d. Vocabulary/Word ID

      ___ e. Comprehension

   2. Mathematics

      ___ a. Computation

      ___ b. Problem Solving

   3. Written Expression

      ___ a. Spelling

      ___ b. Punctuation, Grammar

      ___ c. Portfolio Score

         (Most Recent)_____

   4. Other (Specify)

C. Language Function

   ___ 1. Has difficulty understanding directions, questions, and commands

   ___ 2. Is unable to verbally express thoughts and feelings

   ___ 3. Has difficulty formulating sentences

   ___ 4. Appears to have confusion between dominant and secondary language

   ___ 5. Has difficulty remembering material presented visually

   ___ 6. Has difficulty remembering material presented verbally

   ___ 7. Has poor listening skills

   ___ 8. Speech (articulation, nonfluency, voice disorder)

   ___ 9. Other concerns in this area:

D. Motor Ability

   ___ 1. Difficulty with handwriting and/or printing

   ___ 2. Difficulty copying from the board accurately

   ___ 3. Difficulty in eye–hand movements (cutting, drawing, catching)

   ___ 4. Difficulty performing large muscle activities (run, jump, throw)

   ___ 5. Reversals in reading and/or writing

   ___ 6. Difficulty tracking

   ___ 7. Poor balance, clumsy, poor posture

   ___ 8. Excessive motor activity (tapping, humming, etc.)

   ___ 9. Other concerns in this area:

E. Achievement

   ___ 1. Appears to have average to above-average ability

   ___ 2. Appears to have below-average mental ability

(Continued)

(Continued)

    ____ 3. Appears to be gifted

    ____ 4. Appears to be a discrepancy between mental ability and achievement

    ____ 5. Other concerns in this area:

F. Social Emotional Status

    ____ 1. Inadequate self-concept

    ____ 2. Difficulty with peer relationships

    ____ 3. Behavior:

____ withdrawn	____ acting out/aggressive	____ short attention span
____ impulsive	____ overly restless	____ easily frustrated
____ resists authority	____ destructive	____ poor anger control
____ highly anxious	____ easily distracted	

    ____ 4. Does not complete schoolwork assigned even if it's in ability range

    ____ 5. Does not work independently; insists upon inordinate amount of help

    ____ 6. Other concerns in this area:

Tips for Strengthening the Principal–Parent Relationship

The following tips come from award-winning principals from across the nation who have been recipients of state Principal of the Year Awards, the National Distinguished Principal Award or the Milken Family Foundation's National Educator Award. These are the strategies they successfully used to strengthen the relationship between parents and the principal.

1. Establish a habit of sending thank-you notes to parents throughout the year. Make a few brief telephone calls as well. Express the gratitude felt by you and the school staff for the fine work done by parents in your volunteer program—for their willingness to volunteer, for the time and attention they focus on working with their child on homework assignments, and for their support of the school's overall efforts.

2. One of the most widely read sections of your community newspaper is the "Letter to the Editor" section. You can help foster community interest and support for your school by occasionally writing a letter to the editor explaining what parent participation is all about, what it means to the students, and how it affects their progress.

3. The principal can take pictures of school activities and display them at school for everyone to see. When the display is changed or at the end of the year send the pictures, along with a positive note, home with students.

4. Develop a parent communication advisory committee composed of a cross section of community members to provide a sounding board on critical issues.

5. Have a family day when all of the members of your school staff invite their families to attend school. Schedule a picnic, sports day, or other school-wide activities.

6. Provide opportunities for families to learn together through classes, workshops, and discussion groups. Programs like Family Math, Family Reading, and Family Computers provide wonderful opportunities for parents and students to interact while parents are learning about how and what their children are being taught at school.

7. Regularly prepare a Principal's Recommended Reading List for distribution to all parents. Parents are always looking for new titles of children's books for gifts. You might include a section in the list of "Principal's Hot Hits for Parents" recommending books about various aspects of parenting by authors such as Jim Trelease and Hiam Ginott.

8. The principal can host a Dad's Club. The Dad's Club can provide support for school projects. Schedule Dad's Work Night or Dad's Saturday Detail to build something the school needs. Senior citizens can help too.

9. Try a new approach to increasing participation in parent education workshops by providing a Parent University Day. Conduct a survey of parents to determine topics of greatest interest. On a Saturday morning have school personnel or parents with presentation skills offer a variety of workshops. Run it like an educational conference and have parents register for interactive sessions that provide a wide variety of choices, from parenting skills to school curriculum presentations. You might consider getting local merchants to donate juice, coffee, and donuts. Use your playground supervisors to provide baby-sitting services to make it easier for parents to attend. Supervisors can rotate groups of students through activities such as crafts, story hour, videos, and playground games.

10. Organize book discussion groups for adult and student interaction and discussion. Provide an Author's Day on a Saturday morning, during which student authors share their stories and books in small groups of students and parents. Present special participation awards. Invite a local children's author to speak.

11. Videotape special events or performances at your school and provide several copies in your library for checkout by parents who were working or couldn't attend.

12. Schedule parent coffees with the principal on a regular basis to ask questions and discuss hot topics. Forms sent home in advance help determine the topics parents are most interested in.

13. School Happy-Grams to share positive news with parents about their child are extremely effective. The parents of one student who had been having problems even had the Happy-Gram laminated in plastic.

14. Let parents know the important dates at school. Send home a monthly school calendar that can be posted on the refrigerator.

15. A note by the principal on a student's paper such as "Great Job!" signed by the principal can motivate a child who is having problems and create parent

goodwill by showing that the principal cares. Use Post-it notes for attaching positive comments to the child's report card or to a sample of a child's best work in his or her Open House folder.

16. Schedule an early morning breakfast meeting once a month with fathers to encourage their support and involvement. A personal invitation to "Donuts With Dads" will do the trick. Schedule a "Muffins With Moms" using the same idea.

17. Be visible and accessible! Be out and around the school before and after school. These are times parents are on campus picking up their children and it's important to see you and know that they have a chance to say hello and make a positive contact.

Getting in the Tour Business

Cherishing children is the mark of a civilized society.

—Joan Ganz Cooney

Schools today need to open their doors to the nonparent residents and business members of our school community. As principals we need to step out beyond the four walls of our schools and connect with our community, residents, and businesses. We need to help them see the value and importance of continuing to support public education. When their only information about school comes from what they read in the media, no wonder they become critical of public education. We need to seize the opportunity to give them first-hand information and let them see for themselves the great job we are doing in schools today.

School principals need to invite nonparent residents and business leaders into our schools for special tours of classrooms and programs. We need to take every opportunity possible to get them into our schools to see the great job that we are doing. Our schools today look very different than when most of them went to school and they should be impressed with all the positive changes they will see.

Our community residents need to see how their tax dollars are being spent. What better way than with a small-group principal-guided school tour? Schools can really be impressive when seen from the eyes of a community member being provided a guided tour of classrooms and programs. It can also provide you the opportunity to identify additional needs for your school or areas of community support.

In addition to business leaders and residents, schools might schedule classroom tours for grandparents, retired citizens groups, community service organizations (Lions, Kiwanis, etc.), or employees from your business partnerships.

Parent tours are important also. Send a personal invitation to parents (Treasure Chest Sample #28) to attend a special parent group tour (kindergarten parents, parents new to school, or parents by grade levels). What better way to communicate your successes than to let parents see for themselves by touring the classrooms? It can be a great way to educate your parent community about your instructional programs as well as your program needs.

Begin each school tour with an orientation to the school and describe briefly what they'll be observing. Give them a little pep talk about what makes your school so great. Let them sense your excitement and enthusiasm. End the tour by reconvening for questions, reactions, and praise.

The school principal, leading the tour, can take the opportunity to inservice parents by pointing out teaching strategies for individualizing instruction, excellent curriculum programs, or relating student success stories. Make sure you visit all classrooms and programs to give a complete picture of your school.

Release a teacher from the classroom to help lead the tours. It's a great reinforcement for the teacher and allows him or her to point out the school's successes with pride. The payoff is powerful!

Invite the staffs of the local preschools in your community to visit your school for a tour of the primary classrooms. A tour of your school will give the preschool staff a good feel for your early-childhood education philosophy. Either before or after the tour arrange for your kindergarten teachers to meet with the preschool staffs. Encourage articulation between your primary staff and the preschool for a smooth transition as kindergarten children enter your school.

TREASURE CHEST SAMPLE #28

NEW PARENTS INVITATION FOR SCHOOL TOUR

"Star Vista School—working together for individual excellence and positive self-esteem"

Dear Parents of _____

This is our school motto and we are extremely proud of our school. The Star Vista School program has been designed to meet the wide variety of educational needs of our children. We are committed to the goal of academic excellence and believe that the fundamental skills of reading, math, and language are of the highest priority in the education of our young people. We also believe that a child's self-esteem is the key to success in school and we have created a safe and supportive environment that enhances the joy of learning for our students.

The Challenger School District has been widely recognized for its many outstanding programs and quality education. Star Vista School has received awards and recognition for many of our students, staff, and programs. In 1993, we received the State Distinguished School Award, presented to the top 4% of elementary schools in the state. We believe that the honors and recognition that Star Vista School has received are the result of wonderful students, supportive parents, and dedicated staff working together. Star Vista

(Continued)

(Continued)

School provides quality instruction in the basic skills, and, in addition, offers various enrichment programs by specialists in art, music, physical education, computers, and library media skills.

Naturally we want you, as new parents to our school, to know why the school your child attends is so exemplary. But it is not enough to just know—we believe you must SEE what is happening in the classrooms to fully appreciate the quality programs at Star Vista. I would like to extend a personal invitation for you to attend one of our *New Parent Visitation Days*. We have set aside three dates and hope your schedule will allow you to attend either Wednesday, October 4, Friday, October 13, or Tuesday, October 17, from 10:00 A.M. to 12:00 noon. We have scheduled a special presentation and school tour.

If you are a working parent, we know it is often difficult to arrange schedules to participate in school activities during the day. However, our New Parent Visitation Day is organized to provide parents a unique opportunity to see their child's classroom and school in action. We hope you can make special arrangements to attend this important event. Dads are especially welcomed. A highlight will be a tour of the school, the media center, and all the classrooms, including your child's classroom. Plan now to join us! We will meet in the Community Room for a short overview of the program and then visit the classrooms. As parents new to the school, we feel it is important for you to see the total school program from kindergarten through fifth grade. We do not have accommodations for infants and preschoolers for the tour so you will need to make other arrangements.

Because of the large response in the past, it is necessary to reserve a space for you. Please complete the form below and return it to school with your child as soon as possible. We will need an RSVP and will notify you only if the date you have chosen is not available in order to schedule an alternate time.

PLEASE RETURN RESERVATION BY SEPTEMBER 27

PARENT VISITATION DAY

Parent's Name _____

Child's Name _____   Room #____

NOTE: Please check available dates and return to school by September 27.

_____ Yes, I would like to place a reservation to attend a guided tour of Star Vista School from 10:00 a.m. to 12:00 noon on:

_____Wednesday, Oct. 4 _____Friday, Oct. 13 _____Tuesday, Oct. 17

_____ Sorry, I am unable to attend at this time.

COMMENTS:

Opening the Schoolhouse Doors—Inviting the Community to Open House

A child is a person who is going to carry on what you have started. He is going to move in and take over your church, schools, universities, and corporations. The fate of humanity is in his hands.

—Abraham Lincoln

Spring Open House provides you a great opportunity to reach out to your nonparent residents. Ask each family at your school to bring a neighbor or relative to school with them to Open House. Send home a letter to parents about your VIP invitation and request their help (Treasure Chest Sample #29). Include an invitation that the child can give a neighbor or relative (Treasure Chest Sample #30). Have school volunteers or your PTA set up a VIP Welcome Booth and pass out special Very Important People name tags. What better way to communicate your successes than letting the community, guided by an enthusiastic young child, see for themselves the outstanding quality student work and the many fine programs at your school on the night your school looks its best.

TREASURE CHEST SAMPLE #29

PARENT LETTER TO INVITE VIP TO SCHOOL OPEN HOUSE

Star Vista School Invites You to Our OPEN HOUSE

You and your friends and relatives are invited to attend our annual Open House on Thursday, April 22, from 7:00 to 9:00 P.M.

Many of your neighbors no longer have children in school and are often uninformed about the wonderful things happening in schools today. We would like your neighbors to see for themselves the high quality of education students receive at Star Vista School as well as the outstanding samples of student work on display that evening. The best way for our neighbors to find out how their tax dollars are being spent is to visit Star Vista School.

Therefore, the Star Vista staff is asking for your cooperation in extending to your neighbor an invitation to join us at Open House. We would like to ask you to invite a neighbor or relative to join you as your guests at Open House. Our efforts are especially directed to those friendly neighbors who no longer have children in school. Many people may be unable to attend but will appreciate the thoughtfulness of being asked.

We are proud of our Star Vista students and their accomplishments. Children are our nation's most valuable resource and education is a valuable investment in the future of our country. We believe there is a need to broaden our school community to include not only our families, but our neighbors and businesses as well. These nonparent members of our community need the opportunity to see for themselves what schools are like today. What better way than as guests of your family? We will welcome them that evening as special VIP guests and provide each visitor with a VIP guest badge at a welcome table located outside the school office.

(Continued)

(Continued)

YOU CAN HELP! To make it easy for you we have attached a special Letter of Invitation for each family. Please help us by inviting a neighbor or relative to our Open House. Open House is a time when our classrooms are at their best—sparkling with samples of proudly displayed student work and projects. We believe that a concerted effort by everyone will result in a spectacular evening that will continue to build pride and spark enthusiasm and support for Star Vista School. Bringing together students, parents, teachers, and neighbors can only enhance our strong sense of community here at Star Vista. Thanks for your support and cooperation.

TREASURE CHEST #30

VIP NEIGHBOR INVITATION TO ATTEND OPEN HOUSE

Star Vista School Invites You to Our OPEN HOUSE

Dear Friends:

You have received this letter because you are a friend of a student attending Star Vista School. You are also a resident and taxpayer in this community and your tax dollars support your local schools. Children are our nation's most valuable resource and public education is a valuable investment in the future of our country.

Public schools need the support of parents and members of our community such as yourself. As a friend of Star Vista School, we value your opinions and support.

What's Happening in Schools Today?

You or your neighbors may no longer have children in school and your information about schools often comes from what you read in the newspaper. We believe that you would be very impressed with the high quality of education that the children in your neighborhood receive at Star Vista. What better way to find out what's happening in schools today than a firsthand visit to Star Vista School?

Come See for Yourself!

We invite you to come see for yourself how effectively we are using your tax dollars. It may take an hour of your time to find out, but we believe it may be the most eye-opening and reassuring hour you can spend. We *guarantee* that if you make the effort—take the first step and visit us—you'll leave Star Vista with renewed confidence in public education and the youth of America!

Be Our VIP Guest!

Since many of you seldom have the opportunity to see for yourselves what today's schools are really like, the Star Vista students would like to invite you to join us during our annual Open House on Thursday evening, April 22, from 7:00 to 9:00 P.M. We would like to welcome you as a special *VIP guest* that evening. A special VIP *Welcoming Booth* near the office will have a VIP badge and map of the school for your information. Star Vista School is part of your community. We hope you will be able to join us on April 22 and see for yourself the great job your local school is doing!

Sneak-A-Peek Tours at Middle School and High School

When students transition from elementary to middle school or middle school to high school, parents are usually concerned and anxious. Reduce anxiety and provide a hands-on glimpse of what it's really like at the "big" school. Schedule *Sneak-A-Peek Tours* for parents of incoming students at your school. Use attention-getting questions and statements such as "Do you seem to only get one-word answers from your child about how school is going?" "Ever wonder what goes on at the high school?" "Find out what you always wanted to know about middle school . . . AND MORE!" Then send a personal invitation to all incoming parents to join you for a tour of the classrooms and programs at your school. Provide a question-and-answer session with administrators and teachers to address concerns up front and relieve anxieties.

Tapping the Senior Pool

Sometimes when you think about all the bad things that you read in the newspaper and then you walk inside a classroom and see this you realize that there are so many good things in the world.

—Grandpa Leo—Kindergarten Classroom Volunteer

Each school community has a large pool of untapped talent in the number of retired residents in their neighborhood. By establishing school-based intergenerational programs, schools can build support for their instructional programs while tapping into the concept of having the "elders of the tribe" passing along the traditions and the values of the broader community.

Schools need to explore new ways of getting the message out to this segment of our population that schools are desperate for their volunteer services. Senior citizen volunteers, while contributing to the school, can also find great satisfaction and reward from working with young children. Volunteer work with children can be invigorating and inspiring. However, most of the neighborhood's senior citizens don't know how desperately they are needed. Many are hesitant to volunteer because they are unsure of the commitment and responsibilities.

Here are several ideas for tapping the senior pool:

• **Staff presentations to senior citizen groups.** Senior citizen groups are always looking for guest speakers at their meetings. Ask to speak about your school and the needs of your students. By utilizing videos or slide shows, you can help answer their questions about what's expected as a volunteer and illustrate how important their services are to the school. On the video include kids sharing comments about their special senior volunteer.

- **Photograph one of your current senior citizen volunteers working with children.** Prepare a local newspaper article quoting the senior volunteers' enthusiastic responses to working with kids. This just may be the motivation for others to volunteer. Be sure to highlight the need for more volunteers and include the school's phone number and the name of a contact person.

- **Present the volunteer program as a way to a new career.** Many older volunteers look on their school service as a second career and enjoy acquiring new skills and experiences. Try to match their hobbies, talents, and interests to needs at your school so they can share the wealth of their experiences.

- **Child to neighbor invitation.** This can be the most powerful way to get senior citizens involved in your school. Ask parents to support their children by inviting neighbors, relatives, or grandparents to volunteer in their school. The personal touch is always the best. Even if they decline it's good public relations to have been asked.

PAL-ing Around With Partnerships

Good schools are good for business and businesses are showing that they can be good for schools as well. School–business partnerships have grown significantly in the past few years and are one of the fastest growing strategies for school improvement. Many schools have moved past the "what's in it for me" stage ("Do you have any extra computers for our lab?") to more cooperative and collaborative models. Today, exciting things are happening with school–business partnerships. The focus is shifting to how the partnership can help the school meet the changing needs of the student population, especially those students who are at risk or need extra attention and support.

There are many students in our schools who just need that little bit of extra attention and caring. They are the at-risk students who could succeed if they had someone who really knew what they needed and was there for them. But in today's crowded classrooms their needs often go unmet. We can find the help we need by looking to our business partnerships and our community residents. The PAL Program (Partners at Learning) can help connect businesses, community service organizations, and senior citizens with at-risk students at your school who are in need of extra help and caring. PAL volunteers are partnered with students experiencing academic, social, or emotional difficulties for one-on-one tutoring sessions a half hour each week. To provide the continuity of support the PAL volunteer commits to volunteer for the school year. Students can receive that additional instructional support to strengthen their self-confidence and self-esteem. The extended period of time permits the development of a dependable long-range relationship. For many students, the stability of having someone who cares about them enough to come every week will make the difference. As the PAL volunteers come to know the students, they can really experience that they are having an impact.

One of our business partners releases its employees one hour a week to volunteer to be Partners at Learning. Some give up their lunch hour while other PAL volunteers try to schedule their tutoring session close to lunch so they aren't away from their business for a lengthy time. The PAL Program can be expanded beyond the business partnership to include community residents and senior citizens. If there is a local university nearby, you might post an announcement about the PAL Program to recruit new tutors. University students who are studying to be teachers love the opportunity to get into schools by volunteering for some quality one-on-one time with a student.

In the spring you can schedule a PAL Day and honor all the PAL volunteers with some special activities with the students and their PALs. Have your parent–teacher organization host a special picnic or schedule an exciting field day where students and their PALs can relax and have fun together.

Doing City Business

It is important for schools to play an active role in their city as part of expanding the concept of a school–community partnership. Schools need to explore ways to become involved in city affairs and solicit the participation and involvement of community members and city programs.

• Schools can work with their local police department to provide a police officer in the classroom to support drug prevention programs such as DARE or SANE.

• Work with the city recreation department to provide classes and programs on your campus to keep students involved in a supervised setting after school and during the summer.

• Invite city council members, the mayor, and the city manager to speak to students about city government on Leadership Day or volunteer for special school events such as Read Aloud Day or Career Day. Invite local dignitaries such as the mayor, the president of Kiwanis, or the president of the local home-owner's association to tour classrooms or judge contests.

• Encourage local community service organizations to sponsor school assemblies. Schedule Lion's Club Flag Day where they donate a small American flag for each student or the American Legion's Student Citizenship Award recognition program.

• Contact your local Chamber of Commerce, ask to join, and then volunteer to head up their Education Committee. If they don't have an Education Committee, volunteer to organize one. Solicit committee members from the chamber to join you in looking at school–business partnerships and issues facing public schools in your community.

• Get the chamber's Education Committee to sponsor a Teacher of the Year and Business Partner of the Year awards luncheon where you honor teachers and recognize one of your successful school–business partnerships.

• Request time to address the city council. Present a brief State of Your School talk. Highlight special programs. Invite council members and the general public to visit the school for a personally guided tour. Invite them to volunteer in your school to read to kids or work one-on-one with at-risk students. Thank them for the city's support of youth-oriented services such as their recreation department after-school programs and police in the school programs like DARE or SANE.

Principal for a Day

The single most important person in any school is the principal. You're the instructional leader, you're the coach in the sense that you have a team that you have to bring to its fullest potential.

—Hillary Rodham Clinton

The Principal for a Day Program is a hands-on opportunity to put business and community leaders in school for a day to learn the role of school principal. They learn about issues facing principals daily such as crisis management, curriculum supervision, teaching and evaluation, budget, transportation, school-to-work transition, and discipline. Being principal for a day gives our business and community leaders a realistic view of the day-to-day challenges facing educators. Leaders who participate in this intense day in schools will be empowered with the knowledge of how to strengthen partnerships to improve student learning. Businesses may in turn invite educators to visit their business for a day.

In addition to gaining a better understanding of the challenges school principals face, the Principal for a Day Program will challenge business and community leaders to expand on successful partnership efforts and develop innovative programs for meeting educational goals and ensuring adequate preparation of the future workforce. School boards can proclaim Educational Partnership Week to encourage business and community-leader participation in the program. An Educational Partnership Week Proclamation is a call to business and community leaders to become involved in and make a difference in our schools. The proclamation could identify the goals of school–business partnerships as follows:

- Develop student-focused instruction and ensure student success
- Develop performance-based assessment methods linked to entry-level skills requirements in business
- Strengthen the teaching profession
- Develop and support school autonomy
- Enhance schools' efforts to prepare students for the technology of the 21st century

The Principal for a Day Program begins with an invitation to local business and community leaders to participate, followed up with a contact by the school principal. If the program is adopted by a school district, the day can begin with a district breakfast meeting and orientation. At the breakfast the superintendent of schools can give a short welcome speech and, after breakfast, the Principal for a Day heads to his or her school to begin the day. Individual schools can hold their own Principal for a Day festivities by having the teachers and PTA host a breakfast before school.

The following is a suggested menu of activities for Principals for a Day. However, you can be creative in developing your own activities. The goal is for the business executive to experience as realistic a view as possible of what a day as a principal is like. The principal and the executive should talk prior to the event to discuss plans.

- Take a tour of school campus
- Attend a faculty meeting
- Visit or teach a class
- Give the morning announcements over the P.A. system
- Work with cafeteria workers as they prepare the day's meal
- Meet with student council
- Do lunch supervision or bus duty
- Participate in budget meeting
- Observe a lesson and sit in on a teacher evaluation conference
- Take parent calls
- Review daily attendance reports
- Handle (or advise principal on) student disciplinary problems
- Participate in a student study team for a special education student
- Conduct a fire drill
- Meet with PTA on school issues

Recognizing Community Heroes

What lies behind us and what lies before us are tiny matters compared to what lies within us.

—William Morrow

Schools often benefit from the significant contributions of local community members or service organizations. Schools need to explore how they can recognize these contributions through letters of appreciation or rewards ceremonies. The Heroes of the Heart Award (Treasure Chest Sample #31) is one way for principals to recognize exceptional contributions to the school.

TREASURE CHEST SAMPLE #31

HEROES OF THE HEART AWARD INVITATION

Dear Val Unteer:

Congratulations! Star Vista School would like to honor you for your exceptional dedication and service to the students of the Challenger School District. I am pleased to inform you that you have been selected to receive the Challenger School District's *Heroes of the Heart Award.* This unique award will be presented at a special Awards Breakfast on Friday, May 8, at 7:30 A.M. at the Old Ranch Country Club.

(Continued)

(Continued)

The Heroes of the Heart Award was created to recognize exceptional parents and community members who have had a significant impact on our students, staff, and school community. You have given so generously of your time, talents, and expertise to our school district and we want to honor you in a special way. We know that such generosity and caring comes from the heart

A hero is defined as someone who is recognized and valued for their special achievements. You deserve to be recognized for all you have done for the students of Star Vista School. Your contributions have made a significant difference at Star Vista. We thank you for your caring and support and we honor you for all you have done. You are truly a *Hero of the Heart*!

We hope you'll be able to join us as our special guest to be honored as a Hero of the Heart. Please contact Holly at 555-1234 to confirm your attendance. Thank you very much.

TIPS FOR BUILDING COMMUNITY INVOLVEMENT IN YOUR SCHOOL

Leaders have a significant role in creating the state of mind that is the school. They can serve as symbols of the moral unity of the school. They can express the values that hold the school together. Most important, they can conceive and articulate goals that lift people out of their petty preoccupations, carry them out of the conflicts that tear a school apart, and unite them in pursuit of objectives worthy of their best efforts.

—John W. Gardner

The following tips come from award-winning principals from across the nation who have been recipients of state Principal of the Year Awards, the National Distinguished Principal Award, or the Milken Family Foundation's National Educator of the Year Award.

1. Match several of your teachers with your community and business leaders for a Teacher for the Day program. Hold a breakfast reception with an orientation about your school, hosted by several teachers, and then involve them in the classroom with teachers for the morning. Let them see the challenges we face!

2. Set a goal of hosting one nonparent visitor per student. Have visitors sign a guest book or log of distinguished visitors. Provide each visitor with a school handout or brochure that highlights special programs. Select student hosts to welcome the visitors and show them their classroom or special programs.

3. Begin a Community Involvement Challenge. Challenge a well-known community leader such as a city council member, mayor, police chief, Lion's Club president, and so forth to come to school to read or speak to kids. He or she can then challenge someone else to come another time. Take the leader on a

mini-tour of several classrooms or programs to let him or her see what schools are like today.

4. Get a list of new births at local hospitals and make a visit with welcoming card and a gift of baby's first book. Include some parenting ideas and ways to maintain contact.

5. Contact business or community service organizations and suggest they hold one of their monthly meetings at your school followed by a brief tour of the school.

6. Display student work in shopping centers, hospitals, and other public buildings. Set up art displays in local banks and businesses. Display holiday murals (Halloween, Valentine's Day, etc.) by classes in local supermarkets. Use parent volunteers to coordinate.

7. Have student winners of school speech, poetry, or essay contests read their winning entries at local community service groups' lunch or breakfast meetings. Videotape the winners and have your local cable company show the tape on cable.

8. Invite community leaders to school to judge speech contests, essay contests, poster contests, science fair entries, and so on.

9. Have students invite someone special in their life, other than their parents, to have lunch with them. Provide a brief orientation and introduction. Have a special Grandparents Day or Everybody's Special Day.

10. Send a Welcome to Our School letter to all parents who are new to your school with an invitation to a special tour of the school. Have PTA put together a welcome packet and mail to parents with a follow-up phone call to answer any questions and invite them to be involved in school activities.

11. Contact local community music groups (Chamber quartet, bluegrass group) to perform at a school concert in addition to or with students. Invite community art groups to share their craft or artwork in an art show for the students on your campus.

12. Contact real estate offices in your area and invite them to tour your school and hold their staff meeting there. Provide them with lots of copies of school brochures to present to prospective buyers in the neighborhood. Give them the data to sell your school to parents that in turn will help them make a sale.

13. Invite district or central office secretaries and clerical staff to visit your school. They need to keep in touch with kids and see how their jobs support the schools. Invite them to judge contests or tour classrooms.

14. Add substitutes, many who are residents in your community, to the mailing list for your school newsletter or important notices.

15. Hold a What I Like Best About Our School contest for students and post the winners' stories and artwork in visible areas of your school or put on display at a library or at local businesses.

16. Invite senior citizens who have lived in the community a long time to visit your school and share their memories of the history of the community. Ask your local historical society to visit the school and bring community artifacts. Have students interview community old-timers or have them take oral histories of long-time residents.

17. Have students make Welcome to Our School posters or murals to display at entrances around campus.

18. Compile a listing of staff members and their expertise and provide a speaker's bureau listing and send it to local clubs and community service organizations that are always looking for speakers at their meetings.

19. Give complimentary passes to senior citizens for all school events.

20. Identify any famous alumni and invite them back to school. Ask them to write their impressions of school when they attended. Create a feature article for newsette or local newspaper. Have them meet with children to discuss the importance of an education.

21. Develop intergenerational programs in which adult and senior citizens and your students can interact, share ideas, and learn from each other. Seek out volunteers for sharing a hobby—computers, craft, chess, and so forth—with students as part of an after-school club program.

22. Establish a preschool PTA at your school that networks preschool parents in your community through neighborhood block groups and provides parenting inservices and school-readiness workshops.

23. Reach out to preschools in your area. Offer to provide a kindergarten teacher to speak at a parent meeting. Offer a tour of your school for preschool teachers or directors in the spring before kindergarten registration. They'll be able to more accurately inform their parents about your expectancies and programs.

24. Hold your own education summit to discuss topics of interest to the community such as technology, safe schools, and accountability. Invite representatives from the city, regional, or state legislators, local businesspeople, religious leaders, and community service organizations.

25. Look for special events at school where you can publicly recognize and commend parents, businesses, or community leaders for their support and dedication to children by presenting them special plaques, awards, or certificates.

26. Extend the concept of a school–business partnership by having local businesses each adopt a classroom. Student letters of appreciation or samples of student work could be displayed in the business. A walking field trip for the class to visit its adopted business would enhance the partnership and give the business good publicity.

27. Organize an adopt-a-student program, in which businesspeople would work one-on-one with at-risk students who have learning or attendance problems.

28. Celebrate your school's heritage. Consider holding a special school birthday celebration if the school is to have a major anniversary. Invite alumni back for special programs. Invite speakers to talk about "The Way We Were" (former principals, teachers, PTA presidents, or school board members) and current staff to tell about "Our School Today," giving each group an opportunity to be recognized for what makes your school special then and now.

If civilization is to survive, we must cultivate the science of human relationships, the ability of all peoples, of all kinds, to live together, in the same world at peace.

—Franklin D. Roosevelt

3

MASTERING THE SKILLS OF RENEWAL

RENEWAL

Keeping a Balance in Your Life

You cannot care for your school unless you also care for yourself.

—Richard Ackerman

As school leaders we have chosen a profession in which we give to others. We give, and we give, and we give, but we cannot continue to give to others without renewing our resources. We can easily get caught up in trying to be everything to everybody all the time. Our days become fractured, quickly consuming our time, energy, and resources.

The unending demands upon principals extend beyond the boundaries of the school day into our personal lives. We begin to make compromises and find ways to extend our day to get the job done. We find ourselves coming in early, staying late, and taking work home on weekends. We take home a briefcase full of work to be done.

The reality of the principalship is that it could consume your life. There is always more work to do than there is time to do it. We could literally work 24 hours a day and still not get the job done. It is an open-ended job—there never seems to be an end to our day. As the work piles up, we begin to experience guilt for all the unfinished tasks. Guilt is one of the biggest contributors to stress. So, the principal is racked with guilt, weighed down by the sheer volume of the tasks, and the onset of burnout begins.

You can't create quality on the job if you don't create it equally in your personal life.

—Ann McGee-Cooper

Under these work circumstances we need to recognize we can't do it all. Since we can't know it all or do it all, it's vital that we learn to take the time to contemplate what it is we need to know and what it is we need to do.

Time is the only coin you have in life . . . and only you can determine how it will be spent. Be careful lest you let other people spend it for you.

—Carl Sandburg

Work is only one aspect of your life. We cannot spend a disproportionate amount of time at work to the detriment of our families. You need to make sure you have a full life by keeping a balance between work and a life outside of work. Good leaders identify the need to get away from the job to become renewed and refreshed. Good leaders make a commitment to putting family first. We all need the love and nourishment provided by a significant other in our life. We need to spend time with family and friends to sustain us and renew our energy.

We need to care for ourselves if we are going to have the energy and resources to continue to give to others. We need to take care of ourselves first. Flight attendants tell us that in case of an emergency, masks will drop from the ceiling. If we are traveling with young children we are told to place the oxygen masks over our own face first and then the child's. The message is clear—if we don't take care of ourselves first we are no good to others.

When we truly care for ourselves, it becomes possible to care far more profoundly about other people. The more alert and sensitive we are to our own needs, the more loving and generous we can be towards others.

—Eda LeShan

One of the ways to take care of ourselves is to do those things that nourish and sustain us. We must learn to experience a sense of totality. To experience a sense of totality we must lose ourselves in tasks that we enjoy and cherish. When we are totally involved in a task we enjoy, we often lose any sense of time. Whether it's soothing the soul by listening to music, gardening, cooking, reading a good book, golfing, or painting, these are activities that replenish our spirit. We are so totally involved, we experience pure pleasure and we become unaware of time passing.

Taking Care of Number One

Leaders devote time every day to tipping the scale towards a more balanced life. This means taking care of themselves (exercising, resting properly, eating right); nurturing friendships; spending time with family members; nourishing the spirit; and having fun. If you can't find or make time for these activities, you're not the leader of the organization. You're a slave to it.

—Robert Ramsey

1.   Take a joy break! When you're getting close to physical or mental exhaustion, stop what you're doing, get up, and go out into the classrooms and get your fix. Experience the joy of our job and visit classrooms! When you're working on an intensive or lengthy project, get up from your desk or computer, walk outside, take a deep breath to get oxygen to your brain, and look at the sky. Take at least a 10-minute break every two hours.

2.   Be healthy! Take time for lunch and be conscientious about nutrition.

Don't skip lunch.

Don't eat at your desk.

Don't grab meals on the run.

Avoid cafeteria lunches.

If it's difficult to build a block of time for exercise into your busy schedule you can always get exercise by walking. Whenever and as often as you can, walk! When you're in the middle of a difficult project or at the end of a grueling parent conference, get up and take a brief walk. Walk quickly through the halls or around the perimeter of the school grounds.

3.   Create some *personal quiet time* for yourself. Build in personal quiet time for yourself between work and home. Use this time to make the transition from the principal mode to the family mode. Before getting home, give yourself time to take a walk around the school yard or through a park, drive a different route home, listen to Books on Tape, or park near a bench or trees and take 10 minutes of quiet time before rushing home to begin your "second" job. This should be your refill time—the time when you replenish your energy and resources so you don't burn out and exhaust your reserves.

4.   Get adequate sleep, even if it means putting off the work you feel must be done before the next day. Don't take time away from valuable sleep in order

to make the time to get work done. Work will never be done, no matter how many hours during the night you try to finish it. There will always be more to do.

You might never get sleep if you try to do all the homework from school late into the night. You might be able to cheat on your sleep once in awhile to get something important done, but loss of sleep will catch up with you. Lack of sleep can cause faulty judgment and sluggish energy during the day at school. You begin to become sleep deprived. You don't get enough rest and about mid-day you begin to run out of energy. You make poor decisions. You want to take a nap. Make sure you get a healthy dose of sleep so that you can attack the day with vim and vigor.

Don't want to miss your favorite late-evening TV program? Learn to use your VCR to tape those late-evening programs you don't want to miss. That way you watch the program on your own schedule, and you can fast-forward through those pesky commercials, thereby spending less time watching TV.

5. Develop friends who are not work-related so you can avoid shop-talk. Sometimes we just need to get out of the world of the principalship. We need to talk about other things than education. When you cultivate friends in other professions, you can discuss other exciting and thought-provoking issues.

6. Find a hobby—painting, keeping a daily journal, restoring a car, gardening. Find something that's therapeutic and relaxing as an alternative to your intellectually and physically demanding work as a principal. These are the self-nourishing behaviors you need to keep you balanced and energized.

7. Set boundaries. Let your coworkers and family know when you need time. You can't be all things to all people. When work is beyond overload you need to declare to family and friends that during this high stress-time you need a little extra time and space to get the job done.

8. Take a one-day vacation to Hawaii. When you've hit the bottom, when you're close to physical and emotional exhaustion, it's time for a one-day vacation for yourself. Work will wait, work will always be there, but you may not be there if you don't take care of yourself. Find a place you can go, away from your home and school community, where you can pamper yourself for the day. Use this time to refill your reserves, to reflect on your goals, to renew your spirit, and to reenergize so when you return to work you can continue to give to others.

Enroll in Playtime 101

We do not stop playing because we are old, we grow old because we stop playing.

—Anonymous

Thank you for enrolling in Playtime 101. This basic course is a requirement for renewing your credential and your mental health. No prerequisites are required. Participants will learn how they can help themselves and others who work in schools to relieve stress. A willingness to let go and experience joy and fun is the only requirement. We need to build in a variety of fun things to do within our day. Your grade will be based only on the number of fun things you do from the list below:

1. Hang a sign over the mirror in the bathroom that says,

   "DO NOT TAKE THIS PERSON SERIOUSLY!"

2. Start a Cartoon Board. Designate a bulletin board in the office or teacher's lounge as your Cartoon Board and begin by posting some of your favorite cartoons and invite others to add to the collection.

3. Tap into the creativity of your staff! Have the staff create a mural for the teacher's lounge. Select a fun theme (children, school climate, friendship, etc.), set up some white butcher paper in the lounge with some markers and paints, and see what happens when the staff get started. You can also use this idea as a team-building activity at a staff meeting to add a little variety to your meeting.

4. Have toys and humor props in your office. Include such things as soap bubbles, yo-yos, wind-up toys, and manipulative puzzles for adult play. Keep a red clown's nose on hand to lighten things up and make people laugh.

5. Have someone take a snapshot of you laughing or doing your favorite activity. Post it in your office or keep it close at hand and refer to it often. This picture will remind you to lighten up and that there is more to your life than work.

6. Start a Punch Line Board. Post cartoons without their punch lines and see what creative responses you get. Have the staff vote on the best ones and award a prize.

7. Start a You Must Have Been a Beautiful Baby Board in your staff lounge. Invite people to post their baby pictures without names and have a contest to see who can correctly guess the most.

8. Duplicate inspirational quotes and post them around school. Using your computer, make bookmarks featuring inspirational quotes. Add some great clip art and give them to a parent volunteer to laminate and then give them as gifts to students and staff.

9. Write a list of all the things that are stressing you at the moment on a sheet of toilet paper and then flush it all away!

TIPS FOR KEEPING A BALANCE IN YOUR LIFE FROM AWARD-WINNING PRINCIPALS

One of the characteristics of effective leaders is that they continually find joy in their jobs. This gives them the energy to energize others. They maintain a positive outlook and avoid burnout by focusing on what's right rather than what's wrong, constantly learning and growing on the job, making friends with problems, picking the right dance partners (associating with winners), keeping their sense of humor and getting a life outside of work.

—Robert Ramsey

What strategy do you find most helpful for keeping a balance between the demands and pressures of your job and your personal life? This was the question asked of 200 award-winning principals from across the nation. These are some of the strategies that work for them:

• I have established my priorities and then I more or less "advertise" them so that everyone knows where I am coming from. In fact, I put it right on my business cards under my name—"Steve Woolf—Husband, Daddy, Principal." The check for myself is my time allocation. My staff and even my community will hold my feet to the fire to make sure I keep those priorities. Not only that but my staff and students need to see me model good priorities. I tell my staff, "I love you, but you are third on my list!" *Steve Woolf, Tonganoxie, KS*

• Be well-organized with your time and day. Set aside time each day for yourself. I like to work out 4–5 days per week before work. Develop a personal mission statement about your priorities and goals. It helps guide your decision making in our busy world as principals. *Manuel Valenzuela, Tucson, AZ*

• This is very difficult. Prioritizing is a must. Finding a "pleasure place" daily. It could be through reading a book, sitting on my porch or taking trips. *Oveta Pearce, Enterprise, AL*

• I take a few minutes each day to leave the school. It could be for lunch, trip to the District Office, visit to another school, or just to get a Coke—but at least for 15 minutes, usually no more than an hour, I *leave*! *J. Lynn Jones, Spanish Fork, UT*

• I try to clear all I can off my desk each day before I go home. I feel a sense of accomplishment and can think about my home responsibilities while driving home. I make a "to do" list for the next day of things I can't do before leaving. *Nancy Moga, Covington, VA*

• I walk 3 miles daily very early in the morning. I use the time to reflect and prioritize my day. *Rick Acuncius, Highland, IL*

• I try to delegate certain responsibilities to our assistant principals. My wife and children also visit school during the year to physically remind people I have a personal life. *Kevin McCann, Chicago, IL*

• I take time for fun at least once or twice a week with friends, schedule it in before the week starts. *Lee Schmidt, Tacoma, WA*

• I regularly stay after hours to complete paperwork, but I *never* go to the "office" on the weekend unless a school function is taking place. Weekends are family time. I also keep in mind that family "milestones" only happen once. I do not miss "once in a lifetime" celebrations. Likewise I encourage my staff to attend family awards, etc. *Ronnelle Blankenship, Chattanooga, TN*

• Always *schedule time* for your personal life and *don't* deviate. *George McCullough Jr., South Bend, IN*

• It is an attitude of "Just Do It." I try to run most days. I make sure I get to the theater, read, play music and quilt. I have to keep doing things for myself or I'm no good to others. *Doug Pierson, North Kingston, RI*

• Take time when needed to pamper myself with a relaxing activity. *Glojean Todacheene, Shiprock, NM*

• Wine and an understanding spouse. Actually I didn't do this well initially and I'm reformed now. I've learned to selectively say no to things in the evenings or on weekends. People are understanding when you tell them "That's family time." *Deliece Hofen, Olathe, KS*

• One thing I do is to come to work an hour early for "my time." I am alone, with no interruptions, and can do both work and personal tasks. I can balance my checkbook, make my grocery list, prepare for a meeting, email my Mom and Dad in TN, write notes to teachers and students. I am fresh and alert and get more done in that hour than in any other of the day! It is a great way to start the day feeling great and ahead of the game! *Nancy Varian, Magnolia, OH*

• Reading journals and staff newsletters on the treadmill. *Cathy Bell, Lexington, KY*

• I do not take work home with me. I run at a health club for exercise and stress relief. I go out for dinner on Fridays with friends. Sunday evening is a time for family bonding. *Byron Schwab, West Paul, MN*

• Set a time for quiet work at school, leave, forget the job and go do something fun! *James Rowe, Lovelock, NV*

• My husband and I always stop everything and have dinner together. We review our day and then talk about other matters related to our personal lives. *Susan Van Zant, Ramona, CA*

Enjoy the little things in life, for one day you may look back and realize that they were the big things.

—Author Unknown

Laughter—The Key to Our Survival

• Humor is an antidote for stress. Laughter is like an aerobic exercise. Laughter is a good way to jog internally. Laughter is like a medicine. It increases the heart rate and circulation, and can help heal the body.
• We need to laugh at ourselves and laugh with others. Humor can allow you to cut through a tense situation and help refocus energy in a new direction.

- Put laughter at the top of your daily to-do list.
- Use educational cartoons in bulletins and display them in the teacher's lounge or workroom to spark a smile or create a chuckle. Sometimes we take ourselves too seriously and we just need a good laugh to lighten us up. Besides, laughter helps you live longer—look at the longevity of our comedians.
- Staff meeting starter—Use cartoons without captions and ask staff to create their own punch lines. Hand out treats to the three best captions.
- Keep a *humor journal* to record and savor those hilarious situations we experience every day. By recording them in a journal they will not fade from your humorous story repertoire and will make good material for the book on the principalship you intend to write some day. Start a new tradition at the end of the year when you have everyone tell their favorite humorous story at a staff meeting or after-school get-together.

Most people are as happy as they make up their minds to be.

—Abraham Lincoln

A Smile

A smile costs nothing but gives much. It enriches those who receive without making poorer those who give. It takes but a moment, but the memory of it sometimes lasts forever. None is so rich or mighty that he can get along without it, and none is so poor that he cannot be made rich by it. A smile creates happiness in the home, fosters goodwill in business and is the countersign of friendship. It brings rest to the weary, cheer to the discouraged, sunshine to the sad, and is nature's best antidote for trouble. Yet it cannot be bought, begged or borrowed, or stolen, for it is something that is of no value to anyone until it is given away. Some people are too tired to give you a smile. Give them one of yours, as none needs a smile so much as he who has no more to give.

—Author Unknown

TIPS FOR BRINGING HUMOR TO YOUR SCHOOL CULTURE FROM AWARD-WINNING PRINCIPALS

I have always felt that laughter in the face of reality is probably the finest sound there is and will last until the day when the game is called on account of darkness. In this world, a good time to laugh is any time you can.

—Linda Ellerbee

What is your best strategy for bringing laughter, fun, or humor to your school or the job? This was the question asked of 200 award-winning principals from across the nation. These are some of the strategies that work for them:

• We laugh non-stop! If you can't laugh at yourself and the fun things that happen in the school all day long you are doomed! *Deliece Hofen, Olathe, KS*

• Our team laughs regularly and well. We laugh together at the things students, parents, teachers and we say, do or at times, "goof-up." But we also make sure it's as a team. We are success oriented and we like people. We care deeply about kids. *Wayne Tanaka, Las Vegas, NV*

• The best advice given to me was to take what I do very seriously, but don't take yourself seriously at all. Laughter, fun, and humor have to be modeled by the school's leadership. I have to be the one joking with the kids at appropriate times and I have to be the one to laugh freely. I have found that self-deprecating humor is very effective with my staff. It models for them a way to interject humor in their classroom. *Steve Woolf, Tonganoxie, KS*

• Keep a positive perspective, laugh together, not at one another. We trust. *Mary Jarvis, Littleton, CO*

• At every staff meeting we do "Truth or Lie." Staff have given me two true interesting statements about themselves and one lie. We try to guess the lie. It can get very funny at times. I've learned a lot about the staff. *Patsy Higdon, Candler, NC*

• Building trust amongst the staff, parents, etc. FIRST, and then making a conscious effort to be lighthearted and silly in certain situations when such behavior wouldn't be expected. Funny quotes, cartoons and articles are also helpful. And being humorous all the time so it becomes a normal part of the school culture. *Laurel Telfer, Los Alamitos, CA*

• I share funny stories via e-mail. I show video clips to start every staff meeting. *Denise Potter, Carlsbad, NM*

• I like to seek out appropriate jokes and cartoons to attach to my weekly principal's bulletin. We also try to schedule a monthly staff dinner. Folks are encouraged to share an evening of fun and socializing with colleagues. Family members are also invited. *Manuel Valenzuela, Tucson, AZ*

• We give out raffle tickets to all the early arrivals to our monthly faculty meeting (165 teachers!) and give away logo items, books, new donated items and gift certificates. It always gets us going on a positive note. *Catherine Payne, Aiea, HI*

• Baskets of "goodies" appear on the counter in the lounge during high stress periods. Do the unexpected! Sometimes you have to step out of the role of the "administrator" and break the ice to relieve the stress of today's high-stakes educational forum. For example:

—Send a secret e-mail to your staff. If they read it by a certain date they can get a coupon from a local restaurant by printing out the e-mail and presenting it to you. You can attach this to something important or just use it as a way to get the group on track in checking their e-mail regularly.

—Encourage a staff committee to plan celebrations and activities not related to school (a caravan to the big craft fair, etc.)

—Provide a "first day survival kit" each year on the first student day. A zip-lock bag contains paperclips, note pad, Tylenol, and chocolate!

Ronnelle Blankenship, Chattanooga, TN

• My attitude—I refuse not to laugh. *Gary Burgess, Anderson, SC*

ENHANCING PEAK PERFORMANCE

Kind words can be short and easy to speak, but their echoes are truly endless.

—Mother Teresa

As school leaders, principals must set the tone for recognizing and affirming excellence in the classroom. We need to be profuse with our praise, giving it generously to others. We need to praise each other and do it frequently. Encouragement is oxygen for the soul and we have teachers who are asphyxiating because they never hear the words of encouragement and praise that give them the oxygen to survive. We can enhance peak performance by providing positive feedback and reinforcement. Letting teachers know what a good job they are doing and that you appreciate their dedication and hard work can be a powerful motivator to continue a tradition of excellence at your school. It also serves as an important model for teachers on how they should utilize positive reinforcement to enhance learning in the classroom. We all respond to praise.

When principals step foot onto their campuses, everyone they come into contact with expects something from them. Every student, parent, and staff member expects to be recognized, acknowledged, or affirmed in some way. They seek a smile, eye contact, a hello, words of encouragement, or a pat on the back. They want to know that you care about them as people and the way they measure that caring is through your acknowledging or interacting with them in some way.

Dealing With Difficult Parents

The biggest problem with communication is the illusion that it has taken place.

—George Bernard Shaw

Most of the contacts that principals have with parents are positive and supportive. However, it's the 20% of the difficult parents that often consume 80% of a principal's day. The challenge of communicating effectively with unhappy parents can often bring stress, frustration, and fear to the job. However, one of the most rewarding aspects of dealing with difficult parents is the challenge of finding a solution to the problem and having them leave the conference with a positive attitude or solution.

The best-kept secret about America's schools is the amount of verbal and sometimes even physical abuse that educators experience from angry and difficult parents. The public has no idea the amount of abuse that educators receive. Most parents assume that since they treat you politely and with respect other parents do also. They would be shocked and dismayed at the hostile and angry behavior of some parents toward teachers and principals. Many educators have had to turn to law enforcement and the courts for protection, sometimes even getting restraining orders to keep parents off the campus or away from them personally.

Unfortunately, many principals believe that if they just talk it through with the angry parent they will win them over. When we try to treat the problem logically it doesn't work because we are dealing with illogical people. For many of these parents, it's like rewarding negative behavior—they get the principal's undivided attention with all their shouting and abuse. Their negative behavior begins to escalate to the point of being out of control. So, what should principals do when the "crazies" really do go crazy?

What to Do When the Crazies Really Do Go Crazy!

Principals must not take any verbal abuse or allow any threat or actual physical abuse to occur. Principals must assert their right to be treated respectfully. The following steps can help to prevent the kind of abuse that often occurs when conferencing with a dysfunctional parent.

Step 1. Principals must assert their right to be treated respectfully. You need to make declarative statements like

"I have been respectful of you, now you need to be respectful of me."

"I have listened quietly to you, now you need to listen to me quietly."

"I didn't interrupt you when you were speaking, now you need to let me finish."

Step 2. Principals need to warn disruptive parents that their abusive language or inappropriate behavior is unacceptable. You need to say things like

"There's no need to use profanity."

"Please lower your voice, there is no need to shout."

"Threatening me won't help."

Step 3. Principals need to warn abusive parents whose inappropriate behavior is continuing to escalate that your conversation or meeting will be terminated if the abuse doesn't stop. You need to state strongly that

"If you continue to shout and swear, I'll have to hang up the phone!"

"If you continue to be this upset, it is clear that our meeting is not productive so we'll have to conclude this conference and meet at another time."

Step 4. If the abusive behavior continues, then the principal needs to take action. You need to talk over the shouting and swearing and put these words in your mouth:

"I'm sorry you're unable to stop swearing so I'm hanging up now!"

"I'm sorry but this meeting is over. You need to leave."

If you hang up on the parent, the first thing you do is call your superintendent. You need to get there first! In many cases, the parent will call up the superintendent to report you. Warn the superintendent, so he or she will be prepared, and indicate the nature of the abuse and the actions that you took.

If you conclude the meeting with an abusive parent, then stand up and open the door as you ask him or her to leave.

Step 5. The last step is taken when you are in a meeting and you've stood, declared the meeting over, and asked the parent to leave and he or she refuses to leave your office. In rare instances, some parents become so distraught and out-of-control that they will not leave your office until they get the response they want. Under these circumstances, as a last resort, pick up a tape recorder and start recording the rantings and ravings of the parent. Whenever you know a difficult and angry parent is coming to your office, always have a tape recorder nearby on your desk. Turn it on, hold it up, and say in a strong voice:

"It is (date and time) and I am now recording this meeting with Mr. Blankhead and I have asked him to stop being verbally abusive and to leave my office."

Continue to record the shouting and when the parent realizes he or she is being recorded, in most instances, the shouting will stop. If it does not, then leave your office immediately and call the police for assistance.

BUILDING YOUR DREAM TEAM

There is something that is much more scarce, something rarer than ability. It is the ability to recognize ability.

—Robert Half

One of the most important roles of the school administrator is the selection and evaluation of staff. The ability of the school administrator to hire, supervise, evaluate, and if necessary remediate or dismiss staff is essential to building a successful school team and a culture of excellence at your school. Every school principal would like the opportunity the hire the nation's brightest and best teachers for their school. We'd all like to build our own Dream Team of teachers, including a wide range of experiences from beginning, mid-career, second career, and experienced. The tools, strategies, and sample forms that follow will provide a variety of approaches to interviewing and selecting your Dream Team.

The Teacher Interview

The teacher interview is one of the most important decision-making events for a school. The interview criteria must be clearly established. It is important to involve other staff members in the interview process whenever possible or appropriate. Interview questions need to be carefully prepared and are designed to get at the heart of the candidates' values and beliefs, their love and advocacy of children, and their parent and public relations skills as well as their knowledge of curriculum and teaching strategies. Actual situations or problems need to be posed and probed to assess judgment and problem-solving skills. It's a tall order—but with the right questions and some in-depth probing you will find the next wonderful addition to your Dream Team.

Preparation for the Interview—Gathering Data

In preparation for the interview, thoroughly review the candidate's papers, experiences, transcripts, and recommendations so you can best use the limited time you have to your advantage. Use questions and their responses to probe candidates' thinking or areas of school priorities. Too often valuable interview time is lost the first 10 minutes of an interview by asking simple questions about candidates' background to get information that is already available in their files. Questions like, "Where did you student teach?" and "Where did you go to school?" are designed to set the candidate at ease but waste valuable time that could be used for more in-depth questioning. Most interviews are 30–40 minutes and within this short time frame you want to determine if this is a teacher you want on your staff. You can gather additional in-depth information about the philosophy and beliefs of the candidate through the use of tools or inventories such as the Professional Information Survey (Treasure Chest Sample #32). Have the candidate arrive 10 minutes before the interview and complete the survey. Take a minute before inviting the candidate into the interview to review his or her answers and see if there are any areas that need more in-depth exploration.

TREASURE CHEST SAMPLE #32

PROFESSIONAL INFORMATION SURVEY

To the Applicant: This opinion survey is intended for us to learn some additional insights into your thoughts and philosophy of education. Please record your responses in the spaces provided. Thank you.
Name of Applicant

1. Teachers should
2. Students should
3. Parents should
4. Administrators should
5. Evaluation should
6. The greatest problem facing education is
7. What is your philosophy of student discipline?
8. What methods or practices do you utilize to maintain good student behavior?
9. What kinds of teaching strategies do you utilize in order to meet the individual needs of all learners in a given group or class?
10. What techniques do you use to create a positive learning environment?
11. List three books you have read that you feel have influenced your educational practices.

   Title   Author

1.
2.
3.

12. What do you do to maintain your professional development?
13. Please list any special training you have had as an educator. Examples might include technology, literature, writing, or math problem solving.

The sure way to miss success is to miss the opportunity. Be fearless and bold in your actions. Know what you want and go for it.

—Rupert McCall

Teacher Interview Questions

The following questions are samples to select from when interviewing a teacher candidate (Treasure Chest Sample #33). This is a list of tried and tested questions used by award-winning principals that will enable you to get at the essence of the candidate's beliefs, personality, knowledge, and love of children. Some questions require factual answers, some probe a candidate's values and attitudes, and others ask about educational philosophy or curriculum knowledge. A good interview should contain a mix of these three types of questions.

TREASURE CHEST SAMPLE #33

TEACHER INTERVIEW QUESTIONS

1. What has been the most significant accomplishment in your classroom (or student teaching) this past year? (Look for an answer that is student focused.)
2. How would you respond to parents who complained that their child was not being challenged and that school was boring?
3. Describe your worst discipline problem and how you handled it.
4. What three adjectives would your students use to describe you?
5. What was the last lesson you taught that bombed? What did you do next?
6. Rate yourself as a teacher on a scale of 1–10, and tell us why. What would it take to get to a 10? Do you know anybody who is a 10?
7. In a scale of 1–100, with 100 being highest, where would your supervisor rank you in comparison to all other teachers he or she has supervised?
8. What self-esteem-building activities do you find most effective in working with students?
9. What are your favorite subjects to teach? Is there any subject you'd gladly let a team member teach for you?
10. It's the third month of school and we are standing in the middle of your room during (reading, math, social studies, etc.) time. Paint us a picture of what we would see going on. Describe what we would see happening. What are the students doing? What are you doing? What's the room environment like?
11. If you got the job, what are the first three things you'd want to know?
12. If you could take us on a tour of your classroom three years from now, what would you say is most significant about your accomplishments as a teacher?
13. What kind of behavior in a child pushes your button? How do you respond?
14. What is your philosophy on grading?
15. What is the most exciting thing going on in education today?
16. Describe your ideal math program. Give some examples of how you would incorporate problem solving.
17. What tools have you found most successful in assessing student progress in your classroom? What role do student portfolios play in that assessment?
18. There is much emphasis on writing today. Describe the steps of the writing process and describe when you would use the writing process with students.
19. You have a group of eight students in your class who are experiencing problems with writing and reading and are a year to a year and a half below their grade level. What type of program would you set up to meet their needs?
20. How do you keep yourself abreast of the latest research and instructional strategies?
21. What is the role of full inclusion of special-needs students in your classroom?
22. If we were to phone your former supervisor or master teacher, what would he or she say about you in terms of your strengths and weaknesses as a teacher?
23. Describe your expertise with technology and share how you would utilize technology in your classroom.

(Continued)

(Continued)

24. Describe a conflict you've had with someone in a work setting and share how you resolved it.
25. What is the most frustrating thing facing a teacher in the classroom today?
26. What's the most difficult problem you've had with a parent and how have you resolved it?
27. You have a heterogeneous grouping of students in your classroom. How do you identify the ability levels and then best meet their individual needs?
28. What's the biggest pressure on the classroom teacher today?
29. Describe how you would organize your science program to ensure that students would participate in hands-on experiences and processes.
30. At the end of interview: Would you evaluate this interview and share your perceptions of how you felt you did? Were there any questions that were easier or more difficult than others?

Evaluation Criteria for Teacher Candidate Interview

After each candidate leaves the interview, the panel or principal needs to take time to record thoughts and reactions. There are a wide variety of tools to use for this purpose. The following Teacher Candidate Interview Record Sheet (Treasure Chest Sample #34) allows you to evaluate the teacher by comparing him or her with other teachers. Does this candidate rank in the upper 5% of all teachers, or the upper 30%, or the lowest 50%? This forces the evaluator to consider a very specific criterion designed to identify those teacher candidates who fall in the upper percentile of teachers.

TREASURE CHEST SAMPLE #34

TEACHER CANDIDATE INTERVIEW RECORD SHEET

Applicant's Name_____ Date _____ Time_____
Position Applied for _____Interviewer _____
Credentials Held _____Grade Level/Subject Preference _____
Please rate candidate by comparing with others of comparable training and experience.

	UPPER	UPPER	UPPER	UPPER	LOWEST
	5%	10%	25%	30%	50%

	5%	10%	15%	30%	50%
1. Teaching experience, experience with youth					
2. Enthusiasm, evidence of warmth and caring					
3. Communication skills, clarity of expression					
4. Knowledge of curriculum					
Subject:					
Subject:					
Subject:					
5. Instructional skills, uses multiple teaching strategies that reflect planning and pacing					
6. Classroom management skills, provides environment conducive to learning					
7. Experience and training in technology					
8. Rapport and relationships with students					
9. Rapport and relationships with colleagues					
10. Rapport and relationships with parents					
11. Organizational skills					
12. Attitude, emotional maturity					
13. Discipline skills, positive reinforcement					
14. Growth potential					

Overall Composite Evaluation

Comments:

Overall Recommendation: ____ Exceptional   ____Good Prospect

        ____ Satisfactory   ____ Marginal

        ____ Consider Other Candidates First

        ____ Do Not Employ   ____Hire

Progressive Ranking ____

Reducing the Influence of Others

When using a committee to interview and recommend candidates, you want to get each panel member's individual perception without the influence of other panel members. Often, following each candidate interview, there is a committee discussion in which panel members share their opinions and observations. Sometimes a strong panel member can influence other committee members by swaying their perceptions and the best candidate is not always the one recommended.

The progressive ranking sheet (Treasure Chest Sample #35) is a great strategy for avoiding this kind of influence. After each candidate is interviewed there is a silent period when panel members record their perceptions and reactions on the district's evaluation form and then complete the forced-ranking sheet. Each panel member individually rates each of the candidates without the input of the committee. Concluding each interview, they must rank the candidate in relationship to all the other candidates they have interviewed. This forces panel members to priority rank the candidates immediately without discussion and not wait until they have seen all the candidates.

At the end of all interviews, each panel member can share his or her number one candidate and discussions about the candidates can begin. An example of a progressive ranking sheet completed by a panel member shows that the last candidate, Denise Lamireaux, was her top pick and Raul Ramirez, the third candidate, was her second choice.

TREASURE CHEST SAMPLE #35

CANDIDATE PROGRESSIVE RANKING SHEET

Names	Rank Order						Notes
John James	I	I	2	2	3	4	
Sue Solis		2	3	3	4	5	
Raul Ramirez			I	I	I	2	
Tom Timberlane				4	5	6	
Debbie Lee					2	3	
Denise Lamireaux						I	

The Key to Hiring the Best—The Demonstration Lesson

Once you've narrowed the field down to two or three top candidates, you must take the most important and powerful next step. If you really want to select the best candidate to work with children at your school then you need to invite the finalists back to do what you're hiring them to do—teach. Ask them back to teach a demonstration lesson. Many times candidates can talk a great story in the interview but when hired and placed in a classroom with children, they can't put it into practice. The principal's life just became more complicated as considerable time needs to be directed toward correcting and improving the performance of the teacher. Time will need to be spent in observing in the classroom, conferencing with the teacher to improve performance, and potentially moving toward documentation and dismissal.

So, before you hire a teacher to work with kids, it is imperative that you observe him or her first working with kids. Invite the candidates to teach a 15-minute demonstration lesson. Make it a simple lesson with a good group of kids. The observation of the candidates interacting with students will provide you with the best indicator yet of their potential as members of your team. Following the demonstration lessons, measure their self-evaluation skills by asking them to evaluate how the lesson went to test their judgment and honesty.

Checking References

It is always comforting to validate your perceptions about a teacher candidate by checking on references from those who have supervised or observed the candidate teaching. Make that phone call to confirm your perceptions because we can often be fooled by a candidate's words. With the current fear of lawsuits it can be difficult to obtain honest input and evaluation from prior employers or evaluators. Frequently, it is what they don't say, not what they say, that gives you the clue this may not be the teacher for your school. Look for superlatives and descriptive statements. The Telephone Reference Call Form (Treasure Chest Sample #36) provides a variety of questions to select from that are designed to help you get the information you need to make an informed decision.

TREASURE CHEST SAMPLE #36

TELEPHONE REFERENCE CALL FORM

Candidate's Name: Date:

District Employed: Person/Title Contacted
                                           for Recommendation:

What do you see as the strengths of this candidate?

What do you see as the weaknesses or areas for improvement or growth of this candidate?

Where would you rank this person on a scale of 1–100 in comparison to all other personnel you've worked with? Why?

What one adjective would you use to describe the overall rating of this candidate?

Please rank this candidate on a 1–10 scale (with 10 high) for each of these qualities:

dedication	creativity	good judgment
teaching skills	patience	student relationships
commitment	follow-through	energy
sense of humor	writing ability	communication skills
people skills	initiative	curriculum knowledge
flexibility	leadership	enthusiasm
attendance	discipline	intelligence
team player	personality	health/vitality

Is there anything else I should know or didn't ask about in considering this person for employment?

Would you be eager to hire or rehire this candidate for your school or district or would you want to screen other applicants before hiring this person?

Comments:

ENHANCING PEAK PERFORMANCE

Catch 'Em Being Good is a process like mining for gold. You must literally move tons of dirt to find a single ounce of gold. The Catch 'Em Being Good philosophy means you're not looking for the DIRT—you're looking for the GOLD!"

—Andrew Carnegie

We all respond to praise. However, finding the positive in others is not always easy. As school leaders, we sometimes have to really look hard to find where we can compliment those staff members we perceive as difficult or inadequate.

• Often it may take several walk-throughs in the classroom to catch some teachers at their best. This may force you to "catch 'em being good" in order to find the positives happening in those classrooms. Sometimes you really have to look hard to find something to compliment, but it's important to reinforce the positive for all your staff members, so keep looking!

• Avoid the false positive by making sure that the positive feedback is warranted and sincere. Anything but truthful praise will look like manipulation and both of you will know the praise is not true or warranted.

• If we expect teachers to be troublesome then we will be troubled by them. If you're dealing with a small group of teachers who have "hardening of the attitudes," try to turn them into "positive rays of sunshine." When you walk in the teacher's lounge at lunchtime and see them clumped together in a corner and grumbling and griping, use the element of surprise—join them. Sit right down in the middle of the group and—after the shocked silence—begin to inundate them with positive statements. Repeat this strategy every time you see them clumped together. Try to change the focus of their negative conversations to positive accomplishments at the school. Tell them some of your school's success stories that will convey your enthusiasm and excitement.

• We all know about the research on gifted students where the teacher was given a group of students and told they were gifted even though they were not. Because of her high expectations the students achieved much higher levels than thought possible. What if we, as school administrators, viewed all our teachers as gifted? What would be the result? Would they rise to our expectations? Would they achieve more than we thought possible?

Too often we underestimate the power of a touch, a smile, a kind word, a listening ear, an honest compliment, or the smallest act of caring, all of which have the potential to turn a life around.

—Leo Buscaglia

How to Turn Your Worst Teacher Into One of Your Best!

Every principal faces a wide range of teaching abilities among staff members. Some teachers we see as exceptional or inspirational, while others are seen as dull and deadly for students. How can you turn that worst or most difficult teacher on your staff into one of your best? Here are some strategies that will help you rekindle the passion in those dull and deadly teachers and help you turn them into some of your best!

We're not talking about turning around the incompetent teacher or the marginal first-year teacher that you've decided to dismiss or not renew a contract. We're talking about the teachers who we see in a negative light. They are the ones who push our buttons and irritate the heck out of us. These marginal, difficult teachers are often the best candidates for turning into some of the best teachers on your staff.

The first step is to praise good teaching when we see it. Positive reinforcement is an effective tool for sustaining that which we are praising. We all respond to praise. However, finding the positive in everyone is not always easy. As school leaders, we sometimes have to really look hard to find where we can compliment those staff members we perceive as marginal, difficult, or inadequate.

Principals must acknowledge the power of expectations. Research has shown that expectations often function as self-fulfilling prophecies. If we expect to see a teacher act a certain way, it is more likely that we will see him or her act that way. What we expect is what we get!

When we categorize our teachers as superstars or turkeys, then, when we walk into their classrooms, we see the behavior we expect. We need to stop labeling teachers, and students, and start raising our expectations for them to succeed. We need to change how we look at teachers who irritate us or have retired on the job. With these teachers we need to look for ways we can reignite the passion that led them into teaching in the first place.

When we become conditioned to perceived truth and closed to new possibilities, the following happens:

We see what we expect to see, not what we can see.

We hear what we expect to hear, not what we can hear.

We think what we expect to think, not what we can think.

—John Maxwell

This requires a major paradigm shift on our part. We have inadvertently conditioned ourselves to see that teacher in a certain way—to expect the worst when we enter that teacher's classroom. We need to de-condition our thinking and begin to look for or see the positives that have been clouded by our prejudgments.

TEACHER EVALUATION

The mediocre teacher tells. The good teacher explains. The superior teacher demonstrates. The great teacher inspires.

—William Arthur Ward

The supervision and evaluation of personnel is one of the most important responsibilities of a school principal. The time devoted to the supervision and evaluation of staff is essential to building a successful school. If evaluations are written with care and understanding, principals have a tool that can enhance staff performance, improve classroom instruction, and ensure student success. The process for evaluating teachers and staff will vary greatly from principal to principal, school to school, and district to district. But, whatever the process, principals are always searching for those key ideas or phrases or for just the right words that will help them effectively reflect the attributes, skills, and qualities of each staff member.

Sometimes, in writing our evaluations or letters of recommendation, we get stuck trying to find the right words. What do you say new about the teacher you've been evaluating for a number of years? It seems like you're always repeating words you've used in prior evaluations. Sometimes we're stuck on finding just the right words for that difficult or marginal teacher. To assist us in writing evaluations, we should take advantage of the wonderful word banks or sample evaluations available to us. These resources can spark our thinking, give us just the right phrase, or enable us to put some new life in our writing. Following are a variety of teacher evaluations that can assist you in finding the best words to improve instruction and help teachers create success for students.

(Text continues on page 147)

TREASURE CHEST SAMPLE #37

EXCEPTIONAL ELEMENTARY TENURED TEACHER

Recommendation:

Maria is an exceptional educator who serves as an exemplary model for other teachers. Maria brings to her profession a rich background of experience and expertise and consistently demonstrates the traits of a caring, dedicated, and professional teacher. Maria is an inspiration to others and is highly respected for her knowledge and skills as a teacher by her colleagues, supervisors, and students' parents.

Building on her years of experience in kindergarten, Maria continues to demonstrate enthusiasm and excitement about changes she brings to her classroom each year. Maria is a strong child advocate and that advocacy permeates all decisions she makes regarding her classroom program. Maria has a very strong sense of what makes a kindergarten classroom function effectively.

One of Maria's strengths is her relationships with children. Maria easily establishes a wonderful natural rapport with students that serves as a model for mutual respect between teacher and child. She maintains a special relationship with each of her students and they sense her compassion and caring. She creates a classroom environment that encourages risk-taking and critical thinking. Maria is particularly skilled in eliciting exceptional growth from her students by incorporating high expectations and a challenging curriculum and cramming every minute of the day with new learning. It is a pleasure to take visitors to Maria's classroom as they are always impressed with the incredible learning environment and impressive quality of her instructional program. She has created a print-rich classroom, reflecting student learning through posted class and individual stories, books, and artwork. She created wonderful learning centers that are stimulating and highly interactive. The presentation of student work, in attractively prepared books and folders, is exceptional and they are cherished by parents for years afterward.

Maria continues to expand her leadership skills by sharing her ideas with her colleagues. This year she presented a workshop at the state curriculum conference and has provided early literacy inservices for neighboring school districts. She has prepared an outstanding inservice video, with the assistance of a parent, on the topic of how to teach beginning reading. Her video, highly professional and presented in a knowledgeable and warm manner, serves as an excellent inservice for teachers and parents. Her instructional knowledge and skills are highly respected by fellow staff members and they actively seek out her expertise for ideas and strategies to implement in their own classrooms. Maria is always willing to share with others and is particularly effective in working with those teachers new to the profession.

Maria is one of our trained Reading Recovery teachers, and she has demonstrated exceptional dedication by continuing to teach the program in addition to her regular classroom responsibilities. She effectively incorporates the Reading Recovery strategies in her classroom instruction. Her kindergarten students have benefited greatly from her experiences as she has effectively woven those strategies into her everyday instruction.

(Continued)

(Continued)

Maria provides her students the opportunities to grow in self-confidence and self-esteem. She approaches each student with love and understanding, patience and guidance, and an enthusiasm and joy for learning that results in an exceptional learning environment. This is substantiated by the many positive comments received from parents, students, and fellow staff members. Parents' high regard for her contributions as a teacher were reflected in her selection as a recipient of the Star Vista PTA Honorary Service Award.

Maria is a teacher of exceptional merit and she easily ranks in the top 2% of all teachers I have ever supervised. Maria's zest for teaching, her dedication to the profession, and her ability to enable her students to achieve their highest potential make her a joy to work with. She has my highest admiration and respect!

TREASURE CHEST SAMPLE #38

EXCELLENT HIGH SCHOOL TENURED TEACHER

Recommendation:

1. Professional Attitude, Attributes, and Conduct. Mary Alice teaches American Government and Advanced Placement European History. She is an experienced teacher and conducts herself at a high professional level. She aspires to a high standard of professional conduct in her work ethic, professional dress, and demeanor toward others. Mary Alice could well be characterized as a lifelong learner. This spring she attended the Advanced Placement European History Conference at State University to update her course materials to align with the new frameworks and assessments. She stays abreast of teaching strategies through attendance at inservices and readings such as *Social Education* and *Law Related Journal.* Her most innovative endeavor was the creation of an Internet Web site home page for her Government and European History students, which enhanced resources for her students.

2. Professional Relationships. Mary Alice fosters positive parent, student, and collegial relationships. With parents and students, she communicates classroom progress through the posting of grades, through individual grade conferences with students, through progress and grade reports, and through personal contacts with parents. Mary Alice meets with her colleagues to develop American Political Traditions and Advanced Placement European History course materials. She fosters communication with personnel schoolwide by attendance at staff meetings, department meetings, inservices, and the Faculty Forum.

3. Instructional Techniques, Strategies, and Professional Skills. Mary Alice varies instruction to best convey the objective of the lesson and in a way to best meet the needs of her students. Among the strategies used most are lecture, discussion, group work, writing in class, and writing at home. In designing exams and writing assignments, Mary Alice poses questions that require students to use critical/creative thinking skills of application, analysis, and evaluation. A primary focus of Mary Alice's instruction is concept attainment through applied learning. In one lesson observed, Mary Alice posed a simulation of the jury selection process in which students were asked to analyze a case study, write questions for voir dire, and evaluate potential jurors for exemption. The activity required comprehension of the case; analysis of the position of the defendant or complainant; synthesis in the creation of applicable, indirect questions; and judgment and assessment of the jury pool. Lastly, Mary Alice teaches a sense of civic responsibility to her seniors by encouraging the application of classroom learnings in student behavior. She brings voter registrars to class, she encourages students to volunteer in political campaigns and in political organizations, and she asks students in Government classes to participate in community service projects.

4. Adherence to Curricular Objectives—Preparation and Planning. Mary Alice works with department colleagues in aligning curriculum with that of the framework. In addition, she contributes to the attainment of departmental objectives as follows:

- She supports the inclusion of diversity training in her Government classes.
- She implements the portfolio project in Government.
- She continues to review and recommend curriculum materials.
- She shares and articulates her course content and materials.
- She incorporates the use of technology in her grading, her use of the media center with students, and her creation of a Web site home page

5. Maintenance of a Suitable Learning Environment. Through careful planning and classroom management, Mary Alice maintains an engaging learning environment in her classroom. She is careful to prepare lessons that involve students in interactive lectures of discussion. The students are expected to listen actively, discuss, question, and take notes. She varies a lesson to include group work that involves problem solving. Mary Alice's lessons are rich in content, often building upon students' personal experiences, and balanced with multiple activities to create motivation through interest. In addition, she is good at task analysis—the breaking of content into comprehensible chunks so students are motivated by a sense of success. The feeling tone in the classroom is exceptional. Students exchange ideas in a nonjudgmental yet intellectually stimulating environment of questions and answers. Mary Alice is mindful of fairness and she models this along with an attitude of mutual respect in the classroom. Her learning environment is exceptional.

6. Related Professional Responsibilities. Mary Alice holds to high standards in recording attendance and issuing consequences for attendance violations. She follows through on tardies and truancies with schoolwide means of discipline. Among her extra duties, Mary Alice serves on the PTSA Student of the Week Committee and as lead teacher to a new teacher, member of the School Site Council, and a leader in the Faculty Forum.

7. Pupil Progress. Students in Mary Alice's class succeed. She assesses them by way of essays, homework, class assignments, and exams. She has high passage rates in her classes and on the average her students score above the 80% passage rate on

(Continued)

(Continued)

the AP European History exam. Through frequent testing and monitoring of student homework and classroom assignments, she keeps abreast of student progress and performance. She offers tutorials before and after school for students with a below C grade.

Summary

The learning environment in Mary Alice's classes is engaging, interactive, and high-leveled in terms of thinking skills. Her main focus for the year was to learn to create a home page on the Internet. On it, she has placed assignments, historical links, and communiqués. Students can link to sources that align with the curriculum on the presidency, Congress, the Supreme Court, as well as to other media resources. She is to be commended for her dedication and innovation on this project. With her expertise and with this valuable resource, Mary Alice's next step could be to share this project with her colleagues and provide training and assistance.

In all, Mary Alice is a true professional; always learning and changing to better serve the needs of students. She is a model teacher and a valuable and highly respected member of the staff. It is a blessing to have Mary Alice at our school!

Reprinted with permission from Carol Hart, Superintendent, Los Alamitos USD, California

TREASURE CHEST SAMPLE #39

EXCELLENT ELEMENTARY TENURED TEACHER

Recommendation:

Judy is an excellent second-grade teacher whose zest for teaching radiates enthusiasm and joy for learning and this has a positive effect on all around her, be they children, staff, or parents. Judy approaches each student with love and understanding, patience and guidance, and an enthusiasm for learning. This year Judy has successfully integrated a full-inclusion special needs student in her classroom. The student with special needs is responding to appropriate role models and expectations with considerable success. This is a result of the nurturing, compassion, and understanding shown by Judy who has worked so closely with the student's parents.

Judy is one of those dedicated teachers whose constant mission is the refining of her teaching skills. She continually seeks out new ideas, strategies, and materials that will enhance her instructional program. Judy has established a wonderful learning environment for her second graders that is centers-based and print rich, and reflects the high-quality work of her students. One of Judy's strengths is her willingness to share her ideas with others. She has served in a leadership role as District Mentor Teacher for second grade in several curriculum areas. Judy's creativity and her ability to design lessons and materials that are exciting and challenging have made her one of Star Vista's most respected teachers. Judy has served as an excellent model for those entering the teaching profession. As a master teacher, she has provided excellent guidance and training for her student teachers.

Judy maintains a special relationship with each of her students. She treats each one with great dignity and self-respect. Judy has created a positive environment that is very child-oriented and focuses on building positive student self-esteem. Each year she provides her students the opportunity for creative expression through an impressive dramatic production that is performed for parents. As a result, her students have a wonderful opportunity to grow in self-esteem, self-confidence, oral language-development skills, and dramatic performance skills. These experiences provide her students with memories that will last a lifetime.

Judy is a dedicated and compassionate teacher. She willingly gives of her time out of school to volunteer at hospital wards for terminally ill children where she dresses in costumes and reads stories. Her enthusiasm for teaching, her love of children, and her expertise as a teacher make Judy a highly respected and admired teacher. It is a pleasure to work with such a dedicated and inspirational teacher and I greatly appreciate her enthusiasm, her willingness to grow as a teacher, and her commitment to excellence.

TREASURE CHEST SAMPLE #40

AVERAGE ELEMENTARY TENURED TEACHER

Recommendation:

Middy Middleton is a third-grade teacher at Star Vista School. This is her seventh year in third grade. Middy has created an environment suitable to learning. The room environment is set up to allow for large- and small-group instruction as well as cooperative groups. Student work is displayed around the room and is changed periodically. Classroom routines are understood by all students and discipline procedures are posted in the classroom to facilitate classroom control. On frequent principal walk-throughs of Middy's classroom, it was observed that student discipline was generally handled in a controlled manner. Middy's classroom manner, tone of voice, and discipline techniques with certain children can make it difficult for them to sometimes feel at ease and comfortable. Middy is urged to enhance her rapport with all children by increasing the number of opportunities for positive reinforcement and praise throughout the instructional day.

Middy is open to suggestions that have been made for improving her instructional skills. She continues to work at improving her skill level by exploring new materials and instructional strategies. As part of her professional growth she attended school and district inservices on balanced literacy and technology. She continues to work on ways to implement the instructional strategies from these workshops into her daily routines. Middy continues to explore instructional strategies for breaking

(Continued)

(Continued)

the content down into small pieces of learning that her students can master. Middy is beginning to promote the use of technology in her classroom and is learning to integrate a computer into her classroom instructional program. Middy strives to be more at ease during the observation process and has reduced some anxiety during formal observations by the principal.

Middy, in collaboration with her principal, has established a personal growth objective this year of increasing the effectiveness of her reading instruction through the guided reading process and the diagnostic/prescriptive assessment of student progress using running records. Middy capably covers the third-grade curriculum and this year has implemented math journals to assess student understanding of math concepts and vocabulary. She is prepared in advance with materials, equipment, supplies, and planning to carry out her instructional objectives. It is the responsibility of every educator to help parents understand and appreciate the talents and limitations of their child. Middy is direct in her communications and keeps parents informed of student progress or behavioral problems. She spends considerable time communicating with parents to help them understand and support her instructional program and classroom routines. Middy utilizes some parent volunteers in her classroom to assist her instructional program.

I appreciate Middy's willingness to work cooperatively to enhance her contributions as a teacher and I predict she will continue to demonstrate professional growth.

TREASURE CHEST SAMPLE #41

AVERAGE HIGH SCHOOL TENURED TEACHER

Recommendation:

1. Professional Attitude, Attributes, and Conduct. Avery is an experienced teacher who demonstrates a positive and cooperative attitude. He demonstrates a willingness to continue to grow and learn. His professional growth goal for the year has been to vary his teaching strategies to include simulations and cooperative learning. To accomplish this goal, Avery made inquires of his colleagues regarding their use of cooperative groups. He chose to conduct a lesson on American Family Life that included group research, group writing, and discussion. Groups were divided in common-interest pairings, with some of the work being done in pairs and the rest in larger groups of six to eight students. The activity offered support for the learning in Chapter 15 and was a good technique choice for the lesson due to its research, analysis, and problem-solving nature, lending itself to cooperative learning. Avery is encouraged to expand the opportunities for his students to participate in a variety of teaching strategies as an alternative to the use of only lecturing. Avery attends schoolwide and department inservices to become familiar with information new to the U.S. History curriculum.

2. Professional Relationships. To foster positive parent relations, Avery explains his program to parents during Back-to-School Night and makes telephone calls home when needed. In an effort to foster positive student relations, Avery greets each students with a handshake as they enter class. He is increasing the use of praise and positive reinforcement in response to student effort on homework and in grade performance. With his department, Avery regularly attends team and department meetings and is devoting more time to developing effective working relationships as a member of the department team.

3. Instructional Techniques, Strategies, and Professional Skills. Relatively new to teaching history, Avery is developing a grasp of the subject matter and is still learning to use a variety of teaching strategies in his assessments. He uses lecture to convey the text, term papers to emphasize writing and thinking skills, worksheets for research, maps for the study of geography, term papers for research, and newspapers for comparing current events to past history. Avery needs to increase the number of opportunities for his students to participate in group projects to foster cooperation, competitive games for interest and motivation, cartoons for comparison and contrast, and the use of simulations such as having students research and role-play people affiliated with World War II—Rosie the Riveter, an atomic scientist, a zoot suiter, and a panelist in the pro-con debate on the use of the atom bomb. In using oral presentations, Avery could enhance the learning experience by adding a rubric to the presentation and engaging the audience in rating and analyzing the presentation according to the rubric. While incorporating new strategies, the activities should support a specified learning objective in the lesson.

4. Adherence to Curricular Objectives—Preparation and Planning. Avery uses the U.S. History Guide as a framework for planning his units of study, learning objectives, and activities. From observing his classroom, Avery could benefit from planning cohesive lessons based on a specific learning objective, so that all the activities reinforce stated objectives. Department goals that Avery completed this year were support of community service (he offers it for 5% of the grade), reinforcement of the concept of respect for human diversity, and interaction with team members in articulation of the curriculum.

5. Maintenance of a Suitable Learning Environment. Avery manages pupil control through discipline, motivation, and positive reinforcement. His discipline is progressive, beginning with discussion, then detention, a call home, and last, a referral. Avery follows school policy on tardies and truancy. In observing Avery's classes, students appeared cooperative. Avery has a relaxed style in the classroom, which is workable as long as he is consistent in holding students to strict standards in group work and in testing situations. Avery is working on a goal of planning for the individual differences of students by providing appropriate questions to encourage them to participate in and/or react to the lesson being presented. Avery needs to utilize Bloom's Taxonomy to develop appropriate questions that will encourage and increase student participation.

(Continued)

(Continued)

6. Related Professional Responsibilities. Avery contributes to the school's activities program. He supports the freshman football team, organizes social events that bring the freshman cheerleaders and team together, and he scouts for the varsity football team. He assists with school activities as needed, recognizing that a teacher's responsibilities extend beyond the walls of the classroom.

7. Pupil Progress. Avery uses tests, term papers, writing assignments, and class projects to measure student progress. To assist students, he incorporates pretest study guides, test talk-throughs, and, upon student request, will reteach to enhance student achievement. He allows some oral exams as a testing alternative for students with special needs. He uses multiple assessments to arrive at a grade: essays, matching and completion tests, map quizzes, term papers, and portfolio projects.

Summary

Avery is a veteran teacher who willingly volunteers for sports and activities. He is positive with students in the classroom as well. This year he focused on the use of simulations and cooperative learning. He made strides in this area, and he needs to continue with this goal next year, working toward incorporating varied strategies in a lesson to enhance a specific learning. In addition, the entire class needs to remain actively engaged throughout the lesson. Note-taking and the use of rubrics could assist with audience involvement during oral presentations. Avery is off to a good start with his variation of techniques. His willingness to research, grow, and learn is appreciated. With this professional attitude he will master a wide variety of teaching techniques.

TREASURE CHEST SAMPLE #42

OUTSTANDING ELEMENTARY FIRST-YEAR TEACHER

Recommendation

In his first year of teaching, Scott Morgan was assigned to a third-grade classroom. Scott did an excellent job stepping into the classroom after school had begun to replace a teacher who was promoted. Scott's transition was very successful due to his careful planning and warm personality. Students responded to him immediately in a positive and respectful manner as he quickly established the classroom as his own. Scott is a dedicated, conscientious teacher who is eager to do the best job possible. He has established a warm, supportive classroom environment for his students that reflects his style as a teacher. Scott has a wonderful way with his students and an atmosphere of mutual respect is evident. His enthusiasm for teaching is contagious and the students in his room are challenged and excited about learning.

As a beginning first-year teacher, Scott has been very successful in implementing the third-grade curriculum and expectations. He recognizes the importance of daily and long-range lesson planning and the tremendous amount of time it takes as a first-year teacher. Scott continually evaluates and modifies his lessons and is open to ideas and suggestions to enhance his instructional program. Scott is participating in the district's new teacher program and attends inservices to further develop his level of expertise with curriculum and instruction. He is beginning to utilize a variety of instructional strategies. Instruction takes place in a variety of instructional settings: whole class, small group, paired students, and individual. He has attended district- and school-level staff development workshops in the areas of math and technology.

Scott has established effective classroom management strategies and student discipline is handled in a low-key, consistent manner that sets a tone of fairness and respect. One of Scott's goals is to continue to fine-tune his discipline techniques by exploring a variety of classroom management strategies. Scott is very effective in the natural incorporation of positive reinforcement throughout the instructional day. He demonstrates flexibility and is successful in adapting lesson plans to meet the needs of a variety of students. Scott has a variety of resources available to him such as his new teacher mentor, the learning specialist, the media center teacher, the reading lab teacher, the assistant principal, and the principal. All of these resources can provide advice, direction, suggestions, and assistance in a wide variety of areas, as well as answer those nitty-gritty questions about daily classroom life.

Scott's conscientious efforts and enthusiasm for teaching reflect the attributes of a natural teacher. I've enjoyed working with Scott very much and am excited by his high energy level and enthusiasm for teaching. Scott Morgan is a wonderful addition to the Star Vista Staff.

TREASURE CHEST SAMPLE #43

MARGINAL ELEMENTARY FIRST-YEAR TEACHER

Recommendation

Margie Nal is a first-year teacher at Star Vista School assigned to a first-grade classroom. Margie has made a concerted effort at creating a successful classroom but continues to work on refining her classroom management skills and instructional techniques. Margie is very eager to do the best job possible. As a beginning first-year teacher, Margie is faced with the formidable task of becoming familiar with first-grade-level materials, curricula, instructional strategies, and classroom expectations as she acclimates herself to teaching. She is working to improve her lesson planning to ensure that classroom activities and teacher-directed lessons are well planned

(Continued)

(Continued)

and organized. Margie has participated in district- and school-level staff development opportunities. She has also participated in the district's new-teacher program to further develop her skills in achieving the district's standard of satisfactory performance for a teacher.

Margie has had a wide variety of resources available to her as a new teacher. She has worked with the new-teacher mentor, the learning specialist, the media center teacher, the assistant principal, and the principal in an effort to improve her classroom management and instructional skills. She has had the opportunity to observe other teachers' classrooms and lessons as appropriate models. All of these resources have provided Margie advice, direction, models, suggestions, and assistance as part of the administration's effort to provide her support as a new teacher.

One of Margie's professional growth goals is to fine-tune her discipline techniques and to determine a specific classroom management program in an effort to establish consistent classroom standards. Margie is working on establishing a classroom atmosphere of mutual respect. It is observed that Margie has isolated herself from her colleagues and needs to realize that a teacher's responsibilities extend beyond the walls of the classroom. When problems arise Margie appears to withdraw and ignore the problem, failing to confront it directly with the intent to find resolution. Margie is discovering the tremendous amount of time it takes to be a teacher. Margie is working on refining her instructional objectives so lessons are more appropriate to the ability levels of her students.

She has not been able to consistently utilize diagnostic techniques and test results to provide prescriptive teaching at the appropriate level for each student. It is important for Margie to demonstrate consistent growth in implementing district expectancies in instruction and classroom management skills. In the coming weeks it is expected that the following improvements will be consistently evident and observed:

I. Professional Competence
   • Demonstrate effective instructional planning to meet the instructional needs of each child. Copies of written lesson plans will be provided to the principal weekly and will reflect or include a task analysis for skill lessons with specific outcomes, blocks for small-group directed teaching, and demonstrating student opportunities for active interaction and involvement in learning.
   • Implement varied teaching strategies and lessons to meet the varied instructional levels of students. Specific instruction of concepts must be observed, as opposed to giving student directions.
   • Effectively working with small groups daily, while maintaining quality instruction and effective classroom discipline for those not in the small group.

II. Proper Classroom Control and Suitable Learning Environment
   • Provide an attractive and stimulating room environment conducive to learning and maximize instructional time for students.
   • Establish a climate of classroom management and discipline leading to proper student self-control and self-discipline.

- Establish an atmosphere of mutual respect and handle unacceptable behavior constructively without reducing a student's feeling of worth as an individual.
- Avoid situations in which students feel the teacher is unfair and arbitrary in applying consequences for students not following classroom standards.

The following assistance will be made available:

- Support from the administrators including additional formal observations, frequent classroom visits, and feedback.
- Assistance from the learning specialist and new teacher mentor, which may include demonstration lessons and help with lesson planning and classroom management strategies.
- Provide the opportunity to observe other teachers in the school.

As Margie implements these goals and avails herself of the assistance, it is hoped she will be able to maintain the dedication, endurance, and emotional energy necessary to achieve success as a teacher in our district

In life you are given two ends, one to think with and the other to sit on. Your success in life depends on which end you use the most. Heads you win, tails you lose.

—Conrad Burns

LETTERS OF RECOMMENDATION

As school principals, we are often asked for letters of recommendation. To write a letter of recommendation for an exceptional teacher is a delight, but to write a letter of recommendation for a marginal teacher can be a struggle. Principals, in reading and writing recommendations, soon come to recognize it's not what you say as much as what you don't say. Following are several sample letters of recommendation to assist you in selecting just the right words to convey the message you want.

Let each of us aspire to inspire, before we expire.

—Albert Clarke

Teachers are the important link to the future and the world of knowledge and self-esteem for children. We need to strengthen the chain that brings us together in a worthwhile and noble cause—teaching! Let us continue to strengthen the chain that brings us together. We are a team, but we are only as strong as our weakest link!

—John Blaydes

TREASURE CHEST SAMPLE #44

MARGINAL ELEMENTARY TENURED TEACHER

Recommendation

Jim was transferred to our school two years ago as a third-grade teacher. Jim has had to work at bringing his teaching skills up to the standards of his colleagues at Star Vista School. Jim is a teacher who requires considerable supervision by his evaluator to make sure that his performance level remains satisfactory. Scheduled classroom observations have not always been successful and additional observations were required for Jim to demonstrate his ability to implement the appropriate instructional strategy. His classroom organization, room environment, and instructional program are observably different from other third-grade classrooms. Jim has been taken on principal-guided tours of other classrooms to illustrate appropriate room environments and to gain appropriate models of teaching.

Jim is encouraged to spend more time in the planning and preparation of his instruction. Once Jim was observed in his classroom using his released planning time to read the newspaper and listen to the radio. Jim is encouraged to organize lessons that utilize a variety of instructional strategies that will maximize student involvement and allow for individual modalities and styles of learning. Lesson activities appear to focus on quiet paper–pencil activities and teacher directions are not always clear or correct, resulting in students being unsure of what to do or sometimes completing the wrong tasks. Jim needs to spend less time sitting down and more time walking around monitoring and helping students. Jim needs to create meaningful teacher-prepared activities and rely less on commercially prepared materials.

Jim has continued a program of professional growth attending inservices on math and technology. Jim's classroom environment tends to be stark and uncreative. Student work is posted but often remains up the entire year. Jim needs to display student stories, books, art, and projects throughout the classroom, changing them in a timely manner to reflect current units of study. Jim needs to create a classroom environment that is more nurturing and positive. He needs to praise all students and not just those displaying above-average work. Classroom behavior is tightly controlled and students who misbehave are often isolated for inappropriate periods of time. Once a student who had been assigned time-out at the back of the room was observed hiding under student desks when the principal visited the classroom with school visitors. Parent concerns have been expressed to Jim and to the principal regarding his lack of rapport with students. Due to the large number of parent requests not to have him as a teacher, Jim is working with the principal to begin a campaign to enhance his image in the community.

In order for Jim's performance as a teacher to maintain satisfactory ratings, he will need to demonstrate the initiative and the ability to consistently implement the district and state curriculum guidelines without constant monitoring. It is hoped that Jim will make a concerted effort to demonstrate the necessary energy, enthusiasm, and planning to make his classroom successful.

TREASURE CHEST SAMPLE #45

EXCEPTIONAL HIGH SCHOOL TEACHER

To watch Matt Monet weave history into a story of life in the classroom is to watch the artist and scientist as one. Matt is an exceptional teacher, versed in powerful teaching strategies, including interactive lecture, Socratic seminar, cooperative learning, and technology-based instruction through PowerPoint and the Internet. These are tools, the science of his trade, enhanced by his master's knowledge of history, a carpetbag full of colorful historical and current events, anecdotes, and biographies.

But it is Matt, the artist teacher, who weaves the tapestry of history into a clear and colorful image that comes to life. His boundless energy and enthusiasm, his sense of when to splash the lecture with color, how to excite students into dynamic dialogue, or how to bridge events of the past to problems of the present—these prove his artistry as a teacher. He reads his students well, sensing the ebb and flow of their engagement.

A respected educator once told me that a great teacher is like a great salesman—he or she knows just how far to push, how much information to give, then lets the buyer revel in the thought of being an owner. In Matt's case, he sells a love of history. For example, his students walk in the shoes of the new immigrants to America, they feel the chains of slavery, and they celebrate the courage of Rosa Parks and the inspiration of the American dream. He accomplishes this experience by the use of dynamic multimedia presentations and carefully constructed lessons that involve music, literature, primary sources, art, political cartoons, speeches, student presentations, visuals, discussions, problem solving, and cooperative interactions. In his classroom, history comes alive.

Matt's success with Advanced Placement U.S. History (over 80% passage rate) is his ability to judge the relevance of subject matter and the direction of historiography. His emphasis on social history connects historical themes and instills a sense of social justice in students. By drawing associations between events of the past and present, students are prepared for arguments that demonstrate analysis and cause–effect relationships. Matt balances a chronological approach to history with thematic analyses. The result is a curriculum that engenders rigor and relevance.

In all his classes, Matt succeeds at creating a learning community. He finds ways to relate his students to history through personal approaches. By knowing his students, he creates the link between his students' interests and the events and themes of history. His humor, care for students, and personal love and understanding of the subject of history create a classroom culture that nurtures inquiry, active learning, and a sense of belonging.

Several years ago Matt decidedly stepped up to become not only a remarkable and successful teacher in the classroom, but a major school and community leader,

(Continued)

(Continued)

and eventually a districtwide mentor in the area of human relations. Sparked by a personal desire for racial harmony on campus, a goal threatened by locker stuffings of racial literature, Mark showed initiative, desire, and an innovation unmatched by any other teacher in the school district. He rallied students to join a student club, Harmony, making the group a reputed human relations club; he called together parents, teachers, community agencies, and business owners, and through their fundraising and organization, began a campaign for "Respect for Diversity." As a result, "A Week of Understanding" became institutionalized districtwide, bringing speakers and educational programs to all the schools.

Matt created multimedia presentations on the Holocaust and civil rights movements that were shared districtwide. He organized retreats for all grade levels so that students and teachers learned awareness of discrimination and possessed the tools to combat it. He provided teacher inservices on curriculum from A World of Difference. Art contests, community carnivals, walk-a-thons, and speaker nights helped carry the message to the community. Police, clergy, and businesspeople joined retreats, and elementary through high school students took part in diversity programs under the direct mentorship of Matt Monet. For the past three years, Harmony has sponsored three conventions at which over 75 high schools have shared effective human relations programs. *Parade Magazine* and the National Caring Institute have recognized the impact of Harmony and its power in making a difference.

The remarkable legacy of Matt's work has been his ability to plant seeds and help leaders grow. Throughout the high school and district, human relations student and teacher leaders continue to expand the program with new activities and directions. Matt initiated the expansion of the high school program to include a student-led conflict mediation program that markedly reduced incidents of violence on campus. Behind the energy and growth of Harmony and the conflict mediation program is a man who devotes hours of thought and inspiration to helping students lead and organize. His work as a teacher and school–community leader is a living tribute to the words of Margaret Mead: "Never doubt that a small group of thoughtful, committed people can change the world. Indeed, it's the only thing that ever has."

It is not surprising that Matt Monet was unanimously voted by the district as our Outstanding Teacher of the Year. His humanist values, his limitless energy, and his unfailing belief in his work have inspired an entire school district to create a more caring, respectful, and accepting community for everyone. Matt Monet is a gift to the educational profession.

Reprinted with permission from Carol Hart, Superintendent, Los Alamitos USD, California

TREASURE CHEST SAMPLE #46

EXCEPTIONAL ELEMENTARY TEACHER

It is with the greatest pleasure that I write this letter of recommendation for Mrs. Allison Paige. Allison is a superior classroom teacher who taught the past five years at Star Vista School. She is extremely successful in providing her students with a challenging, creative classroom. Allison is the kind of teacher who is always on the lookout for new strategies and ideas to enhance her instructional program and teacher effectiveness. Her classroom environment is outstanding, often brimming with charts, stories, and samples of student work.

Allison is that rare teacher who can handle a variety of grade levels and assignments. She works well with others and is particularly effective in her relationships with children. When you walk into her classroom you immediately sense you are in a special place. You can feel the nonjudgmental atmosphere of mutual respect and caring. Allison's careful planning and preparation are evident by the high quality of instruction observed in her classroom. She demonstrates flexibility and is always enthusiastic about implementing a new curriculum. She represents first grade on the school leadership team and has worked on district-level committees in social science and math curricula. She is always eager to serve on curriculum committees and is willing to present inservices to her colleagues. She also served as an excellent model for others in the implementation of a full-inclusion special needs student in her classroom. In her third year of teaching, Allison was selected to serve as a master teacher in the training of student teachers.

Allison's enthusiasm for teaching, coupled with her leadership potential, make her an ideal candidate for any school wishing to enhance their teaching staff. It is a loss to our school to lose her services and it would be the gain of any school district able to employ her. With her dedication, humor, and intelligence she brings to education the compassion necessary for long-term success. I extend Allison Paige my highest recommendation, secure in the confirmed knowledge that she will perform in a superior manner, regardless of assignment or task. I use two tests in making such a recommendation: (1) Would I hire this teacher? and (2) Would I want my own children to have this teacher? YES! You have the opportunity to hire an exceptional teacher and I urge you to give her your highest consideration.

TREASURE CHEST SAMPLE #47

EXCELLENT HIGH SCHOOL TEACHER

It is a great pleasure to recommend Luna Noelle for a teaching position with your school district. For the past five years Luna has demonstrated her diverse knowledge and skills, as well as her flexibility, by willingly teaching a variety of subjects, including physical education, health education, physical science, and sports medicine. In addition, she has served as the head athletic trainer, providing primary care for the prevention and care of athletic injuries to 600 athletes in 29 sports.

Having been Luna's principal, supervisor, and evaluator, I speak from personal experience when I confirm that Luna is intelligent, knowledgeable in many subjects, and conscientious. She has met the high level of expectation demanded of this twice-named National Blue Ribbon School.

No matter what new course was given her, Luna created content-rich lessons, and she used the strategies of inquiry, cooperative learning, interactive lecture, and use of technology to approach instruction. In working on standards and assessment, I relied on Luna to lead the health teachers in the development of rubrics and authentic assessment. It was through her leadership that the school built the popular Sports Medicine course with the Regional Occupation Program, thereby increasing career training in health/medical pathways for our students. In her dual role as teacher and athletic trainer, she provided students a valuable hands-on experience in sports medicine. At athletic events her students assisted and observed in real-life situations.

Luna is an institution at student events. As the athletic trainer, her presence on the sidelines ensures student health and safety at all athletic and performance competitions. In many cases, Luna's expertise at diagnosis has provided the injured excellent care as well as prevention of re-injuries. In one case, she insisted that a student seek continued medical advice after being dismissed by a physician, and through her prodding for more testing, the condition was eventually diagnosed as cancer; Luna has literally saved student lives.

Luna's care and interest in students extend into volunteer work. She is eager to chaperone dances, she attends student performances, she serves as the adult supervisor at SAFE Rides on weekends, and she has attended Associated Student Body conferences. She enjoys interacting with teenagers, she has an easy rapport with students, and she supports them through encouragement in their academic and cocurricular activities.

As a colleague, what you see is what you get with Luna. She is honest, straightforward, and candid. She gets along well within several departments, and she is to be commended for her flexibility in taking on a new assignment and a new classroom every year. Being a team player, Luna volunteered to team-teach science and health with a special education teacher, and the program proved to be effective.

It will be a great loss to our high school for Luna to leave; however, she often speaks of moving to a more desirable area. With her breadth of subject matter expertise (she recently added biology to her credential), whoever hires her is fortunate. Luna is a versatile, skilled, and adaptable teacher. She will be a great asset to a staff and a pleasure to work with.

It is with great confidence that I highly recommend Luna Noelle to you. She is truly a dedicated teacher and a model of the finest in the educational field.

Reprinted with permission from Carol Hart, Superintendent, Los Alamitos USD, California

TREASURE CHEST SAMPLE #48

AVERAGE ELEMENTARY TEACHER

I am pleased to write this letter of recommendation for Mr. Ryan O'Kay. Mr. O'Kay taught first grade at Star Vista School this past year. Mr. O'Kay was a caring teacher and demonstrated a strong advocacy and compassion for children. Mr. O'Kay demonstrated a sincere interest in his students and expressed concern and caring for each one of them. He created an attractive room environment that was very appropriate and motivating for first-grade students. Student work was attractively displayed on bulletin boards throughout the classroom. Mr. O'Kay managed the classroom to create an atmosphere where discipline could be conducted effectively.

Mr. O'Kay continued to grow in his knowledge of first-grade curriculum and instructional strategies. As a second-year teacher, Mr. O'Kay was becoming more familiar with first-grade curricula, materials, and expectations. In his first year of teaching, Mr. O'Kay participated in the district's new-teacher program and attended inservices to further learn instructional strategies and grade-level expectations. Mr. O'Kay also attended district- and school-level staff development inservices in the areas of math and technology.

Ryan was open and receptive to suggestions and strategies to improve his instructional skills. He implemented the new math program, with a focus on the use of manipulatives. He continued to work on improving his skills as a reading teacher and utilized a block schedule in order to provide small group instruction. As part of student assessment, he administered running records and the Individual Reading Inventory several times throughout the year and maintained student portfolios to measure student progress.

Mr. O'Kay maintained communication with his students' parents and utilized their talents as volunteers and capitalized upon their strengths and skills to help meet the unique needs of his students. He demonstrated a willingness to assume additional professional responsibilities beyond his classroom, serving on the school's Technology Committee.

I am pleased to recommend Mr. Ryan O'Kay for your consideration.

TREASURE CHEST SAMPLE #49

FIRST-YEAR MARGINAL ELEMENTARY TEACHER

I have been asked to write this letter of recommendation by Mrs. Margie Nal. I can tell you that Mrs. Nal was hired as a temporary first-grade teacher and was under my supervision this past year. Mrs. Nal expressed a sincere interest in her students and strove to be a caring and supportive teacher. Margie worked toward creating a room environment that was appropriate for first-grade students. She managed the classroom in an effort to create an atmosphere where discipline could be conducted effectively.

(Continued)

(Continued)

Margie sought to grow professionally and worked with the school's learning specialist to improve her skills as a teacher. She was open and receptive to suggestions and strategies to improve her instructional skills, as well as the assistance she was provided toward meeting the expectancies of the district. Margie has recognized the need for both long- and short-range planning and the importance of good lesson planning for student success.

Mrs. Nal is anxious to be a successful teacher and is dedicated to the task. With a few more years of experience she may achieve her goal. She strives to grow in her knowledge of first-grade curricula and instructional strategies. As a beginning first-year teacher, Margie was faced with the formidable task of becoming familiar with first-grade curricula, materials, and expectations as she acclimated herself to teaching. She was responsible in carrying out her duties and responsibilities. Margie participated in the district's new-teacher program and attended inservices to further develop her skills as a teacher as well as her familiarity with first-grade instructional strategies and expectations. Margie also attended district- and school-level staff development inservices in the area of math. Margie continues to seek ways to apply the learnings from teacher inservices to enhance her classroom instructional program.

I recommend Mrs. Margie Nal for your consideration for any position for which she may be qualified.

TREASURE CHEST SAMPLE #50

SUBSTITUTE TEACHER

I am pleased to write this letter of recommendation for Hannah Doland. Hannah has served at Star Vista School for the past two years as one of our most requested substitutes. Teachers could always rely on Hannah to do a fine job in their classroom. Prior to her successful experience as a substitute at Star Vista, Hannah completed her student teaching here. She was an excellent student teacher and was successful in maintaining, and in many cases enriching, the classroom program.

Hannah is very conscientious regarding her responsibilities as a substitute teacher and strives to do the best job she can for the students. Hannah was always able to step into any classroom or situation and handle it with skill in a quiet, effective manner. She provided consistency of program and school standards in each classroom due to her familiarity with school and classroom routines. Hannah demonstrates patience in working with children while building student self-esteem with praise and encouragement.

Hannah is a dedicated teacher who is truly committed to the profession of teaching. She is eager and ready for her own classroom. Hannah always strives to do the best job she can for her students. There is no doubt in my mind that she will work extremely hard to establish an effective classroom with a warm, supportive learning environment that focuses on success for *all* children. Hannah has continued a program of professional growth attending workshops and inservices whenever she can. She is very self-reflective and she is open and receptive to suggestions and new ideas.

In summary, Hannah is a conscientious, dedicated, and effective teacher. I predict great success in the classroom and I am very pleased to recommend Hannah Doland for your consideration.

TREASURE CHEST SAMPLE #51

MATH TEACHER AWARD

It gives me the greatest pleasure to bring to your attention an exceptional teacher, Micki Mathman, who deserves recognition for her outstanding services to students and teachers in the area of math. It has been my distinct pleasure to supervise Micki the past eight years she has served as a teacher at Star Vista School. Micki's contributions as a teacher have been exemplary and she is one of the most outstanding professionals I've ever had the pleasure of working with. She is an inspirational teacher who creates a warm, caring relationship with each student and maintains high expectancies for performance and behavior, which students meet with great success. She is highly skilled in motivating students, consistently reinforcing positive behavior and providing immediate knowledge of results. Whenever I visit her classroom it is a pleasure to observe the students' joy of learning and enthusiasm for math.

One of her greatest strengths is her ability to turn students on to math. Student challenge is evident through the variety of problem-solving and critical-thinking activities that she has designed and implemented. Her problem-solving lessons have helped at-risk students find success in mathematics. Micki builds their confidence as mathematicians by giving them the tools to think critically and explore strategies when they are not always successful at learning facts. She has consistently demonstrated exceptional expertise and knowledge in the field of mathematics, not only to her students, but to her fellow teachers and administrators as well.

Micki always seeks new strategies and skills for teaching math concepts and over the years I have observed her incorporate cooperative learning, problem-solving strategies, inquiry skills, manipulatives, and calculator instruction in her math lessons. This year she has been implementing lessons that integrate literature, written language, and mathematics, focusing on the language of mathematics.

In the area of professional skills and curriculum development, Micki's performance is distinguished. Her broad knowledge of mathematics and the state math framework, coupled with her knowledge of learning theories and the ability to apply them to real-life situations for children, has made her a valuable resource for fellow educators.

Micki is to be commended for her leadership in the area of professional responsibilities. She developed a math problem-solving program for her classroom and was so successful that teachers were clamoring to use it. It was piloted at Star Vista School and has now been adopted for use throughout the district. Her math problem-solving program is so practical and useful that she has found instant acceptance from teachers during her workshop presentations.

Over the years she has continued to share her ideas and math expertise by broadening her leadership in math from inservices at the school level, to district workshops and her selection as K–5 math mentor, and finally to presenting math curriculum workshops at state and national conferences. Micki is much sought after as a speaker and consultant, having given workshops for ASCD, ACSA, and the CMC.

(Continued)

(Continued)

She has presented workshops at the last two National Math Conferences. She has served as a math consultant for many school districts in California, providing workshops on math problem solving, teaching for understanding, using math manipulatives and calculators, mental math, estimation, cooperative learning, and classroom management.

Star Vista School has hosted a number of educators who have visited the school expressly to visit Micki's classroom and observe her successful implementation of the math framework and her problem-solving program. She has continued to pursue new ways to integrate math in all curriculum areas in her classroom. Micki enjoys developing and piloting math curriculum, and for the past four years she has been involved in writing a program for teaching calculators through funding by the National Science Foundation.

It is clear that Micki has had a significant impact on mathematics instruction, not only with her students, but also beyond the school at the district, state, and national levels. Micki demonstrates a high degree of integrity and dedication to her profession by continuing as a classroom teacher while providing leadership beyond the classroom in math curriculum development and instructional techniques. Micki's exceptional skills as a teacher, her clear purpose and steady leadership in math curriculum, coupled with her organizational and practical application abilities make her a deserving recipient of the Presidential Award for Excellence in Mathematics Teaching.

TREASURE CHEST SAMPLE #52

SCIENCE SUMMER INSTITUTE

I am extremely pleased to support Bee Green's participation in the Environmental Issues Summer Institute. Bee will be an excellent representative of our upper-grade staff and is enthusiastic about the opportunity to attend your institute. Bee is a leader on our staff and has the ability to translate what she will learn at the Institute into an inservice for our teachers. She will effectively provide a teacher inservice that will create practical lesson plans for immediate teacher implementation.

Bee has been a key force in the implementation of our state science framework and has presented excellent lessons that provide students hands-on, problem-solving scientific-process lessons in the earth, life, and physical sciences. Bee is an excellent teacher and she is very conscientious and dependable regarding her teaching responsibilities. She demonstrates a warmth and caring in her relationships with children and she is patient, understanding, and compassionate. Students respond to her supportive, encouraging manner and there is an atmosphere of mutual respect. She is always focusing on ways to enhance her children's self-esteem. Classroom organization and standards are clearly understood by students and she encourages independent work and study habits. Bee maintains high standards and expectations and she strives to make sure each student experiences some measure of success in science.

Bee is a lifelong learner and is receptive to new ideas and trends in education that will enhance instruction for her students. She selects lesson plans and strategies that reach the needs of the various levels of abilities in her classroom. Bee does a fine job in presenting well-organized, easily understandable lessons, taking the time to make sure all students are successful. Bee keeps records of student progress through portfolio assessments and documentation of student work that show student progress as well as student strengths and weaknesses.

Bee has taken a leadership position with the fourth-grade staff, serving as their representative on the School Leadership Team. She has continued a program of professional growth by attending workshops and inservices. She willingly volunteers to serve on school committees to advance her profession. Her love of science is contagious and her students are provided a science-rich instructional program. It is with great pleasure that I nominate Bee Green for your Environmental Issues Summer Institute.

4

MASTERING THE SKILLS OF REFLECTION

REFLECTION

Enjoy your own company. Learn to welcome solitude and work on your inner being—your character. Solitude allows you opportunity to think deep thoughts. To think about where you've been. To think about where you're going. To think about why you feel so strongly about certain issues. To think about how different your values are from those of other people you know. To think about what all people have in common. To question yourself about why you cling to bad habits. To praise yourself for your strengths. To challenge yourself to follow your dreams. Reflection and solitude feed the soul.

—Dianna Booher

Reflection is one of the most important keys to survival as a school principal. How can principals follow the "whispers of wisdom" within when they are operating in overdrive? We must take time within the day for reflection. But when in your busy day do you have quiet time to gather your thoughts and focus your efforts? With so many demands upon the time, energy, and resources of a principal, it is often difficult not to get scattered and unfocused. Without creating a time within your day to pause and reflect, you continue to perpetuate the problem of feeling out of control. You often feel like a chicken running around with its head cut off. Time to center your thinking is essential!

When angry, dysfunctional parents arrive at our doorstep, we willingly make time in our busy schedule to meet with them. They consume hours of our time and exhaust our energy. We give of our time willingly, with the hope that we can resolve the problem. But we don't have time to close our office door and take time for quiet reflection. Where are our priorities? How we choose to use our time is reflective of what we value. Somehow, the time for reflection is not valued. Yet, the time we spend in contemplation and reflection may be the most valuable use of our time all day. Sometimes sitting and doing nothing is doing something. The time spent staring out the window in contemplation might be the most valuable minutes of the day. The pause that refreshes may just be the pause that helps you refocus or that grounds you, so that when you leave the office you are more productive. Principals often feel guilty going into their office and shutting the door. Shutting out the hustle and bustle of the office may be the only way we can find the time. Inform your secretary that you are going in your office for some thinking time and that you prefer not to be interrupted unless it is an emergency or the superintendent calling. Then, go behind the closed door and use the time to align your daily actions with your vision for the school.

An important survival skill is the ability to be guided by our vision for the school. Our vision for the school needs to be clearly articulated to the students, staff, and parents. It becomes your guidepost. Principals need to stop periodically within the day and align their daily actions with their vision. Without aligning yourself with your vision on a daily basis, you tend to get frustrated and angry and begin feeling out of control.

Align Your Daily Actions With Your Vision

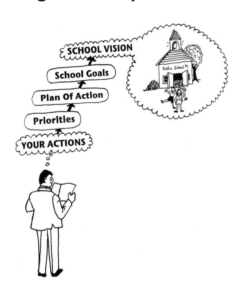

There are six important focus steps to keep you on target and avoid distractions, interruptions, and careening off course.

1. The first step is to create a clear vision for your school and then effectively communicate that vision to your staff, parents, and community.

2. The second step is building a committed coalition dedicated to implementing and achieving your vision.

3. The third step is to establish specific school goals and a plan of action that will help you and your staff to achieve your vision.

4. Make planning the fourth step! Principals must make it a priority to set aside time each day for planning and reflection. Schedule a time for this on your calendar.

5. The fifth step is to set daily priorities for utilizing your time and resources that will enable you to focus on achieving your vision.

6. In the sixth step, you must take the time for reflection to make sure that you align your daily actions with your vision as a guide for weeding out activities that are not directly related to achieving your vision.

TOUCH THE WISDOM WITHIN

I truly believe we should never give up our hopes and dreams. The path may be rocky and twisted, but the world is waiting for that special contribution that each of us was born to make. What it takes is courage to follow the whispers of wisdom that guides us from the inside. When I listen to that, I expect nothing less than a miracle.

—Marilyn Johnson Kondwani

- Take a Joy Break—"The power of the pause that refreshes." Take time each day to experience those things that bring joy to your job. Build in time to experience the joy that you need to sustain and nourish you.
- Build in Some Slack, Jack! Look at your schedule! It is crammed full of appointments, conferences, and meetings. There is not one moment that is just for you! Build in pockets of leisure episodes throughout your day when nothing is scheduled. Allow catch-up time in your schedule where you have scheduled blank spaces to absorb the overload of tight scheduling. Use these moments to gather your thoughts and focus your efforts toward the important work of the principal.
- Self-Appoint. Make an appointment with yourself. Go behind closed doors and establish a no-interruption rule.
- Make Planning a Priority. Good leadership never just happens. It takes careful preparation and planning. Set aside time each day to plan your day. Always keep a notebook or journal with you to record spontaneous planning ideas or inspirations.

Plan ahead. It wasn't raining when Noah built the ark.

—Richard Cushing

- The Power of Self-Affirmation. Make time for self-care, self-reflection, and self-affirmation!

THE M&M GAME—A CULMINATING LEARNING ACTIVITY

The Survival Skills M&M Game (Treasure Chest Sample #53) is a great way to provide a concluding activity for an inservice or training. The M&M Game gives everyone a little snack, creates some fun, and provides an opportunity to summarize the important learnings from the inservice. Pass out a snack baggie with various colors of M&M candies to each participant. Participants sort out the number of M&Ms by color. For the number of each color that they have, they complete the M&M Game by writing down the answers to the question listed for each color. For example, if they have four green M&Ms they'd write down four strategies for reducing stress in their job. Three red M&Ms means they'd write down three strategies for renewing their spirit.

TREASURE CHEST SAMPLE #53

THE SURVIVAL SKILLS M&M GAME

Green M&Ms—List strategies you use for reducing the stresses in your job.
Yellow M&Ms—List the greatest challenges you face in your job as principal.
Red M&Ms—List strategies you use for renewing your spirit.
Brown M&Ms—List strategies you use for keeping a balance in your life.
Blue M&Ms—List those in your life who helped shape your leadership style.
Orange M&Ms—What advice would you give to a principal new to the job?

Green M&Ms

1. _____
2. _____
3. _____
4. _____
5. _____

Yellow M&Ms

1. _____
2. _____
3. _____
4. _____
5. _____

Red M&Ms

1. _____
2. _____
3. _____
4. _____
5. _____

Brown M&Ms

1. _____
2. _____
3. _____
4. _____
5. _____

Blue M&Ms

1. _____

2. _____

3. _____

4. _____

5. _____

Orange M&Ms

1. _____

2. _____

3. _____

4. _____

5. _____

LETTER-RIP!

Put it before them briefly, so they will read it, clearly so they will appreciate it, picturesquely so they will remember it and, above all, accurately so they will be guided by its light.

—Joseph Pulitzer

As school leaders we spend much of our day communicating with others. We communicate through our actions, our spoken word, and our written word. Effective school principals are effective communicators. We spend an important part of our day composing written communications: letters to parents, memos to teachers, parent newsletter articles, requests to district office personnel or businesses, congratulations to students, and staff evaluations and observations. But, it's difficult to find quiet time within our busy day for reflection and composing written communication, so we often take home this part of our job to do in the evenings and weekends. As school principals, we often work in isolation. Each of us sits down at these times to compose letters, forms, and checklists that address the same issues. We've all written parent newsletter articles, letters to parents regarding attendance, and memos to teachers. We seem to reinvent the wheel at each of our schools. The sheer volume of written communication can often be overwhelming and time-consuming. But we do not have to reinvent the wheel! We can share with each other our sample letters, forms, and memos. By sharing, we can cut down on the paper load and save ourselves valuable time by using the samples as a model from which we can easily modify them to fit the particular needs of our school or the individual needs of the student. Word processing allows us to quickly rearrange content or substitute names and specific phrases. This allows us to spend less time on composing, thereby freeing us up to get out into the classrooms and do the important work of the principalship—working with teachers and students in the classroom.

SAMPLE LETTERS

Following you will find dozens of sample letters and memos that are models of both style and content and have been contributed by award-winning educators.

(Text continues on page 182)

TREASURE CHEST SAMPLE #54

**CHANGING CLASSROOM
ASSIGNMENT—NEW TEACHER**

Sept. 12, 200_

Dear Parents of

We have had a very successful opening of school. We have continued to increase our enrollment and some of our class sizes are too large. Our continuing goal is to maintain smaller class sizes by making sure there is equal distribution of students in each classroom. When school begins, the number of students at a specific grade level is not evenly distributed because students have moved in and out over the summer and so some classrooms have uneven numbers of students. At the beginning of each year, once classroom enrollment has been finalized, we need to equalize class size by reorganizing classroom assignments.

We are fortunate to be able to add an additional primary classroom that will enable us to reduce the number of students in classrooms and balance class size throughout the school. The addition of a new classroom requires some school reorganization and student changes. We are fortunate that these changes can be made so early in the school year. Our goal was to create as little movement as possible since many family schedules are already determined.

Beginning Monday, September 12, Mrs. Jack's classroom will become a straight kindergarten and her first-grade students will be assigned to Mrs. Horner's classroom in Room 3. Mrs. Jack will personally escort each student to their new classroom first thing Monday morning. Your child's new teacher will be:

Teacher _____   Room _____

Experience has shown that children adjust quickly to classroom changes, especially with parent support. We look forward to a rewarding and challenging school year. We appreciate your cooperation and understanding and invite you to attend Back to School Night on Thursday, September 29, to meet your child's teacher and become acquainted with the education program designed for your child this year at Star Vista School.

TREASURE CHEST SAMPLE #55

MID-YEAR CLASSROOM TEACHER REPLACEMENT

Dear Parents:

It is with deep regret that I must inform you that Mrs. Sara Smith will need to take a leave of absence for the remainder of the year for health reasons. The loss of her services will be greatly felt by all of us and we wish her a speedy recovery.

We are most fortunate to have selected Mrs. Maria Tomas as your child's teacher for the remainder of the school year. Mrs. Tomas is an excellent addition to our teaching staff. One of the greatest advantages in the selection of Mrs. Tomas is her familiarity with Mrs. Smith's class as well as our school programs. This fall, Mrs. Tomas substituted frequently in Mrs. Smith's classroom. She is therefore very familiar with the students and classroom routines and will provide an extremely smooth transition. Mrs. Tomas will be able to step right in and provide continuity of instruction and program. She will be working in the classroom with Mrs. Smith tomorrow and they both worked together in the classroom today. She will begin on Monday, January 3, when we return from winter vacation.

As I am sure you are aware, a child's success in school is directly related to the quality of the program he or she receives in school and the parent support that program receives in the child's home environment. We find from past experiences that children adjust quickly to a new teacher and that parents play an important role in this transition by their support, understanding, and cooperation. Mrs. Tomas believes it is important to maintain frequent parental communication regarding your child's progress and behavior during the school year through notes, phone calls, student work sent home, and parent conferences. She has scheduled an after-school tea to provide parents the opportunity to meet her and to discuss her goals for the remainder of the year. This has been scheduled for Tuesday, January 4, at 2:30 P.M. We hope you will be able to join us.

We look forward to a rewarding and successful school year. Please call me if you have any questions.

TREASURE CHEST SAMPLE #56

TEACHER LEAVING FOR MATERNITY

Dear Parents:

Tomorrow will be Mrs. Isabel's last day before her maternity leave. She will be returning to the classroom sometime in March.

We are very pleased to inform you that Miss Angel Stocking has been selected as your child's classroom teacher during Mrs. Isabel's leave of absence. We are especially pleased we were able to select such an outstanding teacher who recently graduated from UCLA, where she received an award as one of their most outstanding student teachers.

(Continued)

(Continued)

Miss Stocking has been working in the classroom all this week and is very familiar with Mrs. Isabel's classroom standards, expectancies, and routines and will continue to provide continuity to the instructional program. Miss Stocking spent considerable time planning the transition with Mrs. Isabel and I am confident that Miss Stocking will provide a wonderful program for your child. She has high expectations of performance for her students and will provide the kind of quality program that will motivate and challenge students as she prepares them for the experiences of middle school.

We would like to invite you to meet Miss Stocking at a special Parent Tea after school on Thursday, January 15, at 2:30 P.M. She is very enthusiastic about working with your children and is looking forward to meeting as many of you as possible. She would like to share with you her goals and expectations for the year. Any parents unable to attend will be contacted by phone by Miss Stocking within the next few weeks.

As I am sure you are aware, a child's success in school is directly related to the quality of the program he or she receives in school and the parental support that program receives in the youngster's home environment. We look forward to your support and a successful transition. We know you and your child will enjoy working with Miss Stocking.

TREASURE CHEST SAMPLE #57

ATTENDANCE CONCERNS

Dear Parents:

It has come to my attention that Suella has already had a large number of absences for so early in the school year. She has missed 14 days of school representing approximately 27% of the number of days school has been in session. I'm certain that you understand our desire to cultivate a successful learning climate in the classroom. It is difficult for a student to succeed in school if he or she does not attend regularly. It is essential that students attend school on a consistent basis to ensure continuity of instruction.

When Suella is absent, she misses out on important instructional lessons where key concepts or skills are introduced. This puts her at a disadvantage when she returns because of gaps in her learning and the need to play catch-up to lessons that have already been taught in the class.

Parents have the most influence over their children. Everyone knows this to be true. What a parent believes or values is also important to the child in that family. If you value education and believe it is important, so will your child. I am asking you to pay close attention to Suella's future by seeing that she is in school and on time each day.

Your child's education is our number one priority. In order for us to do our very best for your child, she must be in school every day. The only excused absences are for illness, quarantine, medical appointments, attendance at a funeral of one's immediate family, or exclusion for failing to meet immunization requirements. All other absences will be marked "unexcused."

It is important for the school and home to work together to ensure success at school. We need your cooperation. Please help us improve Suella's attendance. We hope that the rest of this year can be a rewarding and successful one. Thank you for your support.

TREASURE CHEST SAMPLE #58

FOLLOW-UP LETTER—STRONG CONCERNS ABOUT CONTINUING POOR SCHOOL ATTENDANCE

Dear Mrs.

This letter is to inform you of the school's continuing concern about Suella's frequent absences. On October 28, you were sent a letter from my office expressing our concern about Suella's absences and requesting your help in getting her to school. Unfortunately, since that date Suella has been absent an additional six days. As of today, there have been 62 days of school and Suella has missed 20 of those days. This number of absences is nearly 30% of the total days that she has been at school. In addition, she has also been more than 30 minutes tardy on four days. This attendance and tardy pattern is not acceptable.

Suella's poor attendance record is causing her to lose progress in reading and other subjects. Frequent absences from school contribute to a child's feeling of not being a part of the school experience and can set up the serious potential of dropping out of school later on.

Because Suella is our most important concern, this letter will serve as notice that, from now on, you must see to it that Suella is at school every day, and on time, unless she has a fever of over 100 degrees or is seriously ill. If either of these occur, you must call the school the first thing in the morning to inform us of the reason for absence. If Suella has any further absences except for the two reasons mentioned above, I will need to make a formal referral to the district School Attendance and Review Board. The referral will require your attendance at a meeting of school and police officials who will determine the next steps to take.

I would very much like to work with you to avoid having to make such a referral. If Suella's attendance improves as required above, I can assure you that no further action will be taken. I am also certain that we will see Suella's progress improve so that she can experience success in school by working more closely to her potential.

Thank you for your cooperation. If you have any questions, please call me at (222) 123-4567.

TREASURE CHEST SAMPLE #59

CONCERNS REGARDING STUDENT TARDIES

Dear Parents:

It has come to my attention that Eloise is having difficulty arriving at school on time. During the first part of this school year she has had 10 tardies. When a student is tardy, she misses out on the beginning of the day when announcements and lesson plans are discussed or an important lesson has begun in which a key concept or skill is being introduced. This often puts Eloise at a disadvantage, starting her day off with having missed out on important instruction.

School begins at 8:00 A.M. Eloise seems to arrive at school between 5 and 30 minutes late when she is tardy. We feel it is imperative that each student arrives on time after starting the morning off with a good, balanced breakfast. This helps to set a routine of responsibility that can only benefit student success in school. Students may arrive 15 minutes before school starts when there is teacher supervision on the playground. If your child needs to arrive earlier than 7:45 A.M., you will need to make arrangements with day care on our campus for supervision prior to that time.

I must inform you of our concern about Eloise's tardiness. It is important for home and school to work together. Please help us eliminate any future tardiness. We want students to be successful in school and by working together we can achieve this goal.

TREASURE CHEST SAMPLE #60

FOLLOW-UP LETTER—STRONG CONCERNS ABOUT CONTINUING SCHOOL TARDIES

Dear Parents:

I am writing this letter to share my concerns about your son John and his pattern of excessive tardies to school. On October 28, you were sent a letter from my office expressing concerns about the number of John's tardies (10) so early in the school year. We requested your support in eliminating any additional tardies by seeing that John got to school on time. I had hoped that the letter concerning his recurring tardies would help you recognize the importance for students to arrive at school on time. Tardies are such a loss of instructional time and John's progress in school is being affected. I even spoke to John personally about setting his own alarm clock and getting up on his own so he could be at school on time.

(Continued)

Unfortunately, since the October 28 letter, John has been tardy an additional 12 times. Several of these tardies were as late as 11:00 A.M. On one occasion a call was made to your home to inquire about his absence and he was promptly brought to school following the call. Below is a breakdown of the dates and times that John has been tardy so far this year:

Tuesday, Sept. 9	15 minutes	Tuesday, Nov. 18	10 minutes
Wednesday, Sept. 10	10 minutes	Wednesday, Nov. 19	5 minutes
Monday, Sept. 15	5 minutes	Monday, Nov. 24	5 minutes
Wednesday, Sept. 17	45 minutes	Tuesday, Nov. 25	30 minutes
Monday, Sept. 22	60 minutes	Monday, Dec. 1	12 minutes
Tuesday, Sept. 23	25 minutes	Wednesday, Dec. 3	35 minutes
Monday, Sept. 29	10 minutes	Friday, Dec. 5	8 minutes
Monday, Oct. 13	90 minutes	Monday, Dec. 8	10 minutes
Tuesday, Oct. 14	20 minutes	Monday, Dec. 15	50 minutes
Monday, Oct. 27	10 minutes	Tuesday, Dec. 16	5 minutes
Monday, Nov. 17	3 hours	Wednesday, Dec. 17	5 minutes

As you can see, the impact on loss of instructional time has been significant. This is a pattern that must be corrected. I am certain that you understand our desire for John to succeed in school and that it is difficult for him to accomplish this if he does not arrive at school on time.

Therefore, at any time in the future that John arrives at school more than 5 minutes late, he will need to be brought to the office and signed in before being allowed to go to class. If he has more than one tardy over 5 minutes at any time during the remainder of the school year, he will be required to make up the lost time after school or during assemblies at double the amount of time he was tardy.

These measures are not intended as punishment but as consequences to help him become responsible for his actions and to establish a school attendance pattern that is consistent and regular. If the pattern of tardies continues, I will make a formal referral to the district School Attendance and Review Board (SARB). The referral will require your attendance at a meeting of school and police officials who will determine the next steps to take. If I need to make a formal referral to the SARB Board I will be including the breakdown of tardies listed in this letter.

You may wish to contact one of our school support staff to assist you in resolving this problem. At Star Vista School, we are fortunate to have Mrs. Doall, our assistant principal, and Mrs. Fairlady, our school psychologist, as our support staff available to parents. You may call either staff member for help at 123-4567.

I hope this tardy information will be useful for you. We again ask your cooperation in eliminating these excessive tardies, and by working together I feel this can be accomplished.

    cc: Mrs. Doall
        Mrs. Fairlady
        Mrs. Promptly (John's Teacher)

TREASURE CHEST SAMPLE #61

REQUESTING BUSINESS DONATION

Marty Monitor
Allied Technology Corp.
4545 Circuit St.
Techland, CA

Dear Mr. Monitor:

We recently heard from one of your employees, Cindi Wantz, who is a parent at our school, that your corporation has surplus computers. Our schools continue to face budget constraints and we are always on the lookout for ways that local businesses can support our educational programs. We would very much appreciate any surplus donations from your company that would help us expand our efforts to provide our students greater access to computer technology in the classroom.

A school that hopes to achieve excellence is only possible with the cooperation of parents, staff, and members of our business community. It takes the full cooperation of school, parents, businesses, and the community for our neighborhood schools to provide a quality education for our children.

We have identified the need for computers in classrooms to provide students and staff ready access to technology. We wanted to inform you of our need in the hope that you would find it worthy of your consideration.

Please let us know if there is any available surplus technology equipment that we could utilize in our classrooms. Please contact Mary Eager, Star Vista School Technology Leader, at 555-1234 to discuss how we may work together. Thank you for your consideration and support in our efforts to bring our students' technology skills into the 21st century.

TREASURE CHEST SAMPLE #62

THANK-YOU LETTER—BUSINESS DONATION

Dear Friends:

On behalf of the students, staff, and parents at Star Vista Elementary School, I would like to thank you for your generous contribution to the silent auction for our school carnival. We are very fortunate at Star Vista to have such a supportive business community. It is through merchants like you that we are able to put on such a successful Silent Auction. Your contribution will increase the awareness of our parents of your business, products, and/or services.

We appreciate your support of our fund-raising efforts and we hope to support your contribution by patronizing your business in the future. In light of our continuing budget constraints, we can certainly use the funds raised from this event to support our educational programs. Your donation will help us purchase additional computers that will increase student access to technology in the classroom.

The greatest rewards in education are the results we see in children's achievement. I am sure that you must have a feeling of satisfaction in knowing that your donation will assist the school in helping all children achieve. Your donation has given us the inspiration and encouragement to continue to provide the best education possible for our children.

We are very appreciative that you have chosen to support the programs at Star Vista School. We are indeed fortunate to have such a supportive and caring community. On behalf of all the students who will benefit from your generous donation, I offer our most sincere thanks.

TREASURE CHEST SAMPLE # 63

THANK-YOU LETTER—COMMUNITY SERVICE ORGANIZATION GIFT

Dear Mrs. Overstreet:

Thank you very much for your wonderful contribution to our school. We really appreciate the continuing support of the Seal Beach Woman's Club and Arts and Crafts Committee for the arts program at Star Vista School. Through your generous contribution of $1000 to the Arts Program, you have enabled us to purchase some special art materials that have enhanced our art program at Star Vista School. We have been able to purchase several wooden models of the human form that have helped our students when drawing people.

This year we will be able to purchase special drying racks. These racks compactly hold student work that is too wet to stack and needs to dry. Over 400 students visit the Art Lab each week and space to dry their artwork is often at a premium. The drying racks will help preserve the wonderful work of the children. We also are now able to purchase some special art materials for some unique art projects such as scratchboard paper and a good selection of tissue paper and art brushes.

We are so fortunate to have a community service group such as yours that gives so generously to our school. We know that you recognize the importance of community support for your neighborhood schools. We know that as artists you appreciate the value and joy that comes from a strong art program for children. I would like to extend a special invitation for you and your committee to visit our school and tour the classrooms and Art Lab to see the children's artwork. I would love to escort you on a tour of our school. I would like to schedule a visit and school tour on one of the days you have your meeting and schedule it here at the school.

Thank you again for your wonderful support of the arts at our school.

TREASURE CHEST SAMPLE #64

THANK YOU FOR POSITIVE LETTER ABOUT A TEACHER

Good teaching is loving and listening, sharing and supporting. It is being passionately human. That is the point at which a good teacher begins.

—Author Unknown

Dear Mr. and Mrs. Grant:

What a welcome and moving letter you sent me about Cary's wonderful teacher this past year, Mrs. Berniece. Thank you for taking the time to share your kind words and thoughts about our school. You can guess that the types of letters and phone calls we usually receive from parents are often of a different nature. It is important that parents write a letter like yours to their child's teacher once in a while. The kind of letter you wrote can play a key factor in reminding teachers of the impact that they can have on children and reaffirms that they can and do make a difference. I have shared your letter with Mrs. Berniece and I am making it a part of her file here at Star Vista School.

Your letter was a wonderful reminder to all of us of the meaning and significance of teaching. Each child is uniquely and wonderfully different. It is the gifted teacher who can challenge, motivate, and teach to the individual needs of every child in her classroom. Much of a child's attitude toward school and learning occurs in the first five years of life in the home. These formative years are crucial in building a strong foundation of values, self-concept, and responsibility. Your influence as parents is reflected in Cary's success at school.

We feel very appreciative to have had the opportunity to work with such wonderful and supportive parents. The generous donation of your time, energy, and talents to help in the classroom and your support for Star Vista School over the years has been greatly valued and appreciated.

Thank you for your encouraging praise and support and we look forward to another new and rewarding year in the fall.

CC: Mrs. Berniece, Teacher

TREASURE CHEST SAMPLE #65

THANK-YOU LETTER—PARENT DONATION OF GIFT

Dear Mr. and Mrs. B. Gates:

It is with the greatest pleasure that we thank you for your wonderful donation of a computer and monitor to our school. Computer technology is an important part of our school curriculum. We appreciate your contribution to the school as it will help us increase the opportunities for student access to technology. Also, your contribution will enable us to spread out our resources and purchase additional

(Continued)

(Continued)

equipment that we might not have been able to acquire. We hope you will enjoy a feeling of satisfaction, knowing that you have helped support Star Vista's computer technology program.

We are so appreciative of your generous contribution that helps us maintain the exceptional educational programs at Star Vista School. It is so refreshing to know that there are parents like you in our community who value quality educational programs and are committed to making a contribution that supports the best for our students.

We are very appreciative that you have chosen to support the computer technology program at Star Vista School. We wish to express our sincere gratitude and appreciation for your caring and concern for the students at Star Vista. We are indeed fortunate to have such supportive parents and we look forward to a very successful school experience for your son Randy and your daughter Danielle during their years at Star Vista. Support such as yours gives us the inspiration and encouragement to strive for the best education possible for the boys and girls of our community. Thank you very much!

TREASURE CHEST SAMPLE #66

THANK-YOU LETTER—MUSIC TEACHER

Dear Beverly:

Congratulations on an outstanding production of our school musical, "The Mikado." It was a very impressive production! The music, sets, costumes, and particularly the acting were excellent. We are fortunate to have such a large pool of talented children and you effectively showcased their talents. I was very impressed with the quality of the production, especially since it was created in a very short time line of 11 weeks. The production received rave reviews from the parents and staff. Everyone was amazed at the professional quality of the production. Once again you have exceeded everyone's expectations by creating another superb musical experience for the students at Star Vista School. We are so fortunate to have you as our music teacher and I know that students, parents, and staff greatly value you. We all appreciate the wonderful opportunities you provide our school community.

It was obvious that the parents had been very helpful in creating such wonderful sets and backdrops and magnificent costumes. The costumes were very professional and looked wonderful on stage. You obviously spent an immense amount of time outside the school day writing, directing, creating, and supervising the many students, parents, and staff involved in this wonderful production. It was a significant undertaking on your part and you should be commended for the quality of the final creation.

I know that there is a great deal of planning, organization, and preparation that goes into putting on a complex two-hour musical production of this caliber. Your creativity and expertise at staging was quite evident. Last year's production received first place in the County Department of Education Musical Competition, and I'm confident that this production of "The Mikado" will bring additional accolades to you and the school this year.

Thank you for all your hard work and dedication. You have provided our students with an experience they will treasure a lifetime.

cc: Superintendent

TREASURE CHEST SAMPLE #67

THANK-YOU LETTER—TEACHER PRESENTING INSERVICE

Dear Donna:

I want to thank you so very much for the excellent inservice you provided the Star Vista Staff on early literacy last week. Your leadership and expertise in the area of literacy is exceptional. Your presentation was very well organized and provided teachers with a lot of information about the process of teaching children the skill of reading. You organized the workshop so that each of the components was clearly presented and illustrated. You prepared many samples of student work to share. Your introductory statement to the video on literacy acquisition you prepared was excellent and helped teachers get an overview of what they were about to see. Your passion for children and reading came across effectively. The impact of your video was tremendous and some of the teachers were moved to tears. Not only does the video communicate how to teach reading but it touches a responsive chord in teachers, emotionally communicating the power a teacher has in opening the world of reading to a nonreader.

Your leadership on the staff is greatly appreciated. You command great respect from your colleagues for your knowledge, expertise, and professional demeanor and teachers listen closely to what you have to say. I'm hopeful that last week's presentation served as an impetus for our teachers to dedicate themselves to providing an instructional program that will enable all their children to learn to read.

A very special thank you for your willingness to continue to serve students in the Reading Recovery program. How fortunate are the students with whom you will work, for you will truly make a difference in their lives. I hope you will have an opportunity this year to continue to work with our teaching staff by doing model lessons and working collaboratively with them to enhance their reading instruction.

Thank you for all that you do for children. You continue to make a difference in children's lives. I am so lucky to work with talented and inspirational teachers, such as yourself, who truly bring honor to the profession of teaching! Thank you for a great job!

    cc: Superintendent

TREASURE CHEST SAMPLE #68

THANK-YOU LETTER—CONSULTANT PRESENTING INSERVICE

Dear Connie:

Thank you for the excellent inservice on full inclusion you presented to our staff last Tuesday. The response from teachers to the inservice was very positive. Where there had been anxiety and concern, after your inservice our regular education teachers showed a more open and positive attitude toward the benefits of a full-inclusion student in their classroom.

I wanted to express my sincere appreciation for all you have done in guiding us through the process of full inclusion. Your unswerving support for our staff and your understanding and caring manner have made a big difference in helping us to work through our concerns and questions. You have always been there with the reassuring word or the idea that redirected our conversations to the focus of what is best for the child.

How can we not be successful with full inclusion? With your leadership, guidance, and support, I'm confident that we'll find success for our children and our teachers. We are so fortunate to have you as our Special Education Consortium liaison and I look forward to a successful full-inclusion program next year. I appreciate your efforts in helping us secure additional instructional-aide time, teacher training, and additional instructional resources for teachers with full-inclusion students. It is a privilege for our staff to have the opportunity to work with you and to experience your expertise and knowledge. I'm sure that you will continue to serve as a valuable resource for our teachers.

A special thank you for the exceptionally inspirational presentation at our recent staff meeting. It was very moving to have you share with the staff the joys you have found in working with special needs children. These children have obviously touched your life in profound ways and the joy you shared was contagious.

It is a pleasure to work with you and I look forward to our continued collaboration on behalf of special needs children.

TREASURE CHEST SAMPLE #69

THANK-YOU LETTER—CLASSROOM VOLUNTEER

Dear Mrs. Val Unteer:

We just wanted to send a note of thanks for all you have done to make this year so successful for your child and your child's teacher.

Thank you for your wondrous support of Star Vista and all the children it serves.

Thank you for demonstrating to your child how important school is by taking the time off from your important work and busy schedule to volunteer in a classroom sharpening pencils, cleaning paint brushes, and working with our students.

Thank you for making our jobs easier, not harder.

Thank you for wonderful words of encouragement to your child and to us.

Thank you for understanding when things are crazy on our end and for communicating when things are crazy on your end.

Thank you for investing in your child's future.

Thank you for being a partner in instilling a love of reading and learning that will hopefully be a part of your child throughout his or her life.

(Continued)

(Continued)

Most of all, thank you for lending us your incredible child to work with everyday! Not many people can say that they look forward to coming to work each morning. Due to these wonderful children, we have been excited to come to work: to see how they will respond to a story, to watch them interact with each other, and to see concepts take root and imaginations blossom. The amazing progress and changes we have seen in your child throughout the year could not have happened without your immense help.

We value you! We appreciate you! We thank you!

Written by Chris Wilson
Teacher McGaugh Elementary School
Los Alamitos Unified School District

TREASURE CHEST SAMPLE #70

THANK-YOU LETTER—PARENT VOLUNTEER SCHOOL EVENT

Dear Vivian:

Sometimes acts of kindness are not given recognition because of the inappropriateness of words. I will, however, try to express my gratitude for the exceptionally wonderful job you did as Star Vista School's carnival chairperson. Your talents and expertise at leadership, organization, creativity, attention to details, and ability to get others involved combined to make our school carnival the best and most successful ever. It exceeded all others and was highly praised by those who attended. I appreciated your efforts to provide "something for everyone" while keeping the focus on the kids and the creation of a child-oriented carnival.

Your tireless dedication and hard work are greatly appreciated. I remember a proverb which states, "Kindness is something you cannot give away, since it always comes back." I hope that the students, staff, and parents of Star Vista can return such a gift of kindness as graciously as you gave to them. Please know that the boys and girls of Star Vista School will greatly benefit from the incredible amount of funds that were raised in large part to your dedication. You truly have made a difference for the children of Star Vista. Your efforts have been a fine model of commitment and dedication for our parents and a wonderful inspiration to parents and teachers alike.

A school community that hopes to achieve excellence is only possible with the cooperation and dedication of parents, students, and educators. Your contributions as a dedicated parent and advocate of public education are greatly valued and appreciated. Thank you again for your contributions to our school and for making the Star Vista School Carnival our most successful ever!

TREASURE CHEST SAMPLE #71

THANK-YOU LETTER—PTA PRESIDENT

Dear Maria Alicia:

As I was driving home from work last week, I was reflecting on the wonderful job you have done this year as our PTA president and I wanted to write you to express my appreciation for your outstanding leadership. I count myself very fortunate to have had the opportunity to work with you and I greatly respect your leadership as a strong child advocate. You have always been supportive of our efforts to make our school a special place for children. Your organizational skills, your compassion, and your professional manner are evident in your leadership style. I am always impressed with the bountiful praise you give so generously to everyone involved in volunteering at our school. You are such a positive role model for others and they respond to your praise by working harder, donating more, and praising others.

I am so fortunate to be a principal in a community where there are parents, such as you and your husband, who are so supportive of the school's efforts to enhance education. You and John are very special parents and the staff and I are forever indebted to both of you for your many contributions to our school. It's wonderful to see such family teamwork and dedication. It's always a pleasure to look up and see John volunteering, often after a long day's work, at one of our many school events. It is also obvious that he is supportive of your dedication and service to the school. Your tireless support and leadership of PTA has been invaluable to our school. Having such a knowledgeable, articulate parent serve in such active leadership roles is a wonderful gift to the school.

Your selfless service to the boys and girls of Star Vista Elementary School over a continuing period of time has had a significant impact on the success of our school. For that wonderful contribution we want you to know how much we value and appreciate all that you have done. On behalf of the students, staff, and administration I want to thank you again for your outstanding leadership and dedicated support for children.

TREASURE CHEST SAMPLE #72

**LETTER OF CONGRATULATIONS TO
PTA HONORARY SERVICE AWARD RECIPIENT**

Dear Val:

Congratulations on your recognition as a very deserving recipient of the Star Vista PTA Honorary Service Award! You have donated countless hours to our school, whether serving as PTA president, as accompanist for the school musical rehearsals, or as a

(Continued)

(Continued)

volunteer shelving books in the Media Center, and these are only a few of the visible hours. There are many hours spent behind the scenes making sure things are organized and successful. Whether you are handling parent phone calls, conducting efficient meetings, or reading a book to kids in the classroom, you are always giving to others.

It is truly a pleasure to work with you as you are always enthusiastic, dependable, and cheerful. I really appreciate your sensitivity to others, whether they are children, parents, or staff. You listen and respond to their concerns and recognize and praise their talents and efforts. You play an important role in this school as a strong child advocate. You always ask the question, "How does this benefit our kids?" and you provide the leadership necessary to help parents focus on support for the school and the students.

Your dependability, your initiative, and your willingness to get the job done have helped make a difference for kids. I feel very fortunate to be able to work with you in a mutual partnership for the children here at Star Vista. I want to say thank you for all you have done and let you know that the children and staff of Star Vista are fortunate to have benefited from your caring and leadership. Congratulations on your wonderful award! You are clearly a most deserving recipient.

TREASURE CHEST SAMPLE #73

PARENT LETTER—CLASSROOM
VOLUNTEER WHO DIDN'T SHOW UP

Dear Volunteer:

We missed you today!

Parent volunteers are an important and integral part of our instructional program in the classroom. We greatly appreciate your willingness to help in the classroom and we really rely on your support. Since you are so vital to our program, we would request that you please call another classroom volunteer to substitute for you if you are unable to work on your scheduled day. If a classroom parent volunteer is not available to substitute for you, a phone call to the office to report your absence would be greatly appreciated. Thank you very much for your continuing support in the classroom. You are making a difference!

Below is a list of the parent volunteers in your child's classroom and their phone numbers:

TREASURE CHEST SAMPLE #74

PARENT LETTER—CONGRATULATIONS ON STUDENT'S GOOD CITIZENSHIP AWARD

Dear Parents of Sean Superson:

Good citizenship is something that should be honored, recognized, and given status. Anyone can achieve good citizenship—it has nothing to do with academic achievement. The essence of good citizenship is respect—respect for self, respect for others, respect for adults, and respect for rules. It's an attitude that begins at home and is reinforced at school and applied throughout life.

We are pleased that Sean has been chosen from Room 14 as Good Citizen of the Month. This is a special honor here at Star Vista School. We are proud of Sean's good citizenship and we know that you must be, too. As part of Sean's recognition for good citizenship, I have included a complimentary pass to Skate Depot, which is good during any regular afternoon session, plus a gift certificate for a free slice of pizza, a salad, and drink from Pietro's Pizza and a personalized book marker with Sean's name and picture.

We hope that recognizing good citizenship will serve as an incentive and model for others. Congratulations on Sean's selection as a Star Vista School Good Citizen!

TREASURE CHEST SAMPLE #75

STUDENT LETTER—CONGRATULATIONS ON ELECTION TO STUDENT COUNCIL

Dear Morgan:

Congratulations on your election to the office of Student Council President. As a leader in your class, you will have many opportunities to grow and expand your leadership and organizational skills. You have shown us your leadership potential and I'm confident that you will do your best to provide positive and productive service to your school. I know that you will work hard to serve as an appropriate role model for others regarding leadership, behavior, and good judgment.

I am so very proud of how well you handled yourself during your speech to the students and parents at the Election Assembly. You were well prepared and poised. I'm sure that your parents are bursting with pride and are pleased with your accomplishments at school.

Under the leadership of our student council sponsor, Mrs. Allred, I know this semester as Student Council President will be an exciting and rewarding experience for you. Best wishes for a successful semester as Star Vista School's Student Council President!

TREASURE CHEST SAMPLE #76

STUDENT LETTER—CONSOLATION
LETTER, NOT ELECTED TO STUDENT COUNCIL

Dear Celinda:

This letter is to let you know how impressed I was with your Student Council campaign. I was very proud of how well you handled yourself during your speech to the students and parents at the Election Assembly. You were well prepared and poised. How fortunate you were to have your mom and dad, as well as your grandparents, show their support by attending the assembly and cheering you on.

It is unfortunate that every candidate cannot be elected, but every candidate is a winner! You have shown us your leadership potential, and I encourage you to continue to strive for the best that you can be. I know that your parents are proud of your accomplishments at school. We are proud of you and want you to know you have earned the respect and admiration of your principal, your teachers, and your classmates.

TREASURE CHEST SAMPLE #77

PARENT LETTER—FAILURE TO
PICK UP CHILD AFTER SCHOOL ON TIME

Dear Mrs. Later:

It has been brought to my attention that you continue to arrive late to pick up your children from school after they are dismissed. The Star Vista School procedures for picking up children after school have been outlined in the parent handbook that you received with each of your children on the first day of school. These procedures have also been explained to you again on numerous times by office staff when you have arrived late to pick up your children.

I am disappointed to have to contact you again about the continuing late pickup of your children, Sam and Sinda. Your children are dismissed by their teacher at 2:15 each regular school day and we provide teacher supervision in the student pick-up area in front of the school until 2:30. At that time, to ensure safety, any children not picked up are brought to the office to wait or to phone home for a ride. Repeatedly, Sam and Sinda are brought to the office and have had to wait as long as an hour and a half before you arrived. This is unacceptable since it means the office staff at Star Vista must baby-sit your children until you arrive. It is unsafe to have your children remain in front of the school unsupervised for periods up to an hour.

It will be necessary for you to arrange for your children to be picked up at their dismissal time or have them enrolled at one of the day-care programs on campus. I walked through the office several times on the 16th of this month when your children were left for over an hour. Sinda was visibly upset and cried several times during that wait. All attempts to console her were to no avail. This cannot be allowed to continue.

I sincerely hope that you will comply with these regulations. However, it is my duty to inform you that children who are continuously left after school with no arrangements for adult supervision are considered abandoned and can be reported to the local police department as such and further to Children's Social Services. I am sure this will not become necessary.

It is in the children's best interest that you arrange for them to be taken care of after school each day. It is important for home and school to work together to ensure that students be successful at school.

TREASURE CHEST SAMPLE #78

PARENT LETTER—SUSPENSION OF
DISRUPTIVE PARENT FROM COMING ON CAMPUS

REGISTERED MAIL—RETURN RECEIPT REQUESTED

Parent Name _____   Date _____

Street Address _____

City/State/ZIP Code _____

The provisions of the penal code and the policies of the school district allow me to protect our school campus from unwarranted disruptions or confrontations. Specifically, my concerns are that on November 17, you behaved in an intimidating and disruptive manner in the classroom of Mrs. Hunter and in the school office.

I am further exercising my rights under this code and directing that you refrain from being on our school premises for the next seven (7) days; after that, you are only permitted back on campus if you can maintain composure and avoid similar behavior such as occurred on November 17. Any violation of this authority will be immediately reported to the City Police Department with a request to enforce the penal code that carries a first offense of a fine not to exceed $500.00 and/or imprisonment in county jail.

I regret the need to resort to this measure, but I am directed by my supervisor and the Board of Education to protect the students and staff of this public school. It is the hope of the school staff that all future contacts with school personnel will be dealt with in an appropriate and professional manner. We appreciate your cooperation.

If you have issues with this or any other decision at the school, there is a simple process for filing a complaint without resorting to the behaviors noted above. If you wish to appeal this directive, you may do so by filing a Complaint Form in the Superintendent's Office within two (2) school days after receipt of this letter. Complaint forms are available from school offices and the Superintendent's Office.

MEMO-ABILIA

The following are samples of memos that a principal sometimes writes throughout the year.

(Text continues on page 187)

TREASURE CHEST SAMPLE #79

STAFF MEMO—WELCOME BACK TO NEW SCHOOL YEAR

Dear Staff:

Welcome back! It's hard to believe that the warm, wonderful days of summer have passed so quickly and are beginning to blend into the warm, wonderful days of a new school year. It must be true, since you're receiving this annual welcome back-to-school letter from me. Summer is an important time for relaxation, thought, and infilling. We give so much of ourselves throughout the year that it is essential we take this time to reenergize our bodies and restore our spirit. Teaching is a very giving profession. Summer is a time for educators to take instead of give— take in fresh air, take in new ideas, take time to read, and take time to just contemplate. How many of us have learned that doing nothing is doing something?

The beginning of each new year brings a measure of excitement and anticipation. It is also a time of rejoicing and rededication. We are excited about what lies ahead for our students for the coming school year. We are energized by the changes of a new class of students, a new grade level, or, for some of you, a new school. We begin the year with fresh ideas, exciting plans, and great anticipation.

Teaching reinforces the ideas and beliefs that each of us has about making a difference in our student's lives. We are fortunate to have chosen a profession that allows us to be of service to others. We have the incredible opportunity to help students learn how to learn—and learn how to live. The glory of education is the joy that comes from helping others. In the next 10 months you have the opportunity to influence and motivate students with diverse personalities, strengths, and talents. That is our challenge! It's a big job, but one that is part of what we do as caring and dedicated teachers.

I am confident that the coming year will be filled with rich and rewarding experiences that will reinforce the ideals and beliefs that each of us has about the importance of being a teacher. As we are bombarded with the changes and challenges of teaching, we need to keep that as our focus. We need to enjoy and appreciate the opportunity we are given each year to teach children. This is our privilege and our joy!

If we are ever to enjoy life, now is the time—not tomorrow or next year. The best preparation for a better life next year is a full, complete, harmonious joyous life this year.

—Thomas Drier

TREASURE CHEST SAMPLE #80

STAFF MEMO—OPEN-HOUSE EXPECTATIONS

To: ALL STAFF
From: Your Principal
Regarding: Open-House Expectations

Open House is scheduled for Thursday, April 18. This is an important event for students, parents, and staff. It is traditionally the one time of the year when parents and the community turn out to see what our schools have accomplished and to evaluate our "product." It is important that all classrooms reflect the same standard of student work presentation. Certainly individual teacher personality and personal units of study will be reflected in each classroom. However, it can create unnecessary opportunities for comparison between teachers if there are great differences between the qualities of student work displayed. You may want to meet with other teachers in your grade level to discuss what kinds of student work and products you'd like to display.

I wanted to share my thoughts about schoolwide guidelines for Open House in your classroom now, so you will have plenty of time to prepare for this important public relations event.

- It is important that each child in your class has an attractive folder of sample work displayed on his or her desk. The cover should reflect one of your successful art projects that reflect the student's individual creativity. The folder should contain samples of student work from *every* area of the curriculum. This work should be reflective of the growth throughout the year and not just from the two weeks before Open House.

- Student work that you've saved from the beginning of the school year until now will provide parents a nice comparison of the growth their child has made in your classroom during the year. Usually writing samples will provide a good illustration of growth. As I mentioned in September, I hope you saved work samples from the very first week of school to put with work samples done later in the year.

- Papers included in the folder should reflect the student's *best* work. *Note: No paper should be included in the folder that hasn't been carefully proofread and corrected.* Make sure *each* paper has some mark or comment that indicates it has been evaluated in some way by the teacher. Please avoid large numbers of ditto work, practice or drill sheets, or commercially prepared worksheets. The best example of student work is work that is student generated.

- In addition to the student folders, it is important to make sure that every child has at least two samples of his or her best work displayed somewhere in the classroom. The sample could be from any curricular area but should provide students the opportunity to point with pride to their displayed work. Bulletin boards can reflect units of study but should include samples of student work displayed.

(Continued)

(Continued)

- Please make sure that a variety of student work is displayed and that the work covers all areas of the curriculum. Avoid displaying a large number of the *same assignments,* especially ditto work (10 colored dittos of goldfish or 15 spelling tests with 100's written in the right-hand corner). Work that would be more reflective of the learning would be a sample of a student drawing of a fish with a written story below illustrating the application of correct spelling and grammar. Classroom murals, class projects, class books, or individual assignments in specific areas add variety.

- You may want to select students as classroom hosts or guides. They can invite guests to sign in, explain special projects, or give a guided tour of the classroom. This responsibility can be shared in shifts throughout the evening by some of your class leaders or officers. A good review of what they have learned throughout the year can occur for your students when you model what the classroom tour would look like by reviewing the different projects and assignments displayed in the classroom.

- It's always a good idea to have each student review the papers in the folder as a class to remind them about their work so they can more effectively explain the papers to their parents that evening.

- Open House takes a lot of preparation, but the work displayed should be an outgrowth of what goes on in your classroom throughout the year. Saving samples of excellent student work at intervals throughout the year will save you a lot of last-minute pressure to create papers reflective of student work. With a little thoughtful planning and organization Open House should be a fantastic success!

A special thank you for all you do throughout the year to create a positive and student-oriented learning environment in your classrooms.

TREASURE CHEST SAMPLE #81

STAFF MEMO—CONGRATULATIONS ON SUCCESSFUL OPEN HOUSE

Congratulations on a superb Open House! The classrooms looked fantastic and I never cease to be amazed at the high quality of work on display in every room. You should be very proud of the fine job that you do. I want you to know that I believe that you have had a profound, positive impact on each and every one of your students. Throughout the year, as I visit classrooms, I am always impressed with the high quality instruction and the wonderful affective room environments that I see. Students are actively engaged in learning in a warm, supportive atmosphere that ensures success.

I must tell you that every time I visit classrooms I think of all the wonderful things I observe and I reflect on what a pleasure it is to work with such a dedicated staff. Your compassion and caring for children, reflected so well in your classrooms at Open House, greatly enhance the warm, supportive school climate here at Star Vista School. My sincerest and deepest thanks for always being there for kids!

TREASURE CHEST SAMPLE #82

**STAFF MEMO—THANK YOU, DAY
OF THE TEACHER APPRECIATION**

Teaching Is a Noble and Honorable Profession

*As teachers we have a chance to leave
our thumbprint on a child's life.
Let that thumbprint be that we did make a difference!
Let our goal as teachers be
to reach that <u>unreachable</u> child.
Let us make <u>that</u> our challenge!
Just one unreachable child!
Is there anything more noble or honorable
than making a difference in one child's life?
Teachers can and do make a difference!*

—John Blaydes

On this day of the teacher, when the role of teacher is recognized as a noble and honorable profession, it is important to remember how easily we affect the lives of our children. I know that many of you meet that challenge each and every day in your classroom. Please accept this small token of my appreciation for your significant contributions to the lives of children. These personalized business cards represent the importance of teachers in our society and will hopefully enhance the respect and esteem of the teaching profession in our community. Use them with pride!

TREASURE CHEST SAMPLE #83

STAFF MEMO—PROCEDURES FOR RECESS TIME-OUT

To: All Teachers
From: Your Principal
Re: Time-Out at Recess
Time-out supervision at morning recess is available for teachers to assign students to the lunch tables as a consequence. The time-out area is always monitored by the same instructional aide to provide continuity. This time-out is to be used as a consequence for *behavior only!* It is assumed that each teacher has followed his or her own sequence of consequences and the student's behavior has reached a point where time-out is appropriate. Time-out at morning recess is provided as a service for teachers to use as a consequence for inappropriate behavior in the classroom or on the playground. It is NOT to be used for:

Consequences for not turning in homework
Consequences for not completing work in the classroom
Student choice time to do work or project

(Continued)

(Continued)

If you want to assign time-out at morning recess for anything other than behavior then you must stay in your classroom and supervise the student. Students may not be left alone in the classroom during recess or lunch for any reason. You are placing yourself at great liability in the event something was to happen. When students are assigned time-out for reasons other than behavior, the numbers grow significantly, which makes it difficult for one supervisor to monitor 30 students at the lunch benches. They are each assigned their own bench and it spreads them out too far apart to supervise effectively.

When a student is continually placed in time-out, it is obvious that the consequence is not working. Teachers then need to move to the next step in their sequence of consequences, which is a parent conference or phone call. Students who end up in time-out more than once a week need more effective consequences. The Time-Out Supervisor will keep a record of the number of times a student has been sent to time-out so we can track student behavior. We should not lessen our expectations for student behavior but communicate more effectively with parents to solicit their involvement and responsibility for administering consequences at home. Students can call their parents directly from the classroom and explain their behavior as an immediate consequence if time-out is not working.

Teachers need to send students to time-out with a time-out pass. The pass is then initialed by the Time-Out Supervisor to make sure the student was there during recess. The Time-Out Supervisor will return each initialed individual time-out pass and students are to return the pass to you after recess to verify they reported for their consequence. Thank you for your cooperation.

TREASURE CHEST SAMPLE #84

STAFF MEMO—CLASSIFIED STAFF APPRECIATION WEEK THANK YOU

A TRIBUTE TO ALL SUPPORT STAFF

I can imagine no greater satisfaction for a person,
in looking back on his life and work,
than to have been able to give to children.
They are our hope for a better future.
It is important to affirm that we <u>*can*</u> *and* <u>*do*</u>
make a difference in children's lives.
We, who have the privilege
of guiding children in their formative years,
are blessed with the opportunity

to build and enhance children's self esteem,
and knowledge, thereby empowering them
to reach their highest potential.
Everyday you <u>do</u> make a difference and
I want to express my sincerest thanks
for all your dedication and caring.
Your contributions to building student self esteem
and the impact your positive praise has had on
the children at Star Vista School is immeasurable!

—John Blaydes

During Classified Staff Appreciation Week it is important to recognize and celebrate the significant contributions you make each day to the Star Vista School family. As support-staff personnel you are an important link for our children to the world of knowledge and self-esteem. The classified staff at Star Vista School is exceptional in its ability to enable children to learn and teachers to teach, providing the necessary caring, encouragement, and support. Your dedication and hard work are greatly appreciated and valued. Thank you for all you do for kids.

In recognition and celebration of the great job you do, we are pleased to ask you to join us during morning recess for a Sundae on Friday!

PRINCIPAL'S MESSAGE FOR PARENT NEWSLETTER

An important communication tool is the Principal's Message to parents. The Principal's Message often becomes the "bully pulpit" principals use to communicate information about parenting skills. These articles cover a wide variety of topics and are all designed to reinforce good parenting. These articles begin to consume our time and resources and we struggle with the right words. Why reinvent the wheel? Select from the following parent-education articles for your Principal's Messages that are sent home periodically throughout the school year.

(Text continues on page 215)

TREASURE CHEST SAMPLE #85

PARENT LETTER—WELCOME BACK TO NEW SCHOOL YEAR

Welcome Back to a New School Year

Welcome to the Star Vista School Family! I would like to extend a warm welcome to a new school year. The staff and I are looking forward to working with you and your children this year. We will strive to continue to provide an exciting and rewarding educational program for each and every child at Star Vista School.

We'd like to take this opportunity to acquaint you with some routine schedules and procedures of Star Vista School as well as policies adopted by the Board of Education. The updated Star Vista School Parent Information Handbook is enclosed for Grades K–3 and is found in the Student Planner for Grades 4–5. Please use the handbook for ready reference when you have a question about school policies and procedures. If further information is needed, please feel welcome to call the office at 123-4567. Our school office hours are from 7:30 A.M. to 4:00 P.M.

Star Vista School Office and Support Staff

John Delegator, Principal
Betty Doall, School Secretary
Frank Cleaner, Day Custodian
Sue Reliable, Assistant Principal
Ima Typer, School Clerk
Joe Gardener, Night Custodian

EMERGENCY CARDS! *Important information for your child's safety.* Enclosed are two white emergency cards which are to be completed and returned to school with your child **tomorrow.** The information on this card is most important to the *safety* and *well-being* of your child. Please fill the cards out carefully and *completely.* This information is kept on file in the office in the event of an emergency. Phone numbers are not given out at school so if you have an unlisted phone number, it is kept confidential. We must have a *specific number to reach you in time of need,* so please include this number. If your child is *not* to be released to any specific person, please note on the card. If your child is attending day care before or after school, please send a note to the teacher and complete the release form in the office.

Keeping Emergency Cards Updated. It is essential that parents keep their child's emergency card updated at all times. The school must have a home or work number where the parent can be contacted in the event of an emergency. Important minutes can be lost calling disconnected numbers. When you change jobs, residence, or your phone number, please call the office or send a note with the new information. Thank you for your cooperation in this important matter!

Other Contact People. Please list *local* friends or relatives for emergency who are usually available if you should not be. For your child's safety and protection, *only those people listed on the emergency card will be able to pick up your child during school hours* unless the office receives written permission. Make sure your friend, relative, or neighbor has agreed to this responsibility. Please list any health problems of which we should be aware (eyesight, hearing, etc.).

Note: We appreciate your promptness in returning the EMERGENCY CARDS and other forms to the school TOMORROW! Thank you.

TREASURE CHEST SAMPLE #86

NEW STUDENT SURVEY ABOUT SPECIAL NEEDS SERVICES

Welcome to the Star Vista School Family! We are pleased that you are joining our school family. Please complete the survey below so as we enroll your child we can make the best possible classroom placement at Star Vista.

Student's Name_____ Grade Level_____

Has your child participated in any of the following services?

Date Dismissed

1. _____ Gifted and Talented Education (GATE)   _____

2. _____ Reading Lab (Special Reading Teacher)   _____

3. _____ Resource Specialist Program (RSP)

    (Partial-Day Program—Learning Disabilities)   _____

4. _____ Special-Day Class (SDC)

    (All-Day Program—Learning Handicapped)   _____

5. _____ Speech Therapy _____

6. _____ English as a Second Language (ESL)   _____

7. _____ Counseling Program   _____

Has your child been receiving any other services?

Has your child ever been tested by a school psychologist?
(If you answered YES to any of the above questions, please see the school secretary for a *Confidential Release Form*.)

Are there any special custody regulations regarding your child?

Are there any special medical problems?

Any other essential information the school should know?

Parent's Signature: _____ Date: _____

TREASURE CHEST SAMPLE #87

HOME–SCHOOL COMMUNICATION—
THE KEY TO OUR SCHOOL'S SUCCESS

Communications From School

How many times have you found that important piece of information in your child's backpack the day after the event happened? Unfortunately, you are not alone. This year, weekly school bulletins and announcements will be sent home each **Thursday** in order to make it easier for parents to keep track of school events and important school information. It is our hope that the once-a-week distribution of school materials will ensure that parents receive flyers on school activities, PTA newsletters, and other important notices. If you always check the backpack on Thursdays, you'll be kept in the loop and not miss any important events or school information. In that way, no one will be caught off-guard for a special event, test, or deadline. Flyers announcing local recreational activities and events are sent home for your information only and are not endorsed by the school.

Communication With School Personnel

At times during the school year parents may feel they need to speak to the teacher or principal concerning their children and school programs. We always welcome the opportunity to confer with parents and offer our services. If you are concerned about a classroom situation, you should start with the teacher. The teacher has firsthand knowledge of your child's abilities and classroom behavior as well as the classroom standards and expectations. You can call the office and leave a message for the teacher to return your call. The teacher will then contact you to set up a mutually agreed upon time to meet. Please respect the teacher's busy schedule by setting up an appointment ahead of time. If you drop by the classroom unexpectedly, it is very likely that the teacher's afternoon schedule may already be full.

If your concerns are unresolved after meeting with the teacher and you need to confer with the principal, please call for an appointment. If a parent brings a concern to the principal, the principal makes the concern known to the teacher and works with the parent and teacher to resolve the problem.

In order to preserve the continuity of instruction, classrooms may not be disturbed for personal messages to students unless there is an emergency. If a child needs directions for after school, please make arrangements with your child prior to leaving for school.

Chat With the Principal

Have any questions that need answering? Ask the Principal. Come and have an informal chat with the principal on Monday, October 6, between 8:00 and 8:30 A.M. and every first Monday of the month after that. We will meet in the Community Room. There is no agenda, and you will have the opportunity to ask anything and everything that interests you about school! Just drop by for a chat and ask your question!

TREASURE CHEST SAMPLE #88

THE JOY OF READING ALOUD AT HOME

Just Tell Children the Words When They Stumble When Reading Aloud

When young children are learning to read, they love to read out loud to show off their newly found skill, but often they may run into a word they don't know. The best advice, the experts say, is for parents to wait a few seconds to see if they can decode the word for themselves and, if not, simply supply the missing word. Don't ask your child to sound it out. Don't add it to a word list. Those techniques will make reading at home seem like a chore. They can actually discourage a young reader. Let the teacher assume the major responsibility for teaching the skills of reading and helping students apply those skills. The idea is to make reading at home as much fun as possible for children and parents, too. Reading aloud is a more difficult task than reading silently. Having your child read aloud to you gives them a chance to show how proud they are of being able to read. Don't discourage their joy of reading by making a school lesson out of their mistakes.

As adults we don't often find ourselves in a position where we are reading aloud to other adults. Most of our reading is done silently. How do we handle unfamiliar words when we're reading? As adults, when we are reading for pleasure and we come across a word we don't know we usually skip over it and try to determine its meaning by the context of the story. We don't let the unfamiliar or unpronounceable word impede us from getting through the paragraph to find out what happens next. A few readers, especially if they are reading for information, will get a dictionary and look up the pronunciation and meaning. But most of us will just skip over the word, maybe trying to sound it out in our head, and then continue reading. Usually the stories are so exciting we want to find out what happens next and don't want to interrupt the story line with a trip to the dictionary to discover the word's meaning or pronunciation.

It is vital we teach our children the skills of sounding out words and using context clues to determine meaning. But we also need to build a sense of excitement about reading aloud without building a fear of making a mistake when pronouncing an unfamiliar word. We need to simply supply the word when they get stuck and continue to encourage our children to read to us as part of sharing the joy of reading as a family.

TREASURE CHEST SAMPLE #89

GETTING TO SCHOOL ON TIME IN A SAFE MANNER

Dear Parents:

WE NEED THE HELP OF EACH AND EVERY FAMILY! Please read the following information so we can work in partnership to ensure the success and safety of our students. We need your help in getting our students to school on time! This past week, April 17–21, we recorded an incredible number of student tardies. We had over 114 students in the office for tardy slips for being late from 5 minutes to 40 minutes, averaging over 23 tardy students each day.

Getting to school on time has been a continuing problem at Star Vista School.

The staff and I are very concerned about the messages we are giving our students regarding promptness and responsibility. We want our students to recognize the importance and value of an education and to take their responsibilities as students seriously by arriving on time. It is very important that students arrive at school on time so as not to miss out on any instruction or important announcements. I'm certain that you understand our desire to cultivate a successful learning climate in the classroom and that it often puts the student at a disadvantage when arriving late. They then have to start their day off by playing catch-up or catch-on to lessons or learnings that have already begun.

As I stand outside the bus circle each morning I am amazed at the number of cars hurriedly dropping students off after school has started, sometimes in unsafe ways. Parents need to follow safe procedures and demonstrate patience and respect for other drivers when dropping their children off at school. By leaving a few minutes early you can allow for traffic problems and ensure that your child will be at school on time. *Students should not be dropped off on the east side of the school as it is a major highway and the designated school bus drop-off area.* It is unsafe to drop off or pick up students in the bus circle. The bus circle is for busses only and cars block busses from unloading students! Students who walk between the congestion of cars and busses are in danger of being injured. Parents who drop their students off by stopping in the No Stopping Zone are not only unsafe but illegal and could be ticketed. We need your *cooperation* and *patience* in using "safe zones" for dropping off students. The west side and front of the school are safe and uncongested places to drop off your student.

We feel it is imperative that each student arrives at school on time after starting the morning off with a good, balanced breakfast. This will help set a routine for responsibility and good study habits that can only benefit student success in school. Students may arrive at school 15 minutes before school starts (7:45 A.M.), as there is teacher supervision on the playground at that time. If your child needs to arrive earlier than 7:45 A.M. then you will need to make arrangements with day care on our campus for supervision prior to 7:45 A.M.

Please help us eliminate any future tardies and make the dropping off and picking up of students a safe procedure. We want students to be safe and successful at Star Vista School, and by working together we can achieve this goal. Thank you.

TREASURE CHEST SAMPLE #90

TAKING TIME FOR CONVERSATION AND CONSISTENCY

It's no surprise to anyone that children of all ages need time with their parents. And even though most parents are extremely busy, whether they work outside of the home or not, they do find time to spend with their children. But parents want that time to count in helping prepare their children for the world they will find outside the home.

What counts most is what we *SAY* and *DO AT HOME*, not how rich or poor we are or how many years of school we have finished. When children can count on getting attention at home, they have a greater sense of security and self-worth. This will help them do better not only in school, but also when they grow up.

If you think about it, school, while very important, does not really take up very much time. In the United States, the school year averages 180 days. So, the hours and days a child is NOT in school are important for learning, too. As parents there are some important steps we can take in helping to make the time outside of school as meaningful as the time in school.

Communicating

This is probably the most important activity we can do in our home, and it doesn't cost anything. *Ask questions and listen for answers.* These are no-cost, high-value things you can do. The important part is listening for their answers. If you're used to getting one-word answers in response to your questions, then it's time to teach your child the art of conversation.

Think of conversation as being like a tennis game with talk, instead of a ball, bouncing back and forth. Often our communications with our children are one way. They might be commands, like "Turn off the TV!" "Stop hitting your sister!" or "Put your toys away!" Or they might be questions, like "What do you want for lunch?" "Are you OK?" or "How are you feeling?" Usually there is little or no response from your child that could be called a conversation.

Communication can happen any time in any place—in the car, on a bus, at mealtime, at bedtime—you just have to be ready to listen and respond. But we can't wait for our children to initiate a conversation, as the times when they are ready to talk are too few and far between. We need to engage our children in conversation by asking questions and then listening to their answers. We need to get that ball going both ways!

When our children enter and continue school with good habits of communication, they are in a position to succeed—to learn all that has to be learned and to become confident students.

Communication—Starting Early

Here are some things you can do when your children are young:

- Let them see you read, and read to them and with them. Visit the library. If they are old enough, make sure they have their own library card. Keep books, magazines, and newspapers around the house.

(Continued)

(Continued)

- Keep pencils and paper, crayons, and washable markers handy for notes, grocery lists, and schoolwork. Writing takes practice, and it starts at home.
- Teach children to do things for themselves rather than do the work for them. Patience when children are young pays off later.

Consistency

It makes a difference when parents give their children consistent messages and don't allow tantrums or whining to change the parents' directions or expectations. Children need to know that when you speak you mean it. The way this happens is to take the time to be consistent and always follow through on what you say.

- Help children, when needed, to break a job down into small pieces. Then have them do the job one step at a time. This works for everything—from getting dressed in the morning, doing a job around the house, or completing a big homework assignment.
- Develop, with your child, a reasonable, consistent schedule of jobs around the house. List them on a calendar, day by day. *Reinforce* responsibility when they do the job without having to be asked.
- Every home needs consistent rules children can depend on. Put a plan into action and follow through. Avoid assigning a harsh punishment in anger and then backing down when it's an inconvenience to follow through.
- Give each child an easy-to-reach place in which to put things away.
- Set limits on TV viewing so that everyone can get work done with less background noise.
- And, watch TV with your child and talk about what you see.

The time *parents* spend in conversation, exchanging ideas with their children, is vitally important in setting the tone, the attitudes, and the behaviors that will make the difference in school.

TREASURE CHEST SAMPLE #91

CREATING A CLIMATE FOR LEARNING

Star Vista School is a place where everyone is someone special. Our school is organized and designed to enable teachers to teach and students to learn. The efforts of the staff to create a climate for learning at Star Vista are reflected in the accomplishments and achievements of our students.

Our educational goal is to make learning so exciting that students will experience the joy of discovering new ideas and building new skills, thereby developing a love of learning that will create lifelong learners. Student work and projects are proudly displayed throughout the school and students who complete their work on time are reinforced and praised by teachers.

Positive attitudes toward school and staff and long-term changes in behavior are the staff's behavioral goals for each student. The staff focus on positive, effective approaches in building self-esteem by teaching children respect for themselves and others. Students are provided many opportunities to develop and demonstrate self-discipline and responsibility.

The Star Vista staff are deeply committed to providing and maintaining a strong discipline policy for students. We believe that all students have the right to a quality education. We firmly believe that each student has a right to attend school to learn and play in a positive, safe, threat-free environment.

Respect and responsibility are strong components of our school discipline program and they are evident throughout the school. Star Vista students can articulate schoolwide rules, which are consistently and equitably enforced. Our students participate in conflict resolution strategies. Our schoolwide conflict management program ensures a safe and orderly school environment as well as reinforces positive character development. All of our staff are trained to be fair and consistent in the implementation of the simple rules and guidelines here at Star Vista. Our staff motto regarding discipline is "Catch children being good!"

Positive behavior and performance are recognized through a variety of awards such as Good Citizenship, Reading Star, Math Wizard, and PE awards at monthly Spirit Assemblies, as well as individual achievement recognition in the classroom. Each month the Principal's Award recognizes one student from each grade level who has demonstrated a special attribute or character trait identified as the focus for the school year, such as respect, kindness, or cooperation.

Homework is an integral part of school and helps students develop responsibility and good study habits by successfully completing homework assignments. Emphasis is on the quality of the experience rather than the quantity of the work. Homework is a link between school and home, and Star Vista parent support for homework is an important factor toward building positive attitudes and good study habits.

Star Vista School's learning environment is a school strength. Classrooms and school programs reflect the school's strong emphasis on learning. Students and parents express pride in their school. The school takes every opportunity to recognize and reward students, staff, and parents for their successes and accomplishments. The community's pride in school facilities has resulted in almost no incidences of vandalism. The school community's total support for quality education at Star Vista School is impressive.

Home–school communication provides parents information about their children's school programs and ways they can be involved and supportive of school efforts. With the support of parents and community, the staff and students have created a school at Star Vista where a climate of learning is one of the primary educational goals. We hope we have created a school climate where the love of learning enables every child at Star Vista to experience personal success and develop into a lifelong learner.

TREASURE CHEST SAMPLE #92

A PARENT'S GUIDE TO TEENAGE PARTIES

The following suggested guidelines can be helpful to parents who have concerns about their child attending teenage parties. With the potential for drinking and disruptive behavior, parents need to have set criteria for making the decision if their teenager should attend a party or a sleepover.

1. Parents should know where their teenagers will be.
   - Obtain the address and phone number of the party-giver.
   - Let your teenager know that you expect a phone call if the location of the party is changed.

2. Parents should contact the parents of the party-giver to
   - Verify the occasion
   - Make sure that a parent will be present
   - Be certain that alcohol and other drugs will not be permitted

3. Parents should know how their teen will get to and from the party.
   - Assure your teen that you or a specific friend or neighbor can always be called for a ride home.
   - Discuss with your teen the possible situations in which he or she might need to make such a call.
   - Parents might make a "no questions asked" pact.

4. Teens should know what time they are expected to be home.
   - Parents should be awake or have your teen awaken you when he or she arrives home.
   - Parents should be prepared to listen, as often this is a good sharing time.

5. If your teen stays overnight with a friend after a party, parents should check with the parents of the friend to verify
   - They want your teen to stay over
   - They will be home
   - How many teens are spending the night
   - You both agree on hours and other basic house rules
   - Spontaneous sleepover arrangements should always be confirmed with the host parents

6. You and your teen may want to phone the party-giver the next day to express your thanks.

TREASURE CHEST SAMPLE #93

JUST A LITTLE BIT OF HEAVEN

At the start of each school year I visit every classroom to welcome students back to Star Vista School and another great year. As part of the welcome back talk, I ask all students who are new to Star Vista School to come up and stand by me. I then ask for a volunteer to come up and introduce me individually to each new student. While making new students feel welcome, it also gives all students the opportunity to model and practice proper etiquette for introductions.

In a first-grade classroom, when I asked who would like to introduce the new young man standing by me, nearly everyone raised their hand. As I was trying to choose among the sea of waving hands, one boy was politely but energetically waving his hand back and forth. I could tell he wanted to be called on in the worst possible way. When I picked him to introduce the new student, he jumped up and proudly announced to the world, "He's already my best friend."

Later that day, I was in a second-grade class and after introductions of a new student I asked the class, "Why is Jeff the luckiest kid in the world?" Hands shot up immediately and the student I called on answered, "Because he's at the best school!" Everyone nodded their heads in agreement—Star Vista School was the best school and that's just what they all had intended to say. Then one little boy raised his hand and proudly informed everyone with the greatest sincerity, "Star Vista's just like heaven—a little bit."

"Star Vista's just like heaven—a little bit." What a wonderful feeling this seven-year-old boy has about his school. The teachers and administrators at Star Vista often feel we are the ones who are in "a little bit of heaven." We have the privilege of working with the best and brightest kids. Not only are they bright and eager to learn, they are articulate and hard workers. We feel fortunate to work in a school community in which the kids are great, the parents are tremendously involved, and the community is generously supportive.

We had a very smooth opening of school and all the teachers had worked hard to decorate their rooms and create a welcoming learning environment. With the increase in enrollment and the addition of three new portable classrooms we want to thank our dedicated custodial staff, the district administration, and the district's maintenance crew for working long and hard this summer to get the new classrooms ready for the start of school. They thought of every contingency—additional furniture was ordered, new text books and instructional materials purchased, and equipment delivered. When school opened September 5, we were ready!

Thank you, parents, for all your help and support in getting our students off to a great new school year. We look forward to your continued involvement in your child's education and your participation in school events throughout the coming year. Our goal is to strengthen the home–school relationship by building a strong partnership with parents. Parents have an open invitation to volunteer, to participate in, and to share in the setting and achievement of our school's goals for our children. Working together, maybe we can just achieve a little bit of heaven at Star Vista School.

TREASURE CHEST SAMPLE #94

CHARACTER EDUCATION—TEACHING OUR CHILDREN THE ATTRIBUTE OF PERSEVERANCE

It is important for home and school to work together to build strong character in our children. Clearly, when it comes to character building, the family is the key. There is simply no substitute for a mother and father who form a loving and supportive circle around the child, provide loving guidance, and define for their child, by both what they say and how they live, standards of good conduct. Schools have a supportive role to play in character building. Schools must not only help children become literate and well informed, but they must also help them develop the capacity to live responsibly and to be able to judge wisely in the matters of life and conduct. School can reinforce those universal values we all cherish and which we hope our children will demonstrate when we are not around. We want them to demonstrate character traits such as responsibility, honesty, respect, caring, kindness, perseverance, tolerance, and initiative in their everyday lives. These character traits will enable them to be successful in life.

Each year at Star Vista School we select an important attribute to recognize and reinforce in our students. In past years we have focused on respect, cooperation, kindness, and responsibility. This year the staff have selected the attribute of perseverance as the character builder on which we will focus. To help our children learn about these attributes it is important that as adults we identify for our children the behaviors that we expect, by both teaching and modeling.

Perseverance is a big word and we will need to break it down so that our students understand what perseverance means and how they can demonstrate it to others.

Perseverance: Sticking to a purpose or an aim; never giving up what one has set out to do.

When someone demonstrates perseverance, that person is diligent, with the inner strength and determination to pursue well-defined goals. It does matter that a task is completed once begun, and everyone acknowledges that to persevere not only teaches discipline, but brings rewards as well. Each child pushes hard to complete assignments, and members of the school community support children in their work. The Olympic athlete is a great example of goal setting, perseverance, and reward. We need to provide our children models and examples of where perseverance pays off.

Perseverance is often hard for us as adults. We want instant results. How many of us would love to lose weight by just exercising five minutes of each day? We admire the discipline of the Olympic athlete and yet are often overwhelmed and lacking perseverance when learning a new skill or taking on a new responsibility. Remembering the feelings generated when we were overwhelmed can help us realize how important it is to break down learning something new into small achievable steps so we can reach our goal.

We can help children understand perseverance by helping them determine a "big job" that they want to get done—tying shoes, learning to rollerblade, riding a bike, or memorizing their multiplication tables. As adults we can help them see they can achieve their goals by breaking the task or learning into small steps so they can master or complete each step or task. Parents can serve as cheerleaders for each small step achieved and encourage their child to persevere until all the steps are learned and the goal achieved.

Read or reread to your child the great children's book, "The Little Engine That Could." The lesson of perseverance is clearly illustrated by the Little Engine's words, "I think I can, I think I can, I think I can." Discuss with your child difficult tasks that he or she has already learned or achieved and help your child celebrate his or her successes. Point out that your child didn't just jump out of the crib and start walking. Your child took baby steps—a few small steps at a time. Your child took a few steps, staggered, tried to regain balance, fell, and then got up and tried again. And there you were as a loving, supportive parent who held out your arms—just out of reach—to encourage him or her to take that next step just a little bit further. And when your child took six steps in a row without falling you cheered, laughed, and reinforced success by hugging and praising. This encouraged your child to try, try, try again and again until he or she finally mastered the skill of walking.

Many children take up a challenge and persist until they've achieved or completed their goal or task. Some children give up at the first sign of difficulty. We want to avoid having children give up too soon. When some children come across a problem in their homework that they don't know the answer to right away they guess, skip it, or give up. We want to see children respond with a stick-to-it-iveness attitude that reflects their willingness to try, try, try again until they get it right.

We need to help our children set simple, achievable goals and work hard to accomplish them. Parents need to be cheerleaders on the sidelines encouraging their child to continue toward his or her goals and pointing out the successes along the way. Praise is a strong motivator. Remember each step achieved is a step higher.

To reinforce perseverance students will be encouraged at school to use phrases such as "I'm doing my best work," "I'll try again," "I'm going to begin by . . . ," "I can achieve my goal," "Let me try it one more time," and "I can do it!"

In order to reinforce perseverance, as a desired behavior, teachers will recognize students in their classrooms who have demonstrated perseverance. All students nominated will have their name published in the monthly PTA Newsette and one student from each grade level will be selected to be recognized at our Spirit Day assemblies by receiving the Principal's Award.

It is our hope that home and school can work together to reinforce these important attributes. Please take the time to talk with your child about the importance of not giving up when a task is too difficult and encouraging your child to always do his or her very best. Praise perseverance!

TREASURE CHEST SAMPLE #95

AVOID INTERRUPTING CLASSROOM INSTRUCTION

One of our goals at Star Vista School is to enable teachers to teach and kids to learn. In order to accomplish that goal, we are always looking for ways we can protect the valuable instructional time in the classroom from unnecessary interruptions. Parent requests to get messages to their child or the teacher during the instructional day can have a significant interruption on the teacher's ability to keep a concentrated focus on instruction. In an effort to cut down on classroom interruptions, we are asking you, our parents, to help us by making every effort to set your day's plans with your children before sending them off to school each day.

Every time a request is made for a message to be relayed to a student or teacher in a classroom, the secretary in the office must relay the message by calling the classroom and interrupting the class. Since there is no way to determine if it is a time that would not disrupt learning in the classroom, sometimes these calls are made during important lessons or tests, or even when there are guest speakers. These calls are the ones we are trying to eliminate. Therefore, we are asking you to help eliminate any unnecessary classroom interruptions.

- Please do not call the office to relay messages to your children unless it is an absolute emergency.
- Inform children, before they leave for school in the morning, of any plans for after school that they may need to know such as:
    - Who is picking them up after school?
    - Do they need to ride the bus or are they walking home?
    - Who are they to go home with?
    - Do they need to go to day care today?
    - What are they to do if it rains?
    - Do they have their homework?

- Make sure lunch is taken care of by
    - Seeing that they take their lunch with them to school
    - Seeing that they have enough lunch money or tickets for that day
    - Seeing that they have extra tickets on file in the cafeteria as insurance in case of a forgotten lunch or an emergency

If you are going to be picking your child up before his or her regular dismissal time or during the day for an appointment, please send a note for the teacher to your child with the specific time you plan to pick him or her up. *Then come to the office, not to the classroom*, at the designated time and sign out your child. The office will then call your child out of instruction. These are a few suggestions that can help us to eliminate classroom interruptions. Thank you for your cooperation in helping to preserve valuable instructional time!

TREASURE CHEST SAMPLE #96

CELEBRATING OUR SCHOOL YEAR—A SPECIAL THANK YOU

Star Vista School Continues a Tradition of Excellence

Our outstanding school programs and dedicated staff continue to bring praise and recognition to our school. This past year has been a year of exceptional achievement. Many of our special school programs as well as many of our dedicated staff have received awards or been recognized for their extraordinary contributions to education. As a result of our reputation for excellence, we continue to host many educators who visit our school to see these programs in action. It is always with great pride that we share with others the outstanding programs we have here at Star Vista School, but we are most proud of the wonderful students and their impressive accomplishments and excellent behavior. Our visitors often share with us how impressed they are with our students' behavior and attitude; the warm, supportive learning environment; and the students' joy for learning that is so obviously prevalent throughout the classrooms.

This past year at Star Vista School has been one of excellence in the quality of educational experiences for our students and one that has resulted in considerable recognition and praise for our school. As the year draws to a close I would like to take the opportunity to express my sincere thanks to the students, staff, and parents here at Star Vista. They have all worked together to build a pride in our school and its accomplishments. Appreciation must be expressed to those who have helped to make it happen.

A Special Thank You

A special thank you to our outstanding PTA! The PTA Board consists of hardworking, positive, supportive, and extremely capable members who always give so willingly of their time, talents, and energy whenever and wherever they are needed. Whether it's organizing the carnival, counting the Reading Incentive program minutes, or working the Book Fair, our PTA is always there to help. Parents have been so supportive of our fundraising efforts and your contributions have been greatly appreciated.

A special thank you to Maria Acosta, our outstanding PTA President! Her dedication and caring for the children at Star Vista School have been an inspirational model for others. Her tireless energy and hard work, her warm, supportive way of getting the most out of others, and her willingness to take on any task and get it done have been signs of her very effective leadership. We all appreciate the hundreds of volunteer hours she has contributed to this school and thank her for her past two years of excellent leadership and strong child advocacy.

(Continued)

(Continued)

A special thank you to School Site Council Chairman Josh Ponds and the School Site Council members for their involvement and leadership in monitoring and evaluating our school's curriculum. Josh's unwavering support and appreciation for the hard work and dedication of the Star Vista staff is greatly appreciated. The partnership between staff and parents is always evident at our School Site Council meetings where ideas are shared and discussed and parents are able to see beyond the needs of their own child and work toward meeting the needs of all children.

A special thank you to our many parent volunteers. Parents who volunteer are a valuable and important component of the success of our school programs. We need and greatly appreciate the thousands of hours donated each year in our classrooms. Parent volunteers are reflective of the excellent partnership between home and school that enhances and enriches the educational opportunities for our young people. Our volunteers help in many ways: working in classrooms; volunteering in special programs like the Media Center, Publishing Center, Science Lab and Art Lab; sharing jobs, careers, or special interests as guest speakers; donating money to support school programs; helping at home preparing teacher materials; donating time at the carnival or other special events; and the list goes on and on. A special thanks to *Allison Jones*, who spent countless hours this year coordinating our Science Lab program. We are thankful for all our many parent volunteers. We could not do what we do without your help!

A special thank you this year to our school–business partnership with CompEd Technology. They have provided an important resource to our school with their special Employee Read-Aloud Days that occurred throughout the school year. Employees were released from their jobs to come to school and visit classrooms as guest readers. Personnel from CompEd also assisted in our Model Rocketry unit with a special rocket launch witnessed by our fourth and fifth graders. They also provided manpower for the behind-the-scenes help moving the sets during our school musical.

A special thank you is in order for those highly dedicated PAL tutors. The PAL Program (Partners at Learning) is a one-on-one tutoring program. Business partnership personnel and Lions Club members volunteer a half hour each week to work with a partner, a specially chosen Star Vista student. The personal relationships that have developed between tutor and student over the year have really helped to make a difference in those children's lives. The luxury of having that personal, undivided attention each week has had a significant impact on our students. Thank you for your dedication, patience, and commitment!

A special thank you to all the highly qualified teachers who have worked tirelessly to provide a productive and positive learning climate where opportunities for quality instruction, creativity, and academic achievement for each student were accomplished. They are among the best teachers the profession has to offer and we are fortunate to have their services here at Star Vista School.

A special thank you to all the support staff and classified staff who consistently demonstrate the highest degree of dedication and professional performance. We are indeed fortunate to have so many wonderful, warm, and caring people to work with and nurture our children.

A special note of appreciation to our school secretary, Simone Franks, and our School Clerk, Mioshi Chang, who make our days brighter and more efficient. They both handle the incredible demands and interruptions of the front office with skill, tact, efficiency, and patience. Parents, staff, and students really value their warmth, caring, hard work, and dedication.

And last, a special thank you and best wishes to Mrs. Rhea Tire and Mrs. Fonda Farewell who are retiring this year. They have been an integral part of our school and contributed to the great success of our school programs. Rhea has done a magnificent job in challenging students intellectually and creatively. Rhea has been an outstanding educator and has been recognized and honored for the impact she has had on hundreds of boys and girls of this community over the years. Fonda has been a dedicated, hard-working media center aide for many years at Star Vista and she provided wonderful service to the boys and girls of our school. They will both be greatly missed.

A special thank you to our wonderful, supportive parents. We greatly appreciate your unfailing support for and involvement in your children's education. The parent–home–school partnership is a key ingredient to the success of Star Vista School. As a staff, we sense your caring, concern, and interest in what's best for the children at Star Vista. This kind of home–school mutual support can only help to enhance and enrich the educational program for your children. Parents who care and who are actively involved in the school do make a significant difference in the success of their children in school!

And a special thank you to our students, who have worked hard and demonstrated fine progress in all academic areas. They have continued to amaze us with their skills, creativity, and performance. Students have willingly served their school by their involvement in student council and cross-age tutoring and by demonstrating general kindness, respect, and consideration for each other. The Star Vista staff cherishes the privilege we have in being able to work with such wonderful children. They provide the joys and rewards that come from such an important responsibility as that of educating children.

All of the above people make up the Community of Star Vista Elementary School. They are the ingredients that make Star Vista such a special place. It is with renewed enthusiasm that I look forward to next year and all that it will bring. I am confident that we will continue to grow and expand our abilities to provide the highest quality education for your children. It is our goal to continue to work with you, as parents and community members, so we can help children be successful and reach their highest potential.

Thank you all and have a great summer!

TREASURE CHEST SAMPLE #97

ONE GOOD PARENT

One good parent is worth one thousand school masters.

—A Chinese Proverb

Administrators and teachers everywhere recognize the important contributions parents make toward a child's success in school. There is no question about it— success at school begins at home! Parents are the *single most important variable* in predicting a child's success in school. Parents model both a silent and a spoken language in front of their children daily. They have taught their children values through how they spend their time and money.

One of the most important components of a good school is the partnership between the school and the parents who work together for the best interest of children. The close partnership between home and school is one of the exceptional strengths of Star Vista School.

Star Vista has a strong tradition of supportive, hard-working parents. Throughout the year parents have the opportunity to develop that partnership in a wide variety of ways. Parents can join the PTA, volunteer in the classroom, help at the carnival, attend School Site Council meetings, read to their children, and help in many other ways. It is important to your child that you are involved in some way at school. It's a way to let your child know that you think his or her school is very important.

As we begin a new school year, we find teachers establishing school standards and rules. In the most successful classrooms, teachers have established specific routines for the children to follow. This means giving the children a specific place to find and keep materials, a set schedule for classroom instruction, and so on. These routines, blended with the teacher's consistent standards, form a smooth-running classroom where the children have the security of understanding their environment and are reinforced positively for their contributions.

At home, it is also important to provide routines. Many families build a daily quiet time when the television is turned off. This quiet time provides students the opportunity for completing schoolwork or for recreational reading if there is no homework. During this quiet time, a suitable place, somewhat free of other distractions, should be available. The routine of a daily quiet time provides an opportunity to develop self-discipline, stimulate imagination, and enhance reading skills.

Routines can also make completing chores easier for both children and parents. If children are consistently expected to complete a routine household duty at the same time on the same day in the same place, it makes it easier and they soon begin to develop a responsibility for their commitment and contribution to the family.

As families establish routines for the new school year, it is helpful to keep in mind that childhood is a special time of learning, exploration, and growth. Children need to be provided free time to explore their world and experience the joy of discovery. Sometimes children's lives are over-programmed every minute of the day with after-school piano or karate lessons, religious instruction, soccer practice, and then, crammed in-between, homework.

Hopefully we can provide time for our children to be children. The realities of the adult world will be there all too soon. As children grow and learn, they can find joy and satisfaction in working closely with their families toward a common goal. Such is the case with the students at Star Vista School. Commitment to the best for our children on the part of parents, students, and staff is the key to our success with the children whom we teach. It is the hope of the staff and the administration that all parents will help us fulfill this commitment to excellence on behalf of *all* children at Star Vista. The school and home can work together to build skills and knowledge, reinforce values, and develop a strong sense of self-worth. We must invest our time and energies in our nation's most valuable resource—OUR CHILDREN!

TREASURE CHEST SAMPLE #98

THE SEASON OF JOY

There is always something very special about this time of year. There is a spirit in the air. Regardless of one's religious affiliation and regardless of the commercialism in our streets and stores, a spirit of joy and sharing always seems to prevail during the holiday season.

The holiday season provides a rich opportunity for sensory experiences—the taste of traditional dishes; the smell of spices used in special recipes for cookies, pies, and other goodies; the sight of beautiful lights, candles, and cards; specially selected gifts to give and receive; the sound of bells, music, fires crackling, and popcorn popping; and the special warm feeling of being close to loved ones and appreciating our families and our heritage.

Our children bring us a special joy during this season, as we share meals with friends and relatives, share gifts with our loved ones, and share time together as a family. As the year draws to an end, nearly all of us in most occupations are fortunate enough to receive some extra time off.

The best thing to spend on your children is time.

The gifts we give our children provide momentary pleasures that fade in the distance and are insignificant compared to the time and love we give each and every day throughout the year. That is the foundation we build in shaping the kind of adults our children will become. Children bring us their special gifts and we can build their confidence and self-esteem during those crucial formative years if we as adults

- Remember people, not things, matter most
- Love and accept our children from the day they are born
- Respect our children's individual differences and appreciate their unique gifts, talents, and capabilities

When we think good thoughts about our children, we should tell them. Stop being slaves to the tyranny of the urgent in our daily lives and make time to do the important things we value most. We need to make time to spend with our children. The demands on our time, energy, and resources and the urgency of our lives often interfere with our relationships with our children. Too quickly time passes, they grow older, and we lose the wonderful opportunity to really get to know our children as individuals.

We need to get in touch with how our children see and experience the holidays. Let their joy, excitement, and sense of wonder inspire us to keep the spirit of the season with our family throughout the year. Cherish the moments of the season of joy with your children, family, and friends. These are the experiences that give richness and meaning to our lives and are to be treasured and fondly remembered in years to come.

TREASURE CHEST SAMPLE #99

EMERGENCY PREPAREDNESS BULLETIN

Dear Parents:

Together with the leadership of our district and the support of the PTA, we have developed procedures and preparations in the event of an emergency while students are at school. The purpose of this bulletin is to apprise you of our procedures and lists of supplies your family should send to school with your child. Our school staff has been assigned and trained to be members of an Emergency Team. We have acquired equipment and supplies to care for students in an emergency situation. Students have been instructed in and will continue to practice procedures for fire, earthquake, flood, civil defense, intruder, smog, and local disasters.

In order to put our Emergency Plan into effect, we need your cooperation. We are asking you to send the supplies listed below to school in a one-gallon Zip-loc bag for your child's own personal survival kit. This kit will be returned to you at the end of each school year, resupplied, and returned to school again in September of each year. This procedure allows for us to have food at the school that is rotated yearly. We have purchased plastic trashcans with wheels to store the supplies in the classroom. Please be sure that your child's full name is clearly marked on the bag.

Items for the Zip-loc bag are as follows:

2 8 oz. Canned Fruit Juice With Pop Top and/or 2 Water Packs
2 4 1/2 oz. Canned Fruit With Pop Top
2 3 oz. Cans Tuna or Other Canned Lunch Meat With Pop Top
2 Peanut Butter or Cheese and Cracker-type Snack Packages
2 Granola Bars
2 Plastic Spoons
1 Package of Tissues
6 Individually Wrapped Moist Towelettes
1 Solar Blanket (optional—available at sporting goods stores)
1 Miniature Flashlight With Batteries Wrapped Separately (Optional)
1 Note From Home

It would be wise to check the expiration dates on foodstuffs for shelf life. Our storage inside classrooms is limited and prohibits anything larger than a one-gallon Zip-loc bag. If your child requires a specific prescription daily, please contact the school health clerk.

Please return your child's personal survival kit to school this week. Your prompt attention to this very important matter is greatly appreciated. Thank you for your cooperation.

TREASURE CHEST SAMPLE #100

MIDDLE SCHOOL REPORT TO PARENTS

Kids are number one at McAuliffe Middle School in Los Alamitos, California!
McAuliffe is located in a suburban area of north Orange County and is in the
northeast corner of the city of Los Alamitos.

The McAuliffe Middle School Vision is "The mission of McAuliffe Middle School is to
educate its students in a nurturing environment to their highest level of achievement, to
produce autonomous citizens with a lifelong respect for learning and democratic values,
and to teach students to be sensitive to others and to have respect for human diversity."

With a dedicated, caring, and involved administrative team, staff, parents, and
community, a commitment is made to provide an enriching and rigorous educational
experience for every student!

When visitors enter McAuliffe's 22-acre campus, they soon realize they have
come to a special place. They are attracted to the park-like quad area with tables, a
patio cover, grass, trees, and a bright, tropical ocean mural. The California
Distinguished School flag flies proudly at the front of the school. Visitors walk in awe
through a hallway art gallery that displays a promenade of eighth-grade students'
painted canvases. They observe a heterogeneous group of students reading a Civil
War play with a special education resource teacher, students conducting
experiments with paper airplanes, and math students taking a survey during passing
period. They watch students choosing a sport to participate in during physical
education, designing and cooking a healthy meal in Healthy Living/Teen Living, singing
and dancing in Spanish, and writing and thinking across the curriculum.

Proceeding further, visitors are made aware of our commitment to technology
as a vital learning tool as they view our Media Center, Macintosh computer lab,
keyboarding lab, and also see many classroom computers being used by the
community of learners (teachers and students). Video technology, Internet, graphic
calculators, and the newly built Exploring Technology Lab actively engage students
in a wealth of technological advances. Visitors comment on the sense of purpose our
students display as active, involved learners. Quality student work, displayed in every
classroom, is the source of great pride and accomplishment. The visitors have
observed what can be described simply as *a rich academic environment and a great
place to learn for all students.*

McAuliffe Middle School was built in 1967 as Pine Junior High. The school was
recreated in 1987 when the two district middle schools, Pine and Oak, combined to
form one new school—Christa McAuliffe Middle School. Subsequently, in September
1995, the Board of Education reopened Oak, greatly reducing McAuliffe's student
population. Staff members were able to choose to stay at McAuliffe or transfer to Oak,
which has created at McAuliffe a very dedicated and happy staff committed to a vision
of excellence. Currently, McAuliffe is one of two middle schools in the Los Alamitos
Unified School District serving Grades 6–8. McAuliffe's student body of 965 includes 166
gifted students and 64 special education students. The student ethnic breakdown is 65%

(Continued)

(Continued)

Caucasian, 13% Hispanic, 5% African American, 11% Asian American, 2% Filipino, .5% Pacific Islander, and .5% American Indian. Our students speak 29 different languages; there are 28 English-language learners.

The culture of the school is centered in pride, which is mutually shared by parents, students, staff, and the community, that McAuliffe is one of the best middle schools in California. Many parents move into the district specifically for their student to attend school here. In addition, the parents of 410 students (42% of the enrollment), living outside the school district's boundaries, withstand inconveniences to transport their students to McAuliffe on interdistrict transfer permits.

The district's Education Foundation has committed to raise 1.5 million dollars to enhance technology in the schools. The PTA volunteered more than 3,105 hours last year to enrich the educational experiences for our students. Our partnership with Orange County Teachers Federal Credit Union, Los Alamitos Medical Center, Print'n Copy, Sander Engineering, and Boise Cascade have provided McAuliffe with funds, materials, expertise, and service. Golden West Community College and Rockwell/Boeing have provided field-trip experiences and speakers for our students. Our partnership with Orange County Mental Health has provided mental health services for our students, parents, and community. The Outpost, McAuliffe's extended day care center, provides the only known school-sponsored day-care for middle school students in Orange County.

McAuliffe's goal is to be on the cutting edge of quality educational innovation in order to produce high achievement and the best program for its students. The curriculum is developed with the philosophy that all students can learn and deserve equal access to a quality education. There is also a strong commitment to academic integrity while making emotional connections with students. McAuliffe has strong cocurricular activities that involve our students in programs such as intramural sports, student government, Show Choir, Studio Singers, Jazz Band, instrumental music concerts, theater presentations, Peer Assistance League (PAL), PEACE Club, Academic Pentathlon, Science Olympiad, Math Field Day Competition, Club Live, Ski Club, O Club, International Club, and School Site Council.

McAuliffe has a tradition of excellence equaled by few middle schools. In 1996, McAuliffe was selected as a California Distinguished School. In 1997, McAuliffe was recognized with a Building Bridges Award from Orange County Human Relations. As one of the original California Partnership Schools, an original 6–8 California School Improvement Program school, a pilot school for the new Program Quality Review (PQR), a Goals 2000 school, and a Vision 2020 school, McAuliffe has experience in evaluating student work and instructional delivery systems based on California's frameworks, model curriculum guides, and the Program Quality Review criteria.

McAuliffe's outstanding teaching staff has historically been at the forefront of curriculum development and instructional change. Nine teachers have been mentor teachers in the district. The staff has served on a variety of curriculum committees, piloted new materials, and presented at conferences and workshops. Three teachers have been selected as the Los Angeles Unified School District representatives for Orange County Teacher of the Year. Five teachers have been honored by Who's Who in America's Teachers and John Hopkins University California Teacher Recognition Program. Two teachers have been selected as Seal Beach Lions Club Teacher of the Year.

Two administrators, a counselor, six teachers, and three classified employees have been recognized as Honorary Service Award recipients by McAuliffe's PTA. In 1996, our principal was honored by the District's PTA with a Golden Oak Service Award. She has also been recognized as the 1998 Orange County Middle School Principal of the Year. Recognition is flattering, but McAuliffe's greatest achievement is when a student emerges with the highest achievement possible and strives to be successful and a responsible citizen of tomorrow.

Christa McAuliffe once said, "Reach for the stars." As a team of professionals, parents, students, and community, we reach for the stars by recognizing that the only way to move forward in improving instruction, student achievement, and professionalism is to move forward together.
Be yourself, try your best, and never be afraid to dream.
Christa McAuliffe

Reprinted with permission of Karen Lovelace, Former Principal
McAuliffe Middle School, Los Alamitos, California

TREASURE CHEST SAMPLE #101

PARENT SURVEY—A SCHOOL EVALUATION TOOL

The purpose of this questionnaire is to learn how parents and the community feel about our school. We hope you will give your honest opinion. Our goal at Star Vista School is to continue to evaluate and refine all programs so we can offer the best education to our students. Let me thank you in advance for taking the time to provide us your opinions. Since experiences are different for each child, we'd appreciate you completing a survey for each of your children. The results of this survey will be shared with you in a newsletter.

Person completing the survey: __ Mother   __ Father   __ Both   __ Other

Circle grade level of your child: Pre-School   K   1   2   3   4   5

Number of years your child has attended Star Vista School:

____ Less than 1   __ 1   __ 2   __ 3   __ 4   __ 5   __ 6

(Continued)

	Excellent	Good	Average	Unsatisfactory
1. The school meets my child's needs in the following areas:				
Language Arts				
Mathematics				
History/Social Science				
Science/Health				
Physical Education				
Art				
Music				
2. My child is encouraged to participate in an instructional program that helps to realize his or her highest potential, interests, and talents and maintain high standards.				
3. Special programs such as the media center, art lab, computer lab, and music center enhance my child's learning program.				
4. My child is provided opportunities to use technology as a learning tool (e.g., computers, video equipment, laser discs, CD-ROMs)				
5. My child likes school.				
6. The school provides a safe, clean, and pleasant environment for my child.				
7. The discipline standards are high and problems are dealt with in an appropriate manner.				
8. My child feels that he or she is welcomed and valued in a way that acknowledges cultural diversity, learning styles, and unique needs.				
9. The school is providing opportunities for my child to develop a positive self-image.				
10. Positive communication exists between myself and school personnel, and they are receptive to my concerns and suggestions.				
11. The homework assigned my child is teaching responsibility and good study habits and is reflective of the curriculum.				

	Excellent	Good	Average	Unsatisfactory
12. The school Progress Report Card, parent–teacher conferences, and interactions with school personnel effectively communicate my child's academic progress and behavior growth.				
13. The School Site Council and PTA meetings are effective in helping to learn more about the school program and activities.				
I have attendedthe following number of parent meetings and programs this year:		(0–2)	(3–5)	(6 or more)
14. The school provides support and services for students with identified or special needs				
15. Special programs enhance my child's learning:				
Music Program (Grades K–5)				
Art Lab Program (Grades 1–5)				
Media Center Program (Grades K–5)				
REACH Research Program (Grades 4–5)				
Computer Lab Program (Grades K–5)				
16. The school provides my child with opportunities to develop respect, responsibility, and problem-solving skills.				
17. The relationship between my child and his or her teacher is one of mutual respect, warmth, and caring.				
18. I feel welcome at school.				
19. Special activities such as Spirit Days, Good Citizenship Awards, the STAR Reading Incentive Program, and theme days build school pride and positive feelings.				
20. The teacher responds to my child's individual needs.				
21. The school provides a challenging and positive learning environment for students.				
22. The leadership in the school is effective and is shared by parents, teachers, and the administration.				
23. The school maintains high standards and expectancies in school work and behavior.				
24. The overall quality of the instructional program at Star Vista School is outstanding.				

(Continued)

(Continued)

We welcome hearing from you about your child's experiences at Star Vista School. Please use the back of this page if you need more space.

25. In what areas of school life at Star Vista does your child experience joy or success?

26. In what areas of school life does your child struggle or feel unsuccessful?

27. One thing I would like to change about Star Vista School is:

28. As a parent, the thing I appreciate most about Star Vista School is:

Praise, Comments, Concerns:

TREASURE CHEST SAMPLE #102

SCHOOL ORGANIZATION FOR NEXT YEAR

We are currently in the process of organizing the classrooms for next year and we need your help! We need to know if your child will be returning next year to Star Vista School. Please complete the survey on the next page and return it to school by Tuesday, May 1. Also, please urge anyone in your neighborhood with an incoming kindergartner to please let the school office know immediately in order to register for school in September. Last year, parent input from this survey made a significant difference in helping us to organize classrooms more efficiently and accurately.

Projecting school enrollment for each new year is a difficult job. There are three major factors that effect our school organization:

1. The transiency rate—we average about 20% turnover of students each year.
2. The district's and school's intent to maintain balanced class sizes.
3. The budget constraints that limit flexibility in adding new teachers without impacting our funding.

This past year at Star Vista we experienced a transiency rate of approximately 19%, with 149 students moving in or out. Each year, in order to predict next year's school population, we move our current enrollment at each grade level forward and predict the same numbers in kindergarten as those leaving fifth grade for middle school.

(Continued)

(Continued)

This gives us a figure of how many students are at each grade level and enables us to begin to organize balanced classrooms. Keeping classrooms balanced in class size is a difficult task because of the transiency rate. Many times move-outs over the summer aren't replaced with move-ins in exactly the same grade level and class size is thrown out of balance, crowding one grade level and leaving the other light. We often end up starting school in the fall with disproportionate class sizes.

In order to anticipate and plan for any of the three major factors, schools have found that combination classrooms provide greater flexibility in assigning students. Since transiency is an unknown factor causing projected enrollment to fluctuate between spring and the start of school, we will need to provide for more combination classrooms. If we have a Grades 1–2 combination classroom then we can enroll either a new first or second grader. Our goal is to balance our class sizes throughout each grade level by keeping approximately the same enrollment in each classroom. We don't want to go over the state limits for class size and pay a penalty, yet we can't afford a teacher when only half her class shows up in the fall. Therefore, combination classrooms give us the greatest flexibility in assigning new students who enroll in the fall.

Because of the possibility of unbalanced class sizes, schools also need to consider reorganization of classrooms after school has started. Each year as enrollment figures finalize in the first three weeks of school, final class sizes tell us where we are over- or underenrolled. Reassignment of students to balance class size, if done early in the year, causes only a minimum disruption. Once students are reassigned to their new classroom and teacher, they adjust quickly and move smoothly into new classroom routines and programs. We appreciate your continuing support and understanding. Thank you very much.

Please Return to Star Vista School By May 1st. Thank you.

_____ 1. My child(ren) will be returning to Star Vista in the fall.

_____ 2. My child(ren) will not be returning to Star Vista in the fall.

_____ 3. My child(ren) *may not* be returning to Star Vista in the fall.

If you check either Question 2 or 3, please comment below:

Are you considering a move out of the school attendance boundaries? Are you considering placement in a private school? Or are there other reasons? If you're not returning, please let us know where your child(ren) will be attending school next year and we can forward their school records.

ANY information you can provide will be helpful. Even share your tentative plans. If you can give us a percentage as to the possibility we would appreciate it. (For example, There is a 60% chance my husband will be transferred back east. There is a 30% chance we'll be able to sell our house, which has been listed on the market for two months.)

COMMENTS:

PARENT'S NAME _____

CHILD'S NAME _____ ROOM ___

CHILD'S NAME _____ ROOM ___

CHILD'S NAME _____ ROOM ___

CHILD'S NAME _____ ROOM ___

TREASURE CHEST SAMPLE #103

WHEN REPORT CARDS DON'T MAKE THE GRADE

Does your child hide out at the neighbor's house when report cards come out? Before you go looking for him or her, read these five tips for dealing with the less-than-perfect report card.

1. Don't Lose Your Cool. Though many people see report cards as motivating, they can also be demoralizing. "They can sap a child of his confidence," says Dr. Kenneth Shore, school psychologist and author of the *Parent's Public School Handbook*. "The report card is not a measure of your child's worth or your parenting skills." But grades can have an impact on a child's future. Make this point constructively.

2. Look Behind the Grade. The report card only indicates there is a problem. Compare your child's papers over the year to see his or her progress. Discuss whether he or she is involved in too many extracurricular activities or a part-time job is taking time away from studies. "Kids need time just as adults do to get their work done," says Dorothy Rich, president of the Home and School Institute. If your child is trying his or her hardest and still not understanding the material, contact the teacher immediately.

3. Accentuate the Positive. Point out where your child is doing well, whether it's in an academic subject or an extracurricular activity. "Children need to know where they show motivation because they may not be aware of their strengths," says Dorothy Rich. If your child does poorly in math but enjoys figuring out basketball player's free-throw averages, make the connection for him.

4. Set Goals for Improvement. Goals help us get motivated, but be realistic. If a child is getting all C's on his or her report card now, expecting all A's the next reporting period may not be a realistic goal. He or she may need to get a few B's first.

5. Contact, But Do Not Attack, the Teacher. "If a parent has any questions at all, the first thing he or she should do is call the teacher for clarification—not the guidance counselor or assistant principal," says Martie Fiske, a White House Distinguished Teacher. "A parent's first question should be, 'What's going on?'" Fiske suggests gathering more information before charging that something is wrong with the program or the teacher.

To avoid further report card surprises, parents, students, and teachers should keep the lines of communication open all year long.

Reprinted with permission of Karen Lovelace, Principal, McAuliffe Middle School, Los Alamitos, California

TREASURE CHEST SAMPLE #104

PARENT LETTER—RESPONDING TO PARENT REQUEST FOR A SPECIFIC TEACHER

Dear Parents:

The staff and I are beginning our planning for next school year and soon we will be sitting down to make up classes, based upon our best estimate of the enrollment projections for next year. About this time of the year, we begin to hear from some parents who want to request a specific teacher for their child for next year. They want "the best teacher" for their child and they believe they know who that is based on what they've seen and heard.

As the principal, I visit classrooms almost every day for the purpose of observing teachers teaching and students learning. I know the instructional skills of every teacher better than anyone else in the school or the community because I have observed various aspects daily. I could not, in all honesty, tell you who the very best teacher on the faculty is, because there is no one teacher who is the best in everything. In talking about the "best teacher" one must specify "best in what area?" Teaching is made up of hundreds of subskills, and no one is the *best* at all of them. Also, I have seen the instructional level of teachers vary significantly depending upon the makeup of the class and the type of children the teacher has to work with.

When we assemble classes we try to make them heterogeneous. The major factors we consider are the child's demonstrated achievement in reading on a daily basis; if the child is a fast learner, an average learner, or slow learner; the quality of the student's citizenship; the child's work and study habits; whether he or she is a discipline problem; if he or she is a leader or follower; how a child's personality will fit in with the others in the class; if his or her leadership potential will have an opportunity to develop in the class; and the boy–girl ratio in the class. You can see this is a complicated process and is based upon our best assessment of each child.

We do NOT consider social factors such as the number of friends the child will have in the new class who came from his or her former class, or what classroom his or her best friend is in. Children are adaptable and will make friends wherever they are placed. We do know that parents sometimes have preferences for teachers; however, we cannot place children in classes only on the basis of the parents' preferences or the teacher's reputation in the community.

We group children for *instructional purposes*, and placing them in class based on any other factors would defeat this purpose. In the past, some parents have made requests for a certain teacher, and their child was placed in that room. The parent concluded it was only because of their request, but it was because the staff also felt it was a good placement based upon our criteria. Now to the main question "How to get the best teacher for my child?" Provide us with the kind of classroom environment you want for your child if you feel you need to and then trust us to do the best grouping we can. The key ingredient in this process is trust. You need to trust the staff to make the best placement possible with all the information at our disposal. We will do the best job of placement we can, because it is important to us that every child has a good chance for success. We appreciate your trust and support.

SUMMARY

Steps to Mastering the Skills
of Resiliency, Renewal, and Reflection

1. Keep a balance in your life. Schedule in time for family and friends on a daily and weekly basis. Tell people, "This is the time for my family."

2. Create your own professional support group that you meet with at least every other week. Meet early for breakfast before going to your school.

3. Recruit a mentor whom you respect to coach you through stressful times and to serve as a sounding board.

4. Take a joy break. Get out into the classrooms and visit with kids and staff.

5. Delegate to others and then trust them to do the best they know how.

6. Build in slack time. Don't overschedule your day. Give yourself some breathing room by allowing for processing time between appointments or meetings.

7. Don't spend time reinventing the wheel. Share sample letters, forms, and programs with your fellow principals.

8. Periodically get away from it all. Take a long weekend or vacation, leave town, and DON'T TAKE WORK with you!

9. Watch out for burnout and the tyranny of the urgent.

10. Take time away from your job and family responsibilities to care for yourself. Do something just for yourself that gives you joy, expresses your creativity, and reenergizes your physical and mental health so you can continue to give to others.

11. Learn to discern what's important from what's not important. Only do things well that need to be done well. Many of the tasks given to us just need to be done—not done perfectly.

12. Lighten up! Don't take things so seriously. Have some fun! Bring humor to your school culture. Laugh! Laugh! Laugh!

13. Build in quiet time. Find some time in the day for quiet reflection. Reflect on how you can align your actions with your goals and vision for the school so you use your time and resources most effectively.

14. Be an inspirational leader through your actions as well as your words. Enhance peak performance in others and help them rekindle the passion to make a difference in children's lives. Be profuse with your praise! Remember encouragement is oxygen for the soul!

In every child who is born, under no matter what circumstances, and no matter what parents, the potentiality of the human race is born again.

—J. Agee and W. Evans

THE LAST WORD

The life of a school principal is a challenging, rich, and rewarding life. We are fortunate to have chosen a profession where we have the opportunity each day to make a difference in the lives of others.

We are faced with hundreds of choices we must make within our day. The choices we make will reflect on our ability to successfully lead others. One of the most important choices we must make each day is to maintain a satisfying balance in our lives. There will always be pressure to do things faster, work harder, and accomplish more. The workload of the principalship, if we allow it, can consume our time and energy. To be an effective leader we must first take care of ourselves before we can take care of others. We have a choice. We must choose to keep a balance between work and a life outside of work.

One of the keys to maintaining that balance is mastering the survival skills of school leadership: resiliency, renewal, and reflection. Without these skills as a guiding framework we may feel fragmented, overworked, exhausted, and on the brink of burnout. We must choose to create for ourselves a sense of satisfaction and well-being and live a full, productive, and joyful life.

The purpose of this book has been to provide you with a principal's treasure chest of easy-to-implement strategies, ready-to-use sample letters, plus short-cuts and time-savers for making the most of your time and energy. These powerful tools are here for you to choose from and to adapt and modify to fit the individual needs of your school. They are based on the day-to-day reality of the job and the experiences of award-winning principals. You can tap into this valuable resource for years to come as a long-term support that will enable you to use your time and resources more effectively, reduce personal stress, spark new ideas and programs, and enhance your effectiveness as an inspirational school leader.

SURVIVAL SKILLS FOR THE PRINCIPALSHIP

A TREASURE CHEST OF TIME-SAVERS, SHORT-CUTS AND STRATEGIES TO HELP YOU KEEP A BALANCE IN YOUR LIFE

Book Now Available On
CD DISK

CD Contains Mac And PC Formats With Word, Works, and ClarisWorks Programs For Word Processing

Are you looking for an easy way to implement the many ideas found in this handbook? Well, you can save countless hours of RETYPING or REPRODUCING the many forms, checklists, and letters found in this valuable handbook. The Survival Skills For The Principalship Resource Handbook is now available on CD Disk that contains both Mac AND PC formats with Word, Works, and ClarisWorks programs for word processing.

Work smarter by using the formatted disks to modify the materials found in the book to fit your school. Don't re-invent the wheel at your school - just select the sample letter, teacher evaluation or check-list form you want and then add your school's name and personalize the information to meet your school's needs.

The CD disk will save you TIME, freeing you up to do the important work of the principalship at your school!

John Blaydes Enterprises Order Form

P O #_____

Name _____   School _____

Home Address _____   School Address _____

City _____ State ZIP   City _____ State ZIP

Home Phone _____   School Phone _____

E Mail Address _____   School Fax _____

Please Send Check Or Purchase Order Directly To:

MAIL TO:	John Blaydes	PHONE:	714 529-8645
	226 Delphia Ave.	FAX:	714 529-1645
	Brea, CA 92821	E-MAIL:	johnblaydes@mindspring.com

Quantity	Description	Price	Total
	CD of Survival Skills Handbook (CD disk contains both PC and Mac Formats with choices of Word, Works or Clarisworks for word processing)	$28.99	
		Sub-Total	
		Calif. Residents Add 7.75% Sales Tax	
		First Class Priority Mail	$5.00
		TOTAL DUE	

Index

**CORWIN
PRESS**

The Corwin Press logo—a raven striding across an open book—represents the union of courage and learning. Corwin Press is committed to improving education for all learners by publishing books and other professional development resources for those serving the field of K–12 education. By providing practical, hands-on materials, Corwin Press continues to carry out the promise of its motto: **"Helping Educators Do Their Work Better."**